John Franklin Jameson

Essays in the Constitutional History of the United States in the Formative Period, 1775-1789

John Franklin Jameson

Essays in the Constitutional History of the United States in the Formative Period, 1775-1789

ISBN/EAN: 9783337723378

Printed in Europe, USA, Canada, Australia, Japan

Cover: Foto ©ninafisch / pixelio.de

More available books at **www.hansebooks.com**

ESSAYS

IN THE

CONSTITUTIONAL HISTORY OF THE UNITED STATES

IN THE

FORMATIVE PERIOD

1775-1789

BY

GRADUATES AND FORMER MEMBERS OF THE
JOHNS HOPKINS UNIVERSITY

EDITED BY

J. FRANKLIN JAMESON, Ph. D.

LATE ASSOCIATE IN THE JOHNS HOPKINS UNIVERSITY, PROFESSOR OF HISTORY IN
BROWN UNIVERSITY

BOSTON AND NEW YORK
HOUGHTON, MIFFLIN AND COMPANY
The Riverside Press, Cambridge
1889

TO THE

PRESIDENT AND TRUSTEES

OF THE

JOHNS HOPKINS UNIVERSITY,

TO WHOM AMERICA IS INDEBTED FOR A UNIVERSITY

UNIQUE IN SCOPE AND IN STIMULATION OF RESEARCH,

This Volume

IS GRATEFULLY AND MOST RESPECTFULLY DEDICATED

BY THE AUTHORS.

PREFACE.

THE five Essays which compose this volume, treating of subjects within the field of our constitutional history during a brief but important period, are bound together not only by community of subject, but by a common purpose and a common origin.

Beyond the obvious purpose of presenting the results of investigation into their respective subjects, the authors have at heart, in the publication of this volume, what they venture, with modesty, to call a didactic purpose. They wish to call increased attention to the desirability of approaching the constitutional history of the United States from certain points of view which they feel to have been unduly neglected in its study. In the first place, they would be glad to see more work and thought devoted to the study of the origins of American institutions, and especially of their historical origin through processes of continuous development. The very thought that modern American institutions of government had such origins at all is unfamiliar to many educated persons. It has been a habit to think of our Constitution as having sprung full-armed from the heads of Olympian conventioners; and the habit has of late been strengthened by the general acceptance of the familiar dictum of Mr. Gladstone, that "the American Constitution is the most wonderful work ever struck off at a given time by the brain and purpose of man." This view, which at times has been exalted almost into a theory of inspiration, is unfavorable to historical investigation, and has in fact discouraged its progress by offering as adequate an independent solution.

We are convinced that this view is a mistaken one. With the progress of historical science, great national acts of settlement, which have solved deep-lying difficulties or successfully laid the bases for national advancement, are being found, in increasing numbers, to have been preceded by numerous steps of tentative solution, or prepared by a long course of slow and gradual development in the nation. We believe that the same laws of development have held true of America, and that the constitutional history of the United States will be most luminous and fruitful when pursued in accordance with this insight and conviction. Such studies as are here presented, upon the early development of the federal judiciary and the federal executive, and upon the process by which a form of government which at first barely secured consent soon acquired universal approval and admiration and the strength that springs from these, may help, it is hoped, to foster a tendency toward fuller research into the historical origins of American constitutional forms and ideas.

In the second place, and perhaps still more strongly, we desire to assist in broadening the current conception of American constitutional history, and in making its treatment more inclusive. Those who live under a written constitution are in danger of using the term "constitution," and by consequence the term "constitutional history," with a reference to that document only. They are likely to forget that the word "constitution" has also the wider sense of form of government, the sense in which we use it when we are speaking of all countries alike. The practice of confining one's self to the more restricted sense has made American studies of even the present aspects of our constitution less comprehensive than they might well have been. It is obvious that the constitutions of our states and our systems of party organization are just as truly parts, and are almost as important parts, of our form of government as anything set down in the Federal Constitution itself. Yet when Mr. Bryce occupied with these two subjects a third part of the great work which he has devoted to our constitution and politics, it is safe to say that the pleasure of many of his American readers was not unmixed with surprise; so little familiar had their own writers made them with conceptions of our constitution in which such elements would, as a matter of course, be included. And yet it would seem as if the mere reading of the Constitution of the United States, a brief document, which makes no mention of democracy, of the Speaker of the House, or of its committees, ought to have shown how much there is which is not embraced within it, nor even within our federal system.

The constitutional history of any country, properly conceived, is the history of its constitution taken in this wider sense. In the case of the constitutional history of England, there is no opportunity to construe the phrase otherwise. In the case of the United States, the adoption of the narrower interpretation has been only too frequent. Writers upon the subject have not seldom confined their attention to the document called the Constitution, its formation and adoption, its amendment and development. Our divergence from these is something more than a difference of opinion respecting the use of terms. We believe that this particular branch of historical work in the United States will be seriously injured if so restricted a use of terms leads to the neglect of the history of elements not embodied in the written Constitution. Those which are embodied in federal statutes, in the constitutions and laws of the states, and even in the practices and usages of the government and the people, are in hardly a less degree deserving of attention and of historical study. If the story of the parliamentary Reform Acts is a part of the constitutional history of England, that of the state acts successively widening the suffrage to complete democracy is a part of the constitutional history of the United States. If the history of the Redistribution Acts belongs to the one, that of the gerrymander belongs to the other.

Or, to speak more especially of the period and the topics to which these Essays relate, the fact that the Constitution of the United States prescribes with some degree of minuteness the organization of the legislative department of the federal government, yet says little of its executive department or of its judicial system, does not justify us in pursuing ardently the history of the development of the former and totally neglecting that of the latter. The changes which our ecclesiastical constitutions underwent during our formative period are not less deserving of the attention of the student of constitutional history than if they occurred in Europe. The effects which that period, devoted to the obtaining and securing of political liberties, had upon the status of the slave, constitute none the less important an object of inquiry because the Constitution attempted to ignore his existence.

In the publication of these Essays, therefore, the presentation of the results of careful investigation has not been the only object proposed; there has also been present, in the selection of their subjects as in the course of instruction in connection with which most of them originated, a definite purpose of directing increased attention to some modes of approaching the study of our constitutional history which, though not the ones most frequently followed hitherto, are believed likely to prove valuable and productive of results.

It has also been the intention of the authors, by the publication of this volume, to commemorate their common connection with the Johns Hopkins University,—a connection from which they gratefully acknowledge themselves to have received expansive and stimulative influences of the highest value. Most of the Essays which compose it, indeed, are the direct outgrowth of work pursued at that University, originating in investigations undertaken in connection with a course formerly conducted there by the editor of the volume.

J. FRANKLIN JAMESON.

BROWN UNIVERSITY,
PROVIDENCE, RHODE ISLAND,
   October 14, 1889.

CONTENTS.

	PAGE
THE PREDECESSOR OF THE SUPREME COURT, BY THE EDITOR. — NOTE: — THE MODEL OF THE FEDERAL COURT FOR TERRITORIAL DISPUTES	1
THE MOVEMENT TOWARDS A SECOND CONSTITUTIONAL CONVENTION IN 1788, BY EDWARD P. SMITH, PH. D., PROFESSOR IN THE WORCESTER POLYTECHNIC INSTITUTE	46
THE DEVELOPMENT OF THE EXECUTIVE DEPARTMENTS, BY JAY CAESAR GUGGENHEIMER, A. B.	116
THE PERIOD OF CONSTITUTION-MAKING IN THE AMERICAN CHURCHES, BY WM. P. TRENT, M. A., PROFESSOR IN THE UNIVERSITY OF THE SOUTH	186
THE STATUS OF THE SLAVE, 1775-1789, BY JEFFREY R. BRACKETT, PH. D.	263

ESSAYS IN THE CONSTITUTIONAL HISTORY OF THE UNITED STATES.

I.

THE PREDECESSOR OF THE SUPREME COURT.[1]

By J. FRANKLIN JAMESON.

IT is frequently, and indeed very justly, signalized as one of the capital defects of the Articles

[1] The sources of this essay are, the printed Journals of Congress, the manuscript Papers of the Old Congress in the library of the Department of State, the manuscript papers of the court herein treated, now in the office of the Clerk of the Supreme Court of the United States, such reports of cases before it as are contained in 2 Dallas, the reports of the Supreme Court of the United States, other reports, statute-books, and other authorities. The Life and Correspondence of George Read, by W. T. Read, is the only biography of a member of the court which gives much information respecting it. Mr. Read's papers, which might have supplied some additional facts, were unfortunately inaccessible to me because of the owner's absence from the country. Those of Messrs. Paca and Lowell, obligingly searched for me by my friend Mr. William B. Paca and by Mrs. S. R. Putnam, the granddaughter of Judge Lowell, yielded nothing for my purposes. I desire also to record my obligations to Theodore F. Dwight, Esq., late librarian of the Department of State; to Mr. Stanislas Hamilton, of the same office; and to the assistants of the Clerk of the Supreme Court.

A portion of this paper was read before the American Historical Association on December 27, 1888. A few days before that date I received, through the obliging kindness of Hon. J. C. Bancroft Davis, Esq., Reporter of the Supreme Court, a copy of a pamphlet privately printed by him, and entitled The Committees of the Conof Confederation and of our federal system in all the years preceding the year 1789, that they provided no federal judiciary of extensive scope. But it is well to remember that the federal government was not wholly without judicial functions and organs during those years. In the first place, Congress could hardly avoid being called upon to pronounce in disputes between states respecting boundary and jurisdiction, and the Articles of Confederation provided an especial process by which Congress was to determine both these disputes and such as concerned the private right of soil claimed under different grants of two or more states.[1]

tinental Congress chosen to hear and determine Appeals from Courts of Admiralty, and the Court of Appeals in Cases of Capture, established by that Body. This pamphlet is a separate issue of an account prepared by Judge Davis for insertion in the centennial volume of the reports of the Supreme Court. Although its purposes are different from my own, and although much the greatest part of the investigations whose results are presented in this essay had been completed at the time of its receipt, I must profess myself much indebted to this admirable pamphlet in such portions of my researches as were not then concluded. Judge Davis has also placed all future students of the subject, as well as myself, under obligations, by having the papers of the court systematically arranged at his own expense.

[1] Articles of Confederation, art. IX., paragraphs 2 and 3. What is believed to be a new view respecting the source of the peculiar constitution of this tribunal is presented in a note which follows this essay. A brief account of all the judiciary functions exercised by the federal government before 1789 is to be found in an essay on the subject by Thomas Sergeant in P. S. Duponceau, Constitutional Law, Philadelphia, 1820, subsequently embodied, as the first chapter, in Sergeant's Constitutional Law, Philadelphia, 1830 (date of 2d ed.).

Of all the judicial organs of the Old Congress, this tribunal for territorial disputes had, or might have, to deal with the most momentous interests. But in point of fact it was called into existence only a very few times (three apparently), and actually convened and pronounced judgment in only one case. This was the important case of the dispute between Pennsylvania and Connecticut respecting the Wyoming region, decided in favor of Pennsylvania, in December, 1782, by a court constituted after the manner prescribed by the Articles of Confederation, and sitting at Trenton.[1] Another judicial function provided for by the ninth of the Articles of Confederation was the trial of piracies and felonies committed on the high seas; but the power which that article conferred upon the United States in Congress assembled, in relation to such trials, was simply the power of "appointing" courts for the purpose, and their ordinance of April 5, 1781, merely designated certain portions of the existing judicial machinery of the states to try such cases.[2]

Decidedly more important to our constitutional

---

[1] The report of its proceedings is in Journals of Congress (ed. in 4 vols.) iv. 129–140. In the other two cases the court was constituted, but did not act, the states amicably adjusting the disputes The first (1784–86) was a dispute between Massachusetts and New York: Jour. Cong. iv. 444–453, 536, 564, 592–594, 787; the second (1785–86), between South Carolina and Georgia: Jour. Cong. iv. 529, 530, 634, 644, 691–697.

[2] Jour. Cong., iii. 606, 607.

history than these occasional tribunals were the old federal Court of Appeals in Cases of Capture, and the committees which preceded it. That court, the one permanent judicial body which the Confederation maintained, is now well-nigh forgotten by most persons. It seems worth while to call it again into remembrance for two reasons. In the first place, it is well to do all we can to set in clear light the antecedents of important American institutions. The most important of them are too often conceived of as having been without antecedents, as having been instantly called into existence by the creative fiat of great statesmen. Although the most august and powerful tribunal in the world has derived little of its splendor from its obscure and feeble predecessor, it is well for us to know that it had a predecessor, and that the life of that predecessor did something toward making possible the creation of a comprehensive federal judiciary. In the second place, the history of the committees for appeals, and of the permanent Court of Appeals which eventually took their place, casts light upon the character of the Confederation, and illustrates its weakness in a less familiar aspect.

The outbreak of the Revolution, it is well known, was marked by a great extension of privateering. This occasioned many prize cases, or disputes as to captures. At the same time, the machinery which had hitherto existed for the treatment of such cases seems to have collapsed. In each one of the royal colonies in America, as in each of the other colonies of Great Britain, the commission issued to the royal governor usually invested him with the powers of a vice-admiral. In all these, accordingly, there were vice-admiralty courts, in which it seems probable that in some instances the governor himself acted as judge, while in most a judge was specially appointed. Cases of capture arising in the colonies had naturally gone to these courts. But the vice-admiralty courts were rapidly destroyed by the Revolution. Where the governor had acted as judge, he was now in flight. The admiralty judges, as dependents of the governor, would most likely flee also; and the more so because their courts had of late years become highly unpopular, since a recent act had placed many infractions of the revenue laws under their jurisdiction, so that they were tried without a jury.[1] Nor could judges sit by virtue of commissions from King George to give judgment respecting prizes captured from him. The vice-admiralty courts continued in existence in those places only which were occupied by royal forces.[2]

[1] See the instructions of Boston town meeting, 1769, in the sixteenth Report of the Boston Record Commissioners, pp. 287, 288.

[2] Among the papers of the Court of Appeals, in the office of the Clerk of the Supreme Court U. S., in bundle No. 42, is a privateer's commission issued by Governor Tryon and Robert Bayard,

The paralysis of the former prize courts made it necessary to provide a substitute. The necessity was of course first felt in Massachusetts. During its third provincial Congress, the expediency of maintaining a naval force was considered.[1] The Continental Congress having recommended the same in July, an act was passed on the 1st of November, 1775, which provided for three courts, to be held at different places in Massachusetts, which should have cognizance of captures.[2] The name Courts of Admiralty was studiously avoided,[3] and trial by jury was provided for in every case. The establishment of the privateering system, of which this arrangement was a part, was later signalized by John Adams[4] as having been one of the most important steps toward Revolution, and the court early acquired a large volume of business.[5]

The journals of the Continental Congress show[6] that the first suggestion of a federal court for such purposes came from General Washing-

judge of the admiralty court of New York, dated November, 19 Geo. III. The Miscellaneous Papers, case of The Industry v. The Susanna, Ibid., show Nathaniel Hatch, as deputy judge, acting at Boston in September, 1775.

[1] Acts and Resolves of the Province of Massachusetts Bay, ed. A. C. Goodell, Jr., vol. v. pp. 515, 516.
[2] Ibid., 436–441.   [3] Ibid., 517.
[4] Austin's Life of Gerry, i. 95, 109.
[5] Pickering's Pickering, i. 79, 80.
[6] Judge Davis has interestingly brought out this point in the pamphlet cited, p. 3.

ton. Writing to the President of Congress from the camp at Cambridge on the 11th of November, he says: —

"Enclosed you have a copy of an act passed this session, by the honorable Council and House of Representatives of this province. It respects such captures as may be made by vessels fitted out by the province, or by individuals thereof. As the armed vessels, fitted out at the Continental expense, do not come under this law, I would have it submitted to the consideration of Congress, to point out a more summary way of proceeding, to determine the property and mode of condemnation of such prizes as have been or hereafter may be made, than is specified in this act.

"Should not a court be established by authority of Congress, to take cognizance of prizes made by the Continental vessels? Whatever the mode is, which they are pleased to adopt, there is an absolute necessity of its being speedily determined on."[1]

In accordance with Washington's suggestions, which it will be seen, however, included no suggestion of an appellate court, a committee was appointed by Congress which reported a few days later. After debating their report by paragraphs, Congress, on November 25, adopted a series of seven resolutions dealing with the subject of maritime captures. These resolutions au-

[1] Writings of Washington, ed. Sparks, iii. 154, 155.

thorized the capture of British armed vessels, transports, and ships carrying goods to the army, determined a rate of distribution of prize-money, and recommended the legislatures of the several colonies to erect courts in which all cases of capture might be tried by jury. The sixth resolution, relating to federal cognizance of such cases, went a step beyond the recommendations of Washington; it was as follows: —

"6. That in all cases an appeal shall be allowed to the Congress, or such person or persons as they shall appoint for the trial of appeals, provided the appeal be demanded within five days after definitive sentence, and such appeal be lodged with the secretary of Congress within forty days afterwards, and provided the party appealing shall give security to prosecute the said appeal to effect, and in case of the death of the secretary during the recess of Congress, then the said appeal to be lodged in Congress within twenty days after the meeting thereof." [1]

Washington, who had meanwhile repeated his suggestion, wrote on hearing of their action, "The resolves relative to captures made by Continental armed vessels only want a court established for trial to make them complete. This, I hope, will be soon done, as I have taken the liberty to urge it often to the Congress." [2]

---

[1] Jour. Cong., i. 184.

[2] Writings of Washington, ed. Sparks, iii. 184, 196, 197. See, also, his letter of December 26 to Richard Henry Lee, Ibid., 217.

This desire of the commander-in-chief was not fulfilled, as we shall see, until a considerably later time. Meanwhile, the recommendation of Congress respecting colonial admiralty courts was soon acted upon by several of the colonies, and eventually by all except New York. Pennsylvania established courts of admiralty, for the trial of cases of capture, before the middle of January, 1776.[1] Rhode Island provided such a court, with trial by jury, in March; New Hampshire, on the 3d of July. South Carolina in April empowered its court of admiralty to have jurisdiction in cases of capture, proceeding under the forms of trial by jury. Connecticut in May gave similar powers, with permission of jury-trial, to her county courts.[2]

Massachusetts, in April, accommodated her practice to the resolutions of Congress, but did so with jealous restriction. She passed an act allowing appeal to Congress in cases of capture by armed vessels fitted out at the charge of the United Colonies; in other cases appeals were to lie to the Superior Court of Massachusetts. New Hampshire made a similar discrimination in her

---

[1] Correspondence of the Revolution: Letters to Washington, ed. Sparks, i. 125; Thomas Lynch to Washington, Philadelphia, January 16, 1776.

[2] Schedules of Rhode Island, Acts of New Hampshire and South Carolina. For the Connecticut measure, a part of the Act for Establishing Naval Offices, I am indebted to the kindness of Charles J. Hoadly, Esq., state librarian.

act of July 3, and even extended the appellate jurisdiction of the Superior Court of the state over cases of capture effected by Continental vessels and vessels of New Hampshire jointly. All these acts, it will have been observed, antedate the Declaration of Independence. New Jersey authorized the establishment of an admiralty court in October, 1776. In the same month Virginia, which already in December, 1775, had provided three admiralty judges to pronounce on seizures of vessels for violating the non-importation agreement, set up an admiralty court, from which prize causes might be appealed in such manner as Congress should provide. The constitutions of Delaware, Maryland, and North Carolina, completed in the autumn and winter of 1776, institute courts of admiralty, or recognize them as already existing.[1] Georgia, which had a prize court in operation as early as November, 1776,[2] by her constitution of February, 1777, provided for the hearing of such causes in future by special county courts, much as in Connecticut.

---

[1] Acts and Resolves of Massachusetts, v. 477; acts and constitutions of other states named. North Carolina passed an act in November, 1777, giving its admiralty court jurisdiction in cases of capture; but the papers of the Court of Appeals, case No. 16, show such a North Carolina court already exercising such jurisdiction.

[2] As appears from the papers of the Court of Appeals, case No. 12.

Most of the states seem from the beginning to have conceded a more or less extensive right of appeal from their courts of admiralty to Congress, or such tribunal as Congress should provide. If South Carolina did not make such concession in its act of April, 1776, it did so in its act of February, 1777.[1] Stray extracts from the proceedings of the North Carolina legislature in April of that year, among the papers of the Court of Appeal, show us the collector of the port of Beaufort applying for the sense of the assembly as to whether he should prosecute an appeal: the Senate votes yea; the House of Commons demurs, but finally consents.[2] Yet as the Revolution went on, and the spirit of '76 declined, and the jealousies of states toward the federal government increased, their legislation in respect to appeals from their own prize courts shows some effort to curtail the powers more generously conceded at the outset. An interesting memorial of this reaction is Rhode Island's act of November, 1780, which, reciting that some states disallow such appeals, and that those who do and those who do not are therefore not on an equal footing, provides that, if any citizen of a state which disallows appeals to Congress is dissatisfied with

---

[1] Cooper gives only the title of this act, saying that the original is not to be found. A printed copy, however, chances to be among the Miscellaneous Papers of the Court of Appeals.

[2] Papers of Court, No. 16.

the judgment of the admiralty court of Rhode Island, he may have an appeal to the Superior Court of the state.[1]

The first appeal which came to Congress from any of these state prize courts was the case of the prize schooner Thistle, which was brought before Congress on the 5th of August, 1776, on appeal from the admiralty court of Philadelphia. This case was speedily referred to a special committee, whose report, reversing the decision of the state court, was approved by Congress in September. After seven cases had been in this manner adjudicated by committees specially appointed in each instance, Congress, on the 30th of January, 1777, appointed a standing committee of five to hear and determine appeals in prize causes, and authorized it to appoint a register. It was this committee, the membership of which was frequently changed, that decided such appeals during the ensuing three years.[2]

It was not until more than five years had elapsed since General Washington's recommendation, that a regular court for the trial of these

---

[1] Rhode Island Schedules.

[2] Journals of Congress, i. 433, 440, 454, 470, 499, 500; ii. 28. The successive changes in the composition of the committee are chronicled by Judge Davis, *op. cit.*, pp. 5, 6. As he also gives, pp. 15-24, a list of all cases decided by the committee and the court, with dates of reference or lodgment and decision, he has made it easy to follow the history of any case. A less correct list is to be found, without details, in Am. Antiq. Soc. Proc., N. S., ii. 120-122.

appeals was in fact erected. How is this preference for trial by committee to be explained? Mainly, no doubt, by that which so frequently made the methods of government under the Old Congress inefficient, namely, the presence of a doubt whether the powers of the federal government extended so far.[1] But as this doubt was in the end overcome, I venture to adduce, in further explanation of the maintenance of the procedure by committee, the example of the appellate prize courts of England. The organization of the court to which, as colonists, they had been accustomed to see prize cases carried on appeal from the colonial vice-admiralty courts, may fairly be supposed to have been in the minds of members of Congress when providing an appellate tribunal for the prize courts of the states.[2]

In early times, appeals from sentences in the English Court of Admiralty were made to the king. In the time of Henry VIII. and Elizabeth

[1] Judge Davis, p. 7, attributes the delay to this cause, suggesting that by January 15, 1780, when the court was erected, the ratification of the Articles of Confederation was *substantially* secured.

[2] The chief source of the ensuing paragraph is a long foot-note to page 293 of F. T. Pratt, Law of Contraband of War, with a Selection of Cases from the Papers of the Rt. Hon. Sir George Lee, LL. D., Dean of the Arches; the note is described as taken from the printed paper in the case of The Bevor, Medina *v.* Morris, January 17, 1735. Also, Browne's Civil and Admiralty Law, ii. 454; Blackstone's Commentaries, iii. 69, 70; Acts 17 Geo. II. c. 34; 29 Geo. II. c. 34.

they were heard by certain judges delegates, appointed by the crown by a commission separately issued for each appeal. At the time of the American Revolution such was still the practice in appeals from the ecclesiastical courts. But in prize cases a change had been effected in 1628. A general commission was issued in that year to the lord treasurer and six other lords of the privy council, constituting them standing commissioners to hear and determine all appeals from the Court of Admiralty in cases of prize. After 1690 these commissions included all the lords of the privy council by name. After 1708 all appeals from the vice-admiralty courts in the colonies went directly to these commissioners to be heard, provided appeal were made within fourteen days after sentence, and security were given that the appeal would be prosecuted.

Accordingly, the most obvious model for those creating a court of appeal from American admiralty courts was the tribunal of the lords commissioners of appeal in prize causes; and one may note, without pressing them too far, the general resemblances between the appellate committee of Congress and the appellate committee of the privy council, — for such the lords commissioners virtually were. Their decisions do not seem to have been reported. But in the library of Brown University there happens to be a large body of papers relating to cases before them,[1] to each of which has been appended a manuscript note of the names of the privy councillors present, and of the decisions rendered. The tribunal appears to have consisted usually of from six to ten councillors, and to have been fairly constant in its composition. The congressional committee seems to have transacted its business in much the same way as this tribunal. Just as the councillors sitting as lords commissioners of appeal did not employ the clerks of the council, but had a registrar of their own, so the members of Congress, sitting as committee of appeals, were authorized, as we have seen, to appoint their own register.[2] It is true that appeals in cases of prize were received and allowed by their lordships without petition to or reference from the king, while the American commissioners seem not to have acted save on reference from Congress. But all that gave importance to this more direct process of the lords commissioners was, that it enabled them to admit new facts, "which is never done in

[1] There is another such collection in the law department of the Library of Congress, and perhaps others elsewhere in old American libraries.

[2] Up to the time of that authorization Charles Thomson, the secretary of Congress, took charge of their papers. Those relating to the second case, that of The Elizabeth, bear the following note from his careful hand: "The papers relative to the trial and appeal of the above-mentioned ship Elizabeth were sent by the post to the secretary of Congress, the postage charged £7 ,, 10 ,, 0, or twenty dollars, which ought to be added to the bill of costs."

the method of proceeding by petition of appeal to his majesty;"[1] and this power the American committee seems to have exercised, in spite of acting only on petition to Congress.[2] And the court which succeeded them acted without such petition and reference.

The bringing of that court into existence seemed for a long time to depend on the fate of the Articles of Confederation, until the complications arising out of one famous case made evident the need of a permanent tribunal invested with greater power and prestige, and caused it to be established some time before the Articles of Confederation were completely ratified. Franklin's draft of those articles, presented in July, 1775, contained no provision in the matter. But a year later the hearing of prize cases had begun, and the need of maintaining a good standing in the eyes of foreign powers by a regular manage-

---

[1] Foot-note in Pratt, Ibid.

[2] Thus, among the papers in case No. 21, White v. The Anna Maria, a Massachusetts case, is a deposition of Timothy Folger, of Nantucket, as to whaling customs, a deposition taken in order to be used before the Committee of Appeals. Among those of No. 28, a Connecticut case, are a considerable number of depositions taken, after the trial in the state court, for use before the commissioners. So in case No. 46. But since the similar depositions in case No. 34 are accompanied by a certificate from Theodore Foster, register of the Court of Admiralty of Rhode Island, to the effect that, after the case there had been concluded, the parties agreed that these evidences should be taken down in writing for use before the committee, it is possible that in the other cases the same was done.

ment of international affairs, was definitely felt. The draft of the Articles, brought in on July 12, 1776, in the handwriting of Dickinson, contains in its eighteenth article the provision that "The United States assembled shall have the sole and exclusive right and power of . . . Establishing the courts for receiving and determining finally appeals in all cases of capture." The committee of the whole reported this clause with no other change than the substitution of "establishing courts" in place of "establishing the courts." On October 23, 1777, during consideration of amendments, the addition of the proviso, "that no member of Congress shall be appointed a judge of the said courts," was moved and carried.[1] In this amended form, the clause became a part of the proposed Articles of Confederation.

Such was the situation with respect to a court of appeal and the power to erect one, when the important case of the sloop Active was brought to the attention of Congress. A case which for more than thirty years continued to disturb the relations between Pennsylvania and the United States deserves a fuller narration than can here be accorded. An outline must suffice. Gideon Olmstead and three other citizens of Connecticut, having been captured by the British and carried to Jamaica, were there put on board the sloop Active, to assist as mariners in navigating it,

[1] Secret Journals of Congress, i. 297, 309, 332.

with a cargo of supplies, to New York, then held by the British. They rose against the master and crew, took command of the sloop, and made for Egg Harbor; but, before they could reach port, they were captured by Captain Thomas Houston, of the Pennsylvanian armed brig Convention, who took the Active into Philadelphia and libelled her as prize to the Convention. A privateersman, cruising in concert with Captain Houston, also claimed a share in the capture, and Olmstead and his fellows interposed a claim to the whole. But the state court of admiralty adjudged them only one fourth, and decreed the rest to be divided between the state, the officers and crew of the Convention, and the owners, officers, and crew of the privateer.

Olmstead and his companions appealed to the federal commissioners of appeal. On December 15, 1778, the commissioners, who at that time were Drayton, Ellery, Ellsworth, and John Henry, reversed the sentence of the state court, and gave judgment in favor of Olmstead and others. Thereupon Judge Ross, of the Pennsylvania Court of Admiralty, recognizing the authority of the Court of Appeals to set aside a decree of an admiralty judge, yet declaring that, as the verdict of the jury in the case still stood, he was unable to disregard its finding, issued an order that the sloop and cargo should be sold, and the proceeds brought into court, to abide its further order;

also a warrant to the marshal to make such sale. The appellants then, on the 28th of December, moved the commissioners that process might issue to the marshal of the admiralty of Pennsylvania, commanding him to execute the decree of the Court of Appeals.

The case was postponed for further argument until the 4th of January, 1779, at five o'clock, P. M. At eight o'clock that morning the court was again convened at the urgent request of Olmstead and others, who informed the commissioners that, in spite of their decree, the judge of the admiralty court had ordered the marshal to deliver the moneys to him at nine o'clock that morning. The day before, at the request of the claimants' counsel, Benedict Arnold, then military commander of Philadelphia, had written to the Court of Appeal a letter, still preserved among the papers of the court, in which he warned them that this plan was on foot, and urged them by all means to defeat it, concluding thus: "Such a daring Attempt as this to evade the Justice of the Superior Court, at a Time too when the Matter is under Consideration, will I doubt not apologize for my troubling you with a Request to meet this Evening at such Time and Place as you may think proper in Order to determine upon what Process shall issue at so early an Hour to-morrow Morning as will tend to the Carrying into Execution the Decree above."

Acceding to the request of the claimants, the court, meeting early in the morning, granted an injunction commanding the marshal to hold the money subject to their order; but he disregarded it, and paid the money over to the admiralty judge. The authority of the United States was thus entirely set at naught. Thereupon the court declared . . . [that] " this Court, being unwilling to enter into any proceedings for Contempt, lest Consequences might ensue at this Juncture dangerous to the public Peace of the United States, will not proceed farther in this affair, nor hear any Appeal, untill the Authority of this Court shall be so settled as to give full Efficacy to their Decrees and Process." They also took steps toward laying the proceedings before Congress.[1]

The details of the subsequent history of this case, interesting as they were, do not fall within the scope of this essay. The moneys having been deposited with David Rittenhouse, Olmstead and others sued his executrixes for them in 1802 in the United States District Court for Pennsylvania. Judge Peters decreed (1803) for the plaintiffs. But the legislature of Pennsylvania passed an act directing the attorney-general to sue the execu-

---

[1] The sources of the foregoing account are, 5 Cranch, 118 et seq.; the papers of the Court of Appeal, case No. 39, and the Papers of the Old Congress, in the library of the Department of State, 29; 351–355. Judge Davis, pp. 11–13, prints Arnold's letter and several other documents in full.

trixes for the money, and the governor to protect them from any federal process whatever. In February, 1809, the claimants having applied to the Supreme Court of the United States for a mandamus to the judge, the matter came before that court in the leading case of The United States *v.* Peters, and Chief Justice Marshall delivered the opinion of the court, that the judgment of the District Court in favor of Olmstead and others must be executed. For some time in the spring of 1809 Pennsylvania troops surrounded the house of the executrixes, to prevent service of the writ. Finally the United States marshal, "with some firmness, much composure, and great address," succeeded in entering the house, afterwards humorously called Fort Rittenhouse, and serving the process.[1] Thus the case of the sloop Active was finally concluded, after thirty years of debate, and with it the long struggle between the authorities of Pennsylvania and those of the federal government.

In 1809 it was easy for the United States to overcome the resistance of Pennsylvania; in 1779 the case presented grave difficulties. The commissioners' report to Congress was successively referred to two committees, and much debated.[2]

---

[1] 5 Cranch, 118 *ss.*; Watson's Annals of Philadelphia, iii. 93; the house was that on the northwest corner of Seventh and Arch streets. Dallas's Dallas, 96. See, also, Ross *v.* Rittenhouse, in 1 Dallas.

[2] Journals of Congress, iii. 195, 219.

The original report of the former of these committees, in the library of the Department of State,[1] differs considerably from the resolutions as finally adopted, especially in stating more strongly than was finally done the incompetence of a state legislature to contravene the supreme executive power of Congress in foreign affairs. The resolutions finally adopted on March 6, with no dissenting voice but that of Pennsylvania and one member from New Jersey, affirmed the right of the Committee of Appeals to examine into decisions on facts as well as decisions on the law; declared that Congress, being invested with the supreme sovereign power of war and peace, and the power of executing the law of nations, must have in prize cases a control by appeal over both judges and juries, as otherwise Congress could not give satisfaction to the complaints of foreign nations; and concluded that the committee in the case of the Active had competent jurisdiction to make a final decree, and that therefore their decree ought to be executed.[2] Three days later the commissioners resumed their sessions, declaring that, Congress having affirmed their claim of jurisdiction, the court, " thereupon having no doubt that their authority would be effectually supported, were now ready to proceed in the dispatch of causes."[3] After conferences, by committee, with

---

[1] Papers of Old Congress, 29 : 356.
[2] Journals of Congress, iii. 219–221.
[3] Papers of the Court, case No. 35.

the Pennsylvania assembly, the latter in the next spring repealed their act as to juries in prize cases.[1]

Meanwhile, public attention had been strongly drawn to the inadequacy of the system. In the report of the committee of Congress a paragraph not finally adopted had read, "Your Committee beg leave to suggest that in the prosecution of the Enquiries referred to them they have discovered some Imperfections in the present system of marine Judicatures, and to recommend to the Congress that the same be revised."[2] This same spring, Spanish remonstrances on the capture of two Spanish ships by privateers of Massachusetts, whose laws allowed no appeal from her courts in such a case, compelled Congress urgently to request the states to conform themselves to its resolutions of March 6.[3] Massachusetts and New Hampshire, with jealous niggardliness, passed acts conceding appeals in cases where subjects of friendly powers were claimants; yet Virginia was meantime restricting appeals to Congress by refusing them in cases between citizens of Virginia.[4]

---

[1] Pennsylvania Act of March 8, 1780.
[2] Papers of Old Congress, 29: 356.
[3] Journal of Congress, iii. 286. The report of a committee, upon which this action was based, is to be found in the Papers of the Old Congress, 29: 371. Its recommendations will be mentioned at a later point.
[4] Massachusetts, June 30, 1779; Acts and Resolves, v. 1077;

In May, moreover, there came a strong appeal from Philadelphia itself, in the form of a petition from many of its chief citizens, forwarded with approval by the council of Pennsylvania. As this petition was doubtless one of the chief causes of the subsequent reforms, and interestingly exposes a phase of public opinion, the latter part of it is here quoted at length. After commending the establishment of a privateering system and of state admiralty courts by recommendation of Congress, the petitioners go on to say:[1] —

"The success of the American privateers exceeded for a time the most sanguine expectation, and in all probability had still continued, if certain causes had not arisen to interrupt it. What these Causes are, we do not mean to enumerate. We shall only suggest one, and leave it to your honors to say what influence it may have had, and to provide a remedy against it in future.

"Certainty in the Laws is the great Source of the people's Security, and an adherence to prior adjudication is the principal means of attaining that certainty. But the Court of Appeals in its present State is continually fluctuating, the same

---

New Hampshire, November 18, 1779, Papers of Old Congress, 44 : 191, 195, 260 ; the legislators say that, until the Confederation comes in, their position, they think, cannot be assailed. On February 26, 1782. South Carolina abolished jury trial in prize cases.

[1] Papers of the Old Congress, 69 : 2: 69; Letter of transmission from President Joseph Reed, of Pennsylvania, to the delegates of Pennsylvania in Congress, May 20, 1779 ; 69 : 2: 65.

Judges seldom acting for more than a few months. In a Court where there is this Constant change and succession of Judges, it is impossible that fixed principles can be established, or the doctrine of precedents ever take place.

"Every obstacle that creates unnecessary delay in the administration of Justice, should be carefully removed, but when the seeds of this delay are sown in the very Constitution of the Court, the People, rather than have recourse to a Tribunal of that kind, will be induced to give up their right. This we apprehend to be the nature of the Court of Appeals. Composed of Members of Congress, it can never sit in any other place than where Congress resides. Hence the parties who attend it are perhaps under the necessity of coming to Congress from the most distant parts of the United States. In the prosecution of a suit under these Circumstances, the expences of the Journey must be enormous, not to mention the time which it must necessarily consume, or the inconveniences to which a person engaged in Trade will be inevitably exposed by an absence from his home. Permit us to add, that a sense of these difficulties may possibly have been the Cause, why the Laws passed in several States, relative to prizes, seem to interfere with the Jurisdiction & Authority claimed by the Court of Appeals, at present established by Congress. In the privateering trade in particular, the very life of which consists in the adventurers receiving the rewards of their Success and Bravery as soon as the Cruize is over, the least delay is uncommonly destructive.

"Sailors soon grow disgusted & quit the Service; whilst the Owners, harrassed with their importunate Demands and unable to comply with them untill the Determination of the cause, are compelled to abandon a Business attended with so many disagreeable Consequences.

"Impressed with these Considerations and others that might be mentioned, [we venture] to point out the propriety of nominating Judges of Appeal, who, not being members of Congress, wou'd have more leisure for the discharge of their employment. We shall only observe that we trust to the Wisdom of Congress to establish the Court of Appeal on a lasting and solid Foundation, and to remove by proper regulations the imperfections that are at present so generally the ground of Complaint."

This petition was signed with sixty-eight names, among which were those of Robert Morris, Blair M'Clenahan, William Bradford, Yelverton Taylor, Thomas Houston, Thomas Fitzsimons, George Ross, James Wilson, and other influential men.

Under the pressure applied in the several ways described, Congress slowly moved toward definite action. It appears that, in the matter of the two

Spanish ships already alluded to, among the resolutions brought in was one recommending that each state pass an act empowering Congress, in advance of the ratification of the Articles of Confederation, to erect a permanent court of appeals; but the resolution does not appear to have passed.[1] Probably Congress felt that they would be taking a stronger position if they assumed the existence of such power, as derived from their "supreme sovereign power of war and peace," in much the same way as the power to hear such appeals by committee of Congress had been; probably also it despaired of securing such action on the part of all thirteen of the states.

This was on May 22, 1779, the same day on which the Philadelphia petition had been read. In December, a draft of an ordinance for establishing a permanent court was finally prepared. It provided that there should be three judges, any two of whom might hold court; that they should have the powers of a court of record in fining and imprisoning for contempt and disobedience; that the court should proceed in accordance with the usage of nations, and not by form of trial by jury; that the state admiralty courts should execute its decrees; that it should sit at Philadelphia first, and afterward elsewhere, provided it were not farther to the east than Hart-

[1] Journals of Congress, iii. 286, compared with Papers of the Old Congress, 29: 371.

ford, or farther to the south than Williamsburgh; that it might appoint a register and a marshal; that appeals should be limited in time, as heretofore; and that a duty of one per cent. should be levied on the appraised value of all prizes coming before the court, out of the proceeds of which, paid into the Continental treasury, each judge should receive a salary of $30,000 per annum.[1]

This draft seems to have proved not wholly acceptable. Probably it was felt that it conferred too high powers upon the court, and assumed too much power in Congress. The draft reported by a committee on January 14, 1780, repeated the provisions for the constitution of the court and its quorum, for the appointment of a register (but not, be it observed, of a marshal), for the observance of the law of nations, and for the arrangement of the places of sessions. It proposed to postpone for a few days the fixing of the salaries of the judges. For the rest, it provided that the states be recommended to pass laws requiring their courts of admiralty to execute this court's decrees, and to decide without a jury in prize cases.[2] In this milder form the resolutions were debated on the 15th. The first four were agreed to. The fixing of the judges' salaries was post-

---

[1] Papers of the Old Congress, 29: 375, "Ordinance for Establishing," etc., endorsed, "December 5, 1779:" a vote, of four states for it and four against, is noted upon it.

[2] Papers of the Old Congress, 29: 379.

poned to July; but in the interim the sum of $12,000 was to be advanced to each of them. The other two resolutions, embodying recommendations to the states, failed of acceptance.[1]

A permanent Court of Appeals was now at last created. On January 22d Congress chose, as the three judges of the court, George Wythe of Virginia, William Paca of Maryland, and Titus Hosmer of Connecticut, and eleven days later adopted a form of commission.[2] Writing to the judges elect on February 1st, Samuel Huntington, president of Congress, after informing each of his election, says: —

"By reason of the present State of the Currency the Salary of the Judges is not yet fixed, yet there is no doubt their Salaries will be decent and satisfactory; at present twelve thousand dollars is to be advanced to each of them for support, that they may immediately enter upon the Business of their Office. . . .

"I hope the Business may not employ so much of your time as to interfere with your other Engagements and deprive the public of your Service in this important Station, as it may be in the power of the Court to state the Time of their session convenient for themselves without Injury to the public.

"I have only to add, the Election of the Judges

[1] Journals of Congress, iii. 425.
[2] Ibid., iii. 427, 429; Papers of the Old Congress, 29: 383.

was with great unanimity, and I trust will give Satisfaction to all the States."¹

Chancellor Wythe having declined, Congress, on April 28th, chose Cyrus Griffin of Virginia in his stead.² Messrs. Paca and Hosmer accepted, but Mr. Hosmer died in August. The court being constituted, resolutions looking to the transference of cases to it were brought in on May 5th. On the 24th a series of resolutions were passed, repealing the sixth section of the resolutions of November 25, 1775, transferring to the new court all appeals then before Congress, providing that henceforth all appeals in cases of capture should be lodged with the register of the new court, and that all papers relating to such appeals then in the office of the secretary of Congress should be by him delivered to the register. The necessary oaths were also provided. In the original resolutions of May 5th, the new tribunal was entitled "The High Court of Appeals in Maritime Causes." But the ordinance which was finally passed styles it "The Court of Appeals in Cases of Capture."³

---

[1] Papers of the Old Congress, 14: 290.

[2] Journals of Congress, iv. 451; Huntington's letter to Griffin, Papers of the Old Congress, 14: 337.

[3] Papers of the Old Congress, 19: 6: 569; 29: 387, 389, 393. Journals of Congress, iii. 459. As registers of the court we have: Andrew Robeson, appointed June 14, 1780 (Papers of the Court, Miscellaneous), who had been at once register to the Committee and register of the admiralty of Pennsylvania (Ibid., Case No. 39); John Potts, appointed July 30, 1781, who was in office at the time of Griffin's letter of January, 1785, i. e. to the temporary suspen-

On September 13, 1780, the salary of the judges was fixed at $2,250 per annum, apparently the highest of the salaries paid to civil officers by Congress.[1] The committee of appeals seems always to have sat in the State House at Philadelphia, and the new court is not known to have sat elsewhere than at Philadelphia before August, 1783.[2]

Messrs. Paca and Griffin presided over the court during its first two years. "This station," says Mr. Paca's biographer, "was new and arduous; it was a branch of law relative to which he could have had no previous opportunity of gaining more than the most loose and general knowledge. . . . His decisions met with the approbation of foreign governments and jurists, and several of them were so much esteemed as to draw from the Count de Vergennes, at that time prime minister of France, an expression of high admiration, which he directed the Chevalier de la Luzerne, the envoy of that nation, to communicate in his name to Mr. Paca."[3] In November,

sion of the court (Papers, Miscellaneous); John D. Coxe, in August, 1786, who on November 7th resigns the office of "one of the registers" of the court; Benjamin Bankson, at New York, November 18, 1786 (Ibid., cases 90 and 104). In the times of the Committee, we find Drayton subscribing himself "President of the Court of Appeal for the United States of America" (Ibid., No. 36).

[1] Journals of Congress, iii. 518.
[2] Papers of the Court, 14, Miscellaneous, 48, 31, 51, 47, 54; 107, 18, 94.
[3] In Sanderson's Lives of the Signers, iv. 122.

1782, Mr. Paca, on becoming governor of Maryland, resigned his judgeship; and on December 5th, George Read of Delaware and John Lowell of Massachusetts were associated to Mr. Griffin as judges, Mr. Read being given precedence by lot.[1]

Meantime, the Articles of Confederation having been fully ratified, a detailed draft of an ordinance for the regulation of the court had been reported to Congress in June, 1781, when a proposal of tenure during good behavior was negatived. It was recommitted in July, with instructions also " to prepare and bring in an ordinance for regulating the proceedings of the admiralty courts of the several states in cases of capture, . . . and to call upon the several legislatures to aid by necessary provisions the powers reserved to Congress by the Articles of Confederation on the subject of captures from the enemy." It was again reported on March 30, 1782.[2] Such was the leisurely habit of Congress. It was ordered that the next Tuesday be assigned for the second reading. But the Journals of Congress seem to contain no further record of the ordinance.

In the absence of such record of the form in which it finally passed, an interest attaches to the

[1] Journals of Congress, iv. 109, 112, 119; Elias Boudinot, president of Congress, to Read and Lowell (Papers of the Old Congress, 16: 160, 163). The former also in W. T. Read, Life and Correspondence of George Read, 378.

[2] Journals of Congress, iii. 639, 647, 648, 740 (Papers of the Old Congress, 29: 375, 397).

information which George Read's brother sent him from Philadelphia, while his nomination was being talked of. Fitzsimons, he says, who had broached it to him, and who a few days later nominated Mr. Read, "said it seemed to be generally agreed that the Eastern States should furnish one of the judges, and the Middle States the other. . . . The salary is six hundred pounds per annum, and he said it would not require above six or eight weeks at most in the year to perform all the duties. There are three stated sessions annually, viz., one at Hartford, Conn., and at this place, and one in Virginia; but it is very seldom there is business to occasion all these meetings." Again, in response to further inquiries, he writes: "I am told the judges are paid as part of the civil list; all which, I am told, receive pretty regular quarterly payments."[1] In March, 1783, a committee of Congress reported an arrangement of sessions in accordance with which the court was to sit at Philadelphia on the first Monday in May, at Hartford on the first Monday in

[1] Read's Read, 375-378. Mr. Read also had other shrewd apprehensions: "If fixed for the Middle Department, it would fall to my lot to attend at each stated session in the Eastern, Middle, and Southern Department; as, for instance, the Eastern judge would readily find an excuse for not serving in Virginia, and so the Southern judge in Connecticut." It seems strange that he should have to inquire the name of the Southern judge then on the bench. — Six hundred pounds of Pennsylvania or Delaware money would be only sixteen hundred dollars; the salary must therefore have been reduced.

August, and at Richmond on the first Monday in November; and this arrangement seems to have been adopted, at least for that year.[1]

It is obviously impossible to discuss here the various cases decided by the court, though two of them were afterwards important as cases in the Supreme Court of the United States, the cases of Penhallow v. Doane and Jennings v. Carson, the former of which, in 1795, settled the jurisdiction of the Court of Appeals.[2] Judge Davis computes that "sixty-five cases in all were submitted to the Committees of Congress, of which forty-nine were decided by them, four seem to have disappeared, and twelve went over to the Court of Appeals for decision;" and that "fifty-seven cases in all, including the twelve which went over, were submitted to the Court of Appeals, and all were disposed of." Eight more of its cases are reported in 2 Dallas,[3] making one hundred and eighteen in all. In its mode of proce-

[1] Papers of the Old Congress, 29: 397. The court sat at Philadelphia in May, 1783 (Papers of the Court, case No. 94); at Hartford in August (No. 89); at Philadelphia in September and October, 1783 (Nos. 102 and 107); at Philadelphia again in May, 1784 (Ibid., case of The Ersten; and 2 Dallas, 40).

[2] 3 Dallas, 54; 4 Cranch, 2.

[3] J. C. Bancroft Davis, pamphlet already cited, p. 14; 2 Dallas, 1-42. There may have been other cases; a few of those upon the list in the Proceedings of the American Antiquarian Society, New Series, ii. 120-122, are not at first sight identical with those now among the papers of the court; but this seems to be owing to errors, easily committed before Judge Davis's arrangement of the papers.

dure, there was nothing demanding mention except, perhaps, its manner of obtaining evidence in certain cases. As in the case of its English prototype, and as had apparently been the case with the commissioners who had preceded it, additional evidence to that heard in the court below was admitted in the Court of Appeals. In one case, at least, witnesses were heard in open court. For other cases, it was the practice of the court to appoint two or three commissioners in each state to examine witnesses upon the interrogatories sent them, to reduce their replies to writing, and to send these depositions to the court.[1]

The business of the court dwindled after the termination of the war. Hamilton, it is interesting to find, during his brief term of service in Congress, made a characteristic attempt to prolong the life of this federal institution, feeling doubtless that any such institution was, for "continental" reasons, too valuable to be allowed to expire. He moved a resolution which, approving in the general case the forty days' limit upon appeals, allowed the judges to entertain an appeal, in cases in which they thought it proper, after the expiration of the forty days, provided it were less than three years after the sentence of the state court. This motion was referred to a committee on June 2, 1783; the committee reported adversely, declaring that in their opinion

[1] Papers of the Court, Nos. 88, 92, 93, 104.

the measure would work more injustice than it would prevent.[1]

The remainder of the history of the court is characteristic of the Confederation. At the end of their May session at Philadelphia in 1784, the judges informed Congress that all the cases submitted to them had been disposed of. The letter, written after May 24th, failed to reach Congress, which adjourned at Annapolis on June 3d. It reassembled at Trenton at the end of November, and on December 23d Mr. Griffin and Mr. Lowell addressed to its president the following letter:[2] —

"SIR: We had the Honour immediately after our last Sitting to inform Congress by a Letter directed to the President that all the Causes which had been brought before the Court of Appeals were determined, & altho some Motions had been made for Rehearings, they had not been admitted; Since that Time no farther Applications have been made to us; of this we also think it our duty to inform Congress, that they may make such Order concerning the Court as they may think proper."

[1] Papers of the Court, case of The Ersten, and Miscellaneous Papers.

[2] Journals of Congress, iv. 447, 448. The court was in session May 24th (2 Dallas, 40). Mr. Griffin writes to Mr. Read, at a later date: "It is very extraordinary that Congress never received the joint letter we wrote them upon the subject of the court when they sat at Annapolis. Mr. Lowell and myself were compelled to repeat it at Trenton, without even having an opportunity to consult you." Read's Read, 419. The December letter is to be found among the Papers of the Court, Miscellaneous.

This letter seems to have been at once referred to a committee, consisting of Messrs. King, R. R. Livingston, Beatty of New Jersey, Monroe, and C. Pinckney. On January 20, 1785, Mr. Griffin wrote from Philadelphia to some one of the members of this committee, Congress having meantime adjourned to New York, the following letter: —

"I take the freedom, my dear Sir, to mention a circumstance which was omitted in the short conversation you did me the honor to hold about the Court of appeals.

"Our register, Mr. John Potts, has been very punctual in the discharge of his duty; no emolument of any consideration or certainty was annexed to the office; the time and abilities of a worthy young man will not be disregarded by Congress; a thousand dollars for some years' services cannot be thought enormous, would be perfectly agreeable, and give pleasure to those who employed him.

"If a probability of war in Europe does not induce Congress to continue the Court of Admiralty, to decide upon prizes which may be brought into the American ports, which probability your superior Judgment and better Information can more clearly establish or reprobate, yet we flatter ourselves the Court of the union will not be abolished in a few months without some little compliment of approbation to the members of it. If we deserve such a compliment for our assiduity, &c., the favorable notice of your illustrious Body will give us particular satisfaction, and must operate greatly to our advantage in adopting some other pursuit of life to maintain our families. I am candid enough to confess my anxiety upon this subject, my personal character is deeply concerned, and being obliged to live in this expensive City during the Contest my slender property is almost annihilated; therefore the honorable opinion of your Committee and of Congress would to me in particular be very highly interesting.

"Will you have the goodness to present me with great respect and esteem to the other Gentlemen upon the same business, and if you can excuse the length and indelicacy of this letter, I hope you will consider me, with the highest regard, your most obedient humble servant,

"C. GRIFFIN."[1]

A motion for putting the court upon an allowance per diem, and several petitions for rehearings, were referred to the same committee. Its report was read and recommitted in April, Mr. Johnson of Connecticut being now substituted for Mr. Beatty. In June it reported, "That in

---

[1] Papers of the Court, Miscellaneous. The prospect of European war, to which Judge Griffin alludes, arose from the aggressions of the Emperor Joseph II. upon the Netherlands. The Empress of Russia notified to the States-General her intention of siding with the Emperor, and for a time a European war seemed inevitable, but it was averted by the Treaty of Fontainebleau in 1785.

the opinion of your committee the present judges of the court of appeal must be still considered as in commission, no information having been communicated to Congress of their intention to resign, and that it will be necessary the court of appeal should remain upon their present establishment, except with respect to the salaries of the judges, which should cease from the   Day of   , and that in lieu thereof they shall be entitled to   dollars per day during the time they shall attend the sitting of the courts, and including the time they shall be necessarily employed in travelling to and from the said courts;" that the judges should be notified, and that they should be authorized to grant the desired rehearings if they thought it right. On July 1, 1785, Congress took up this report, negatived a substitute of Mr. King's abolishing the court, and recommitted the report; but, on motion of Melancthon Smith of New York, resolved that the salaries of the judges should thenceforth cease.[1]

Secretary Thomson communicated this resolution to the judges. Judge Griffin, who afterward intimated to Mr. Read that "a little party business had predominated in the affair," remonstrated in January, 1786, and Congress, in response, on the ninth of February, resolved, —

---

[1] Motion of Mr. Howell, March 28, 1785, and other minutes, in Papers of the Court. Miscellaneous; Papers of the Old Congress. 28: 205; Journals of Congress, iv. 543, 514.

"That Congress are fully impressed with a sense of the ability, fidelity, and attention of the judges of the court of appeals in the discharge of the duties of their office; but that as the war was at an end, and the business of that court in a great measure done away, an attention to the interests of their constituents made it necessary that the salaries of the judges should cease."[1]

This emollient to irritated feelings was not wholly effectual, at least in Mr. Griffin's case, especially when Congress, in the ensuing summer, finding new business arisen, summoned the judges to renew their sessions. On June 27, 1786, they authorized and directed the judges to sustain appeals and grant rehearings and new trials whenever justice in their opinion required it; voted them ten dollars a day during session and travel to and from it; and directed them to assemble for transaction of such business at New York on the first Monday in November. The secretary of Congress was directed to publish these resolutions for the information of all concerned. He did so extensively, taking measures to have the resolutions republished in the newspapers of all the states, and notified the judges.[2] When au-

---

[1] Thomson to Griffin, Read, and Lowell, July 5, 1785, and March 1, 1786; Papers of the Old Congress, 18: A: 106, and 18: B: 31; Griffin to Read, August 29, 1786, in Read's Read, 419; Journals of Congress, iv. 617.

[2] Papers of the Old Congress, 28: 201, 215; 122: 56, 57; Journals of Congress, iv. 656; Thomson to Read, in Read's Read,

tumn came, two of the judges found it seriously inconvenient to attend at the designated time. Mr. Read had been a member of the Annapolis Convention in September. The legislature of Delaware was to meet at the end of October, and he, as the sole commissioner of the state at Annapolis who had a seat in the legislative council, conceived that, in view of the important action recommended by that convention, his presence in the assembly of the state was of great and general importance. Mr. Griffin also, as he had learned from the latter's brother in Baltimore, did not intend to go to New York until after the rising of the Virginia Assembly, which would sit in November, and of which he was a member. Mr. Read therefore wrote to Thomson, begging that, under the circumstances, there might be a postponement until the end of November or the beginning of December.[1]

The secretary replied that the judges must come, as notice of the session had been widely disseminated; and a session of the court was in fact held in November, 1786.[2] Thus again called into activity, the Court of Appeals in Cases of Capture held, beside this, two other sessions. A

416, 417; Papers of the Old Congress, 18 : B : 60, 65. *E. g.*, Virginia Gazette, July 19, 1786.

[1] Read to Thomson, October 7, 1786, Read's Life, 421–423.

[2] Thomson to Read, October 24th, Papers of Old Congress, 18 : B: 103. Bankson's appointment as register (Papers of the Court, No. 104) is of November 18, 1786.

memorandum among its papers enumerates them as follows: "Three several Sittings of the said Court of Appeal have been had to wit The first of them on the first Monday in Nov^r, in the Year 1786 — at the City of New York — the Second on the twenty fifth day of April in the Year 1787 at the said City of New York and the Third on the Eighth day of May then next ensuing at the City of Philadelphia and on the 16th of the same Month the said Court of Appeals finally adjourned without day."[1]

Two days before, the memorable convention had met which provided the United States with a more comprehensive and more effective judiciary. Some three months after the new government had been inaugurated, Secretary Thomson delivered into the hands of Washington, along with the great seal of the federal union, the "Seal of the Admiralty."[2] By Act of Congress, May 8, 1792, it was provided that all the records and proceedings of the Court of Appeal should be deposited in the office of the Supreme Court of the United States. It would appear that some of its judicial experience, also, had been handed

---

[1] Papers of the Court, No. 89; also, case of The Ersten. The second session, at New York, continued to May 3d; case of The Chester, in which Hamilton appeared for the appellants, 2 Dallas, 41.

[2] Washington to Thomson, July 24th, Thomson to Washington, July 25, 1789, in the New York Historical Society's Collections, 1878.

over to the new court. In a foot-note to Mr.
Harrison Gray Otis's remembrances of Judge
Lowell, printed in 1847 in the Law Reporter, Dr.
Charles Lowell says of his father: "I have the
sketch of a letter of his on the judiciary system
of the United States, about which his opinion and
counsel had been asked, as I think, by a committee of Congress."[1] It is matter of great regret that this paper is apparently no longer in
existence, for it is altogether probable that the
occasion of its preparation was the deliberation
in 1789 respecting the organization of the judiciary under the new government, and that thus
the experience gained in the conduct of the earlier federal court had an influence upon the formation of its more comprehensive and more powerful successor.

However this may be, it cannot be doubted
that the Court of Appeals, though, as remarked
by counsel in Jennings v. Carson,[2] "unpopular in
those states which were attached to trial by jury,"
had an educative influence in bringing the people
of the United States to consent to the establishment of such a successor. It could hardly be that
one hundred and eighteen cases, though all in one

---

[1] Law Reporter, xi. 429. The Massachusetts Archives formerly contained a letter written by Senator Caleb Strong to Lowell in 1789, now missing, which may very likely have been the one which elicited his letter above mentioned; for Strong was a member of the Senate committee which framed the Judiciary Act.

[2] 4 Cranch, 9.

restricted branch of judicature, should be brought by appeal from state courts to a federal tribunal, without familiarizing the public mind with the complete idea of a superior judicature, in federal matters, exercised by federal courts. The Court of Appeals in Cases of Capture may therefore be justly regarded, not simply as the predecessor, but as one of the origins, of the Supreme Court of the United States.

NOTE.

THE MODEL OF THE FEDERAL COURT FOR TERRITORIAL DISPUTES.

The ninth of the Articles of Confederation provides that, in cases of dispute between states respecting boundary and jurisdiction, and of dispute between individuals concerning the private right of soil claimed under different grants of two or more states, the agents of the parties shall first be directed by Congress to appoint, by joint consent, judges or commissioners who shall, as a court, hear and determine the matter. When the parties cannot thus agree upon arbiters, " Congress shall name three persons out of each of the United States, and from the list of such persons each party shall alternately strike out one, the petitioners beginning, until the number shall be reduced to thirteen; and from that number not less than seven nor more than nine names, as Congress shall direct, shall, in the presence of Congress, be drawn out by lot; and the persons whose names shall be so drawn, or any five of them, shall be commissioners or judges to hear and finally determine the controversy."

It seems obvious that we have here a reproduction of the machinery provided by Mr. Grenville's famous Act of 1770 for the trial of disputed elections to the House of Commons. Up to that time, disputed elections had for nearly a century been passed upon by the whole House. The natural result of such a procedure was a scandalous disregard of justice, those contestants who belonged to the majority party being uniformly admitted, their competitors as uniformly rejected. To remedy this abuse Mr. Grenville's act provided that forty-nine members should be chosen by ballot, and that from this list the petitioner and the sitting member should strike out names alternately until the number was reduced to thirteen, — a process which later became known, in the slang of the House, as " knocking out the brains of the committee," each contestant excluding any able man likely to assist the cause of his opponent. These thirteen, with an additional member nominated by each contestant, constituted the authoritative tribunal. The act, celebrated at the time, was of course perfectly well known to lawyers in America six years after its passage. It seems plain that, with the natural substitution of thirty-nine for forty-nine, we have, in this peculiar process established shortly before in England, the model on which Congress framed its scheme for constituting temporarily a judiciary body when one was required for land disputes.

THE MOVEMENT TOWARDS A SECOND CONSTITUTIONAL CONVENTION IN 1788.

BY EDWARD P. SMITH.

"The American Constitution," says Mr. Gladstone, giving utterance to what is probably the common impression respecting its origin, "is the most wonderful work ever struck off at a given time by the brain and purpose of man."[1]

These words suggest unanimity; they give no hint of strenuous struggles to secure, or of unremitting efforts to change, that Constitution; they ignore the fact of its speedy amendment.

Of unanimity there was a painful lack in the Federal Convention. It was needful for Franklin to remind the delegates that they were sent "to consult, not to contend, with each other." In his celebrated "Letter to the Maryland Legislature," Luther Martin mentions " near a fortnight, during which we were on the verge of dissolution, scarce held together by the strength of an hair, though the papers were announcing our extreme unanimity."[2] The delegates were not agreed as to the real work before them, or as to the extent of

[1] "Kin Beyond the Sea," North American Review, 126: 185.
[2] Elliot's Debates, i.: 358.

their powers. When a decision was reached as to their work, they differed in respect to the measures to be employed for its performance; and as to the nature of the instrument they at length framed and adopted, they held widely divergent views.

The differing opinions of the delegates concerning the extent of their powers and the real task before them were at the outset disclosed and embodied in two rival propositions, — the national or Virginia plan of Governor Randolph, and the federal or New Jersey plan of Mr. Paterson. Between these rival plans there could be no compromise, and no effort was made to blink the square issue between them in the debate that for five consecutive days ranged about them.

The decision of the Convention in favor of Randolph's resolutions did not secure full acquiescence. The governor of New York, George Clinton, had unreservedly declared that no good was to be expected from the deliberations at Philadelphia; and after the Convention had decided in favor of the Connecticut compromise, Messrs. Lansing and Yates, who shared Clinton's views, withdrew, and declared in a public letter to their governor that they could take no further part in the proceedings without exceeding their delegated authority, and assenting to measures which they conceived destructive of the political happiness of the people of the United States.[1] Luther Martin of Maryland held these same views with even more intense feeling, and with an almost fanatic energy, but he remained in the Convention till near its close, and ably lifted up his voice for the Confederation. At last, leaving the body forever with one of his colleagues rather than sign the Constitution, he told the Maryland legislature, in the "Genuine Information" he laid before them, that the delegates "appeared totally to have forgotten the business for which they were sent."[2]

The work of the Convention was revolutionary. In a secret conclave, the ablest men of the nation were seeking to invest the central government with those sovereign powers which the individual states had usurped. Yet these men, whom Jefferson called "an assembly of demigods," while framing revolutionary measures, were not revolutionary in spirit. In setting their faces toward the future, they showed no forgetfulness or disdain of the past. They did not break with their own history. The Federal Convention had assembled on the recommendation of Congress. That Congress was in session, and some of its members were at the same time delegates to the Philadelphia Convention. The members of the

---

[1] Letter of Lansing and Yates to Governor Clinton, Elliot's Debates, i.: 480.

[2] Luther Martin's Letter, Elliot's Debates, i.: 389.

Convention sat as delegates of the states and voted by states, the majority of the delegation casting the single vote of the state. Some of these delegates had assisted in framing the Articles of Confederation. Nevertheless, this council of the states, this Federal Convention, in providing for the future, did not hesitate to repudiate the very basis upon which itself was formed. It refused to admit the principle of a confederation of states; it declared for a national union. The success of the proposed plan would give the *coup de grace* to the sinking Confederation. This change from a treaty of states to a national constitution was made with the utmost deliberation, and with opposition at every step by the adherents of the old system. This change was no *coup d'état;* it was peacefully accomplished, but it was none the less a revolution.

To recount the diversity of the views among the delegates, as to the measures they should devise to achieve their task, would require an account of the long, earnest, and passionate debates, the compromises, the reconciliation of conflicting aims, and the surrender by the different states of one cherished scheme after another, till the Constitution as embraced in its seven articles emerged. As it came from the hands of its framers it completely satisfied none of them. Just before it was signed Hamilton said: "No man's ideas are more remote from the plan than mine own are known to be."[1] Franklin and Washington, like Gouverneur Morris, considered the plan "the best that could be obtained, and took it with all its faults."[2] The majority of the signers felt, as Hamilton expressed it, that it was a choice "between anarchy and convulsion on the one side and the *chance* of good to be expected from the plan on the other."[3] Within a week after adjournment Madison wrote: "I hazard an opinion that the plan, should it be adopted, will neither effectually answer its national object, nor prevent the local mischiefs which excite disgust against the state governments."

If unanimity did not prevail among the delegates as to their powers, their task, their measures, or the results they had wrought; if "the Father of the Constitution," as well as the majority of the signers, felt so little satisfaction in the instrument, — it is not singular that persistent efforts were made to change it. These efforts began in the Philadelphia Convention itself. When the Convention had decided not to suspend the plan of the Convention upon the approbation of Congress, Randolph, whose resolutions had been the basis of the Convention's work, began to speak of the Constitution as a plan which would end in tyranny. He proposed that the state conventions, on receiving it, should have

---

[1] Madison Papers, iii. 1601.   [2] Ibid., 1600.
[3] Ibid., iii. 1601.

power to adopt, reject, or amend it; after which another general convention should meet with full power to adopt or reject the proposed alterations, and to establish finally the government.[1]

This motion Franklin seconded, and out of respect to its authors this, the first distinct proposition for amendments and for a second federal convention, was allowed to remain on the table. This action on Randolph's part was due to changes which his resolutions had undergone in the Convention, and to the anti-republican shape which he believed the Constitution was assuming. His efforts to make the state and federal powers distinct and unmistakable the Convention withstood. Yet he remained at his post, secured modifications that have been generally approved, and occupied a vantage-ground from which he could powerfully urge future amendments. He agreed to sign if provision for a second convention were made after the new instrument had been discussed. He again moved "that state conventions might have power to offer to the Constitution to be laid before them as many amendments as they pleased, and that these amendments, together with the Constitution, should be submitted to another general convention"[2] for a final decision.

Randolph's motion was warmly seconded by his colleague, George Mason, who was greatly

---

[1] Madison Papers, ii. 1512.
[2] Ibid., iii. 1593.

discontented with the grant of power to a bare majority of Congress to pass navigation acts. "A second convention," said Mason, "will know more of the sense of the people, and be able to provide a system more consonant with it. It is improper to say to the people, 'Take this or nothing.' The government established by this Constitution will surely end either in anarchy or in a tyrannical aristocracy. As it now stands, I can neither give it my support in Virginia, nor my vote here. With the expedient of another convention I could sign."[1] Charles Pinckney shared Mason's objections to the power of a majority of Congress over commerce, yet expressed his readiness to sign the instrument and opposed the calling of a second convention. "The states," he said, "will never agree in their plans, and the deputies to a second convention coming together under the discordant impressions of their constituents will never agree. Conventions are serious things and ought not to be repeated."[2] Elbridge Gerry could not subscribe to a Constitution giving the legislature the general power to make "necessary and proper" laws, to raise "armies and money without limit," and to establish "a star chamber as to civil cases," and he conceived that the best that could be done was to provide for a second convention.[3]

[1] Madison Papers, iii. 1593. [2] Ibid., 1591.
[3] Ibid., 1595.

The nature of the Constitution, and the form in which it was to be submitted to the people of each state, made it necessary that they should accept or reject it as a whole. As provision had been made in the instrument itself that amendments might proceed from the people as represented in the legislatures of the states, or from the people as represented in Congress, or from the people as present in a convention, a second general convention seemed unnecessary to the delegates. For when the vote was taken on Randolph's motion for amendments by the states, and for a second federal convention, all the states answered "No."

On the day of adjournment, Franklin, who had seconded Randolph's original motion for another convention, made a final effort to win over the dissenting delegates. He said he doubted whether any convention that could be obtained could make a better Constitution, and offered a form of attestation put into his hands by Gouverneur Morris.[1] It contained no personal approbation of the system, but was a simple statement that the Constitution had received the unanimous consent of all the states present. To this members could append their names without relinquishing their personal scruples. But this ample concession failed to secure the signatures of Randolph, Mason, and Gerry. The delegations from Massachusetts and

[1] Madison Papers, iii. 1598, 1599.

Virginia had cloven apart, and the prestige that would have been gained for the Constitution by actual unanimity among the delegates in signing was lost.

To Congress, as a matter of form and respect, the Constitution must be submitted before it could be acted upon by the states. Three days after its signature, September 20, 1787, the Constitution, together with the resolutions of the Federal Convention and a letter from its president, George Washington, was laid before Congress in New York. This body, whose sanction of the new Constitution would have greatly facilitated its adoption by the states, owed its continued existence to the Articles of Confederation. The new system of government proposed by the Constitution would not merely alter, but would abolish and supersede, the Confederation. It was a ticklish procedure to ask Congress to countenance measures the success of which would put an end to its existence. Fortunately, eighteen of the delegates to the Federal Convention were members also of Congress, and were not, therefore, much startled by this virtual invitation to Congress to light its own funeral pyre. Before applying the torch, however, there was much for Congress to do.

On their return from Philadelphia, Madison and his fellow-delegates found the technical objection raised that Congress could with no propriety countenance any measure designed to change the form of government they were appointed to administer. To this flimsy objection answer was fittingly made that the necessity which had justified Congress in recommending the Federal Convention, "as the most probable means of establishing a firm national government," justified now the countenance of the new plan presented by that Convention; and that necessity existed, if any faith was due to the representations of Congress themselves. The delegates were, however, content to secure the unanimous passage of a resolution by Congress to transmit the new Constitution without either approval or disapproval to the state legislatures, to be in turn submitted by them to state conventions. But the unanimity thus secured had reference, as Richard Henry Lee significantly indicated in his letter to Governor Randolph, only to the transmission to the state legislatures.[1]

For in Congress the Constitution met with instant opposition and a new proposal for amendments. Richard Henry Lee, the mover of the Declaration of Independence eleven years before, wished to insert a bill of rights, a provision for trial by jury in civil cases, and the requisition of more than a majority to determine commercial regulations, in conformity with the objections of

[1] Letter of Richard Henry Lee to Edmund Randolph, Elliot's Debates, i. 505.

George Mason in the Federal Convention.[1] Fatal as these amendments would have been to New York's commercial prosperity, Melancthon Smith of that state nevertheless warmly supported Lee's motion, and insisted that Congress had the undoubted right and duty to amend the plan of the Convention, in which the essential safeguards of liberty had been omitted. Congress could, indeed, propose to amend the Articles of Confederation, but such proposed amendments must be ratified by the state legislatures, while the Constitution was to be ratified by the state conventions.

It was chiefly by Madison's skill and address that this motion to amend in Congress was defeated. Had Lee's effort succeeded, it would probably have brought to nought all the anxious toils of the Federal Convention. Two instruments, one the work of the Federal Convention, the other the work of Congress, would have been before the state legislatures and conventions for their ratification, and the acts of these bodies would have related to different instruments. From such a scene of chaos and collision, Mr. Madison said, " confusion and disappointment would be the least evils that would ensue." [2]

The Constitution having passed unscathed these perils in Congress, had now to run the still more

---

[1] Madison Papers, ii. 644.
[2] Rives's Madison, ii. 480; Madison Papers, ii. 645.

dangerous gauntlet of the state conventions. In his letter transmitting the Constitution to Congress, Washington had written: "That it will meet the full and entire approval of every state is not perhaps to be expected." There was abundant justification for this statement. Rhode Island had taken no part in the Federal Convention. Ten of the delegates elected to that assembly had never taken their seats. Early in the Convention, Messrs. Yates and Lansing from New York had withdrawn, and toward the close Luther Martin of Maryland had retired in disgust. Messrs. Randolph and Mason of Virginia, and Mr. Gerry of Massachusetts, had refused to put their names to the instrument. More than one fourth, sixteen out of the fifty-five members, had refused or neglected to sign the Constitution. One morning, in a desultory conversation before taking the chair, Washington had observed how unhappy it would be if any of the members of the Federal Convention should oppose the system when they returned to their states. Luther Martin replied that he was confident that the system under consideration was of such a nature that he could never recommend it for acceptance, and thought the State of Maryland never ought to adopt it, and expressed his firm belief that it never would.[1]

There was little doubt that these dissenting

---

[1] Letter of Luther Martin in the Maryland Journal of March 21, 1788.

delegates would endeavor to justify themselves and seek to win public opinion in their favor. The battle which had been fought out in the Federal Convention was to be renewed in the state conventions, and in some of them to rage with peculiar violence. For in spite of the widely felt need of a stronger central government, the majority of the people in the United States in 1787 probably held views more in consonance with the ideas of state sovereignty. There were many who regarded federal authority in the light of a foreign government, and transferred to it the hostility they had felt toward the mother country under the colonial régime; others confounded a central with a consolidated government; still others were in favor of the establishment of three or more distinct confederacies, believing that the economic interests of the different sections could only in this way be best promoted. Those debauched by paper-money tender laws, and other fraudulent expedients for avoiding their obligations, regarded with disfavor a constitution proscribing in advance such inventions. It was among these various opponents that the project for a second federal convention found favor.

Washington was intensely anxious for the adoption of the new Constitution. On his return to Mount Vernon from the Federal Convention he had promptly transmitted copies of the Constitution to Patrick Henry, Benjamin Harrison, and Thomas Nelson, each of whom had been governor of Virginia.[1] By an appeal to their own experience as governors, he sought to secure their favor for the new instrument. Each of them in his answer, while avowing great respect for Washington, had expressed his repugnance to the new Constitution.[2] Patrick Henry, Nelson, and Richard Henry Lee had all refused to be delegates to the Federal Convention. Richard Henry Lee in Congress had waylaid Gerry on his return from the Federal Convention, and had helped him in the preparation of an official letter explaining to the Massachusetts legislature his refusal to sign the Constitution. Lee also wrote to Samuel Adams, "that dear friend with whom he had toiled so long in the vineyard of liberty," and to his wisdom and patriotism submitted objections to the Constitution.

Nor did Lee's efforts end here. Baffled in his attempt to amend the Constitution while in Congress, Lee had appealed to the public through the press in a series of "Letters from the Federal Farmer." These were circulated by thousands in the central states. They were designed to counteract the powerful impression the papers of Publius were producing, and to delay the decisions in Pennsylvania and Delaware.

In a letter to Washington written October 11,

---

[1] Sparks's Washington, ix. 265–267.
[2] Rives's Madison, ii. 532.

1787, Lee expressed the wish "that such amendments as would give security to the rights of human nature, and the discordant interests of the different parts of this Union, might employ another convention."[1] A fortnight later Lee wrote to Governor Randolph recommending, as a policy open to "no objection and promising great safety and much good,"[2] that amendments adopted severally by the states should all be definitely referred to a second federal convention. In the Virginia legislature resolutions were introduced on the 30th of November, 1787, to carry out this policy, and were strongly supported by Henry and Mason. Into the act calling a convention to act upon the Constitution was introduced a contingent provision for defraying the expenses that would attend representation of the state in another general convention, or communications with the conventions of other states, for the purpose of procuring amendments to the Constitution before its final ratification, if such amendments should be deemed expedient by the convention of Virginia.[3] The success of this measure indicated a marked change in the sentiments of the legislature, due to the influence of Henry, Mason, and Lee. Such a provision looking forward to

[1] Letters to Washington, iv. 180, 181.
[2] Life of R. H. Lee, ii. 81; Elliot's Debates, i. 505.
[3] Hening, xii. 462; Journal of the House of Delegates of Virginia (session of 1787), pp. 77, 81.

another federal convention led Madison to write: "Mr. Henry is the great adversary who will render the event precarious. He is, with his usual address, working up every possible interest into a spirit of opposition."[1]

This law, with its provision looking forward to a second general convention, the Virginia legislature directed Governor Randolph to transmit to the governors of the other states, to be laid before their legislatures. This was to furnish an occasion for an interchange of opinions between the several states. The act was sent to each governor on December 27, 1787. The one mailed Governor Clinton did not reach its destination till March 7, 1788.[2] The delay was fortunate for the Federalists. No explanation has ever been given for an event so momentous in its results. The delay was just sufficient to prevent the New York legislature from acting upon the Virginia letter, and also to prevent Clinton from making any communication to the Virginia Assembly, which had adjourned before Randolph's letter was received. Had this action of Virginia been known in time, New York would have responded with an offer of coöperation, and a second general convention would have been inevitable.

This action of the Virginia legislature was in the line that Randolph had urged in the Federal

---

[1] Rives's Madison, ii. 541; Madison Letters, i. 364, 365.
[2] Conway's Edmund Randolph, p. 110.

Convention, and again in a letter to the speaker of the House of Delegates in Virginia. Many expedients, he said, were proposed to remedy the defects in the Constitution, but none brought forward by the delegates was less exceptionable than this: "that, if our convention choose to amend, another federal convention be recommended; that in that federal convention the amendments proposed by this or any other state be discussed, and if incorporated in the Constitution or rejected, or if a proper number of the other states should be unwilling to accede to a second convention, the Constitution be again laid before the same state conventions, which shall again assemble on the summons of the executive, and it shall be either wholly adopted or wholly rejected, without a further power of amendment."[1]

As Madison had by his arguments and persuasions led Randolph to abandon the belief that the Confederation could be so amended as to possess the requisite energy for the needs of the nation, and had induced the Virginia governor to take a foremost part in the Federal Convention, so it was for Madison to dissuade him from the scheme for a second federal convention. In a letter written to him on January 10, 1788, Madison said: "A second convention would of course be formed under the influence, and composed in a

[1] Governor Randolph's Letter to the Speaker of the Virginia House of Delegates, Elliot's Debates, i. 490.

great measure, of the members in opposition in the several states. . . . The very attempt at a second convention strikes at the confidence in the first; and the existence of a second, by opposing influence to influence, would in a measure destroy an effectual confidence in either."[1]

Washington no less than Madison addressed himself to win Randolph to the advocacy of the Constitution. On the decision of this governor much depended. He hesitated long before finally resolving to advocate unconditional ratification. He saw no possibility of obtaining amendments without endangering the Union. Randolph saw that the Constitution would preserve and strengthen the Union, and when everything was reduced to the question of Union or no Union, he entered the lists as its powerful defender.

New York city, then the seat of Congress, became the centre of the agitation caused by the new Constitution. The party in power in the state was passionately opposed to ratification. They hated the new instrument from beginning to end. It was wise for the triumvirs, Hamilton, Madison, and Jay, to publish in the public prints of New York the articles subsequently published under the title of "The Federalist." Here their greatest efforts were imperatively needed. No other state required a strong general government more

[1] Madison Papers, ii. 662, 663, Letter of Madison to Randolph.

than New York, but under the lead of George Clinton none was more obstinate in its opposition. This state, which had acted with magnanimity through the War of the Revolution, had now fallen under the sway of factious selfishness. Her unrivalled advantages for trade secured her the certainty of ample revenue by imposts, and the power of levying tribute on her neighbors. Clinton had long been at the head of affairs in the state, and he wished to retain these advantages for New York. By his social prestige and official patronage, he had dealt a staggering blow to the feeble Confederation in preventing New York from ratifying the impost amendment of 1783. Only six days before Congress issued the call for the Federal Convention, New York had rejected the application for the impost for the third or fourth time.[1] The selfish refusal of New York had been the proximate cause of the recommendation of the Federal Convention, and the Constitution to which that Convention had given birth had no more implacable foe than George Clinton.

Under the name of Federal Republicans, the opposition in New York promptly organized. General John Lamb, the collector of the port of New York, was their chairman, and their electioneering headquarters the custom-house. Correspondence was opened with leading men in the

[1] Rives's Madison, ii. 186.

various states to concert measures to prevent ratification of the new Constitution.[1] Rawlins Lowndes and Judge Burke of South Carolina; Bloodworth of North Carolina; Patrick Henry, Grayson, George Mason, and Richard Henry Lee of Virginia; Samuel Chase of Maryland; and Joshua Atherton of New Hampshire, entered vigorously into the scheme of the Clintonians. Their temper and attitude may be read in the following utterances. Rawlins Lowndes, who had persistently opposed the Declaration of Independence, and who was a stanch believer in negro slavery and in paper money, was warm in his eulogies of the government of the Confederation. Like the Virginians he recommended a second convention. Single-handed he contended for three days in the South Carolina legislature against calling a state convention to act upon the Constitution. He declared that he could wish when dead no other epitaph than this: "Here lies the man that opposed the Constitution, because it was ruinous to the liberties of America."[2]

For his intensely partisan devotion to Federalism at a later date, Jefferson christened Luther Martin "the Federal bull-dog." When summoned by the Maryland legislature to give an account of the proceedings of the Federal Convention, Luther Martin rehearsed to them, and later pub-

---

[1] Leake's Life of John Lamb, 306.
[2] Elliot's Debates, iv. 311.

lished to the world, his three days' arraignment of that body for having exceeded its authority. Hardly foreseeing the time when the legislature should decree that every lawyer in the State of Maryland should annually pay a license fee of five dollars for the use of Luther Martin,[1] he closed his paper with these words: "So destructive do I consider the present system to the happiness of my country, I would cheerfully sacrifice that share of property with which Heaven has blessed a life of industry; I would reduce myself to indigence and poverty; and those who are dearer to me than my own existence I would entrust to the care and protection of that Providence who hath so kindly protected myself, — if on *those terms only* I could procure my country to reject the chains that are forged for it."[2]

Joshua Atherton of New Hampshire wrote to General Lamb: "To ratify and then propose amendments is to surrender our all, and then ask our new masters if they will be so gracious as to return to us some or any part of our most important rights and privileges."[3]

Five states, however, promptly ratified the Constitution. New Jersey, Delaware, Connecticut, and Georgia were all small states. The compromise granting equal representation in the Senate was

---

[1] H. P. Goddard's Luther Martin, the Federal Bull-dog, p. 28.
[2] Elliot's Debates, i. 389.
[3] Leake's Life of John Lamb, 312.

bearing good fruit. In the states whose interests were commercial, ratification was easy, while in those in which agricultural interests were predominant ratification was difficult. A line fifty miles west from the coast would have pretty accurately divided the friends and the foes of the Constitution. In the agricultural districts west of the Susquehanna great dissatisfaction was felt with the Constitution. The unseemly urgency, not to say violence, of the Pennsylvania legislature in calling a state convention, had called forth a remonstrance from the minority in the western districts, among whom Richard Henry Lee's objections had found a fruitful soil.

Intense anxiety was felt about the conventions to be held in the large states of Massachusetts, Virginia, and New York. Upon the issue in these states the fate of the Constitution hinged. As the result proved, the change on the decisive ballots of ten votes out of three hundred and eighty-five in Massachusetts; of five votes out of one hundred and sixty-eight in Virginia; and of two votes out of sixty in New York, would have been enough to reject the Constitution in these states and to throw the country into anarchy. It was exceedingly desirable that each of these important states should ratify. The refusal of any one would bode ill to the aim for "a more perfect union."

In each of these states there was at least one

man whose opposition to the new Constitution was believed to be formidable. They were Samuel Adams, Patrick Henry, and George Clinton. Each had long been known for his conspicuous zeal in the cause of independence. Each was a delegate to the convention called in his own state to act upon the Constitution. Each was the natural nucleus of the opposition in his own state. Clinton and Henry were acting in as much concert as the circumstances would admit, and Clinton was the most bitter hater of the Constitution to be found anywhere in the thirteen states. Samuel Adams in the North and Patrick Henry in the South had been the great leaders of public opinion in the Revolutionary War. But the issues in 1787 and 1788 were of a widely different nature from those in 1776. The talents and energy most valuable in promoting revolution were not the most useful in fostering union.

Samuel Adams, "the Palinurus of the Revolution," had already wrought a great work, but at this crisis the ship of state needed another hand at the helm. His hands, so powerful in pulling down royal tyranny, had not been trained to the more difficult task of rearing the political fabric for a national government. His unfitness for this task may be read in the Articles of Confederation, if, as reported, they were largely his work. The recent insurrection of Shays had shown alike the weakness of the Confederation and the need of a central power that could guarantee the states in their freedom. Though the great representative of home rule had firmly upheld Governor Bowdoin's energetic measures, he was nevertheless startled when he found that the new Constitution proposed "a national government instead of a federal union of sovereign states."[1] In a letter to Richard Henry Lee, December 3, 1787, he had admitted that he had "a poor opinion of the political structure."[2] Adams, whose noblest efforts in youth and manhood had been in behalf of the most sacred and invaluable privileges of man, must have felt a deep discontent with an instrument that wholly omitted a bill of rights. To this omission, one who had done so much to secure the Declaration of Independence, and who had signed that document, could not be indifferent, or sure that the form of the proposed government would preserve the thought of the Declaration.

The Massachusetts convention met earlier than the conventions of New York and of Virginia. It was a large body of delegates. They had been chosen when the country districts, still in the throes of the suppressed insurrection, were bowed down with debts. Hancock, the governor, was chosen president, partly as a tribute to his eminence and official position, but still more because of his neutral position with respect to the new

[1] Wells's Samuel Adams, iii. 251.   [2] Ibid., 253.

Constitution. Like Adams, he had disapproved of it, but both had maintained a cautious reserve. They were the most generally popular men in the state, and doubtless supposed that, united, their opinion would, as in the past, be all-prevailing. Gerry, who had been defeated for Cambridge, was invited to sit in the Convention to answer questions of fact, but with no power to join in the debates. The Clintonians sent their emissaries to attend the proceedings of the Convention, and, if possible, to frustrate its acceptance of the union. "The decision of Massachusetts in either way," wrote Madison from Congress, "will involve the result in this state,"[1] and there was great reason to fear that the voice of the state would be in the negative. The minority in Pennsylvania was very restless under its defeat, and rejection by Massachusetts would rouse it to a stubborn resistance. Langdon, from New Hampshire, and men from Newport and Providence, who had come to watch the proceedings, declared that adoption by Massachusetts would lead to acceptance by New Hampshire and Rhode Island. The rank of this state in the Confederation, her importance in population and in wealth, her Revolutionary fame, and the influence her example was likely to have on the other states, made her action a matter of great public interest and anxiety.

It was known that the Convention was not

---

[1] Letters, Madison, i. 370 ; Madison Papers, ii. 666.

evenly divided in opinion, and the advocates of the Constitution avoided every question which would have shown division of the house, till the Constitution had been discussed from beginning to end. The opposition comprised eighteen insurgents in Shays's insurrection, who did not yet feel sure of amnesty, and who knew that the new government, if established, would be certain to repress violence; delegates whose hearts were set on paper money; and delegates from Maine who had always disliked annexation to Massachusetts, and desired a government of their own far more than entrance into the Union as a part of Massachusetts. These men, it was estimated, made up four sevenths of the Convention. The cause of the Constitution was championed by the late Governor Bowdoin, Messrs. King, Gorham, and Strong, who had been delegates to the Federal Convention, three Supreme Court judges, fifteen members of the Senate, twenty-four among the most respectable and eloquent of her clergy, ten or twelve of the first members of the bar, judges of probate, sheriffs of counties, Generals Heath, Lincoln, and Brooks of the Revolutionary army. The commercial, the cultivated, the conservative elements favored the adoption of the Constitution.

The opposition had no powerful speakers. Their minds were made up: they were eager to conclude their business and go home. Had debate been silenced and the question hurried to a vote early in the session, the fate of the Constitution would have been sealed. The advocates of the new instrument had before them a hard task. They had not merely to answer, but even to bring forward and state, the objections of their opponents. It was not well-founded convictions, but deep-seated prejudices, that were to be overcome. The opposition was suspicious that some injury was plotted against them. Their real objection, as Rufus King said, was not to the Constitution, but to the men who made it. They instinctively distrusted a system that was the production of the cultured, the rich, and the ambitious. They complained that the lawyers, the judges, the clergymen, the merchants, and the men of education, were all in favor of the Constitution, and were able to make the worse appear the better reason. "But," said they, "if we had men of this description on our side, we should alarm the people with the imperfections of the Constitution, and be able to refute the defence set up in its favor." Against such a position what could argument and persuasion avail? One of the delegates, Randall, said: "A good thing does not need praise. It takes the best men in the state to gloss this Constitution, which they say is the best that human wisdom has invented. If these great men would speak half as much against it, we could complete our business and go home in forty-eight hours." "All the good men we read of," said another delegate, " have failed ; I would not trust a flock, though every one of them should be a Moses."

As they heard such remarks, the advocates of the Constitution must have felt, as Schiller said : " Gegen die Dummheit kämpfen die Götter selbst vergebens."

But they knew well there were no votes to lose by ridicule, by temper, or by careless management. The utmost tact, gentleness, and courtesy were needed to persuade these reluctant delegates to their good. Seeing that they made little or no impression upon a prejudice and stolidity that baffled all arguments and " were proof against demonstration itself," they resorted to other means. They knew that the votes necessary for ratification would be secured from the opposition, not by argument, but because those who gave them would yield to the judgment and persuasion of those in whom they had confidence. There were but two such men in the Convention, Hancock in the chair and Adams on the floor; both very reserved, but believed inwardly to be deeply hostile to the Constitution.

These men must, if possible, be won to its support. Tactics worthy of Adams himself were employed. Fortunately Adams had always approved of granting the general government power to regulate commerce. This had sharply separated him from Clinton and the opposing Virginians. Richard Henry Lee had written to Gerry urging that Massachusetts should not adopt the Constitution without insisting on sundry amendments, and to consider these it was suggested that there should be another federal convention. Gerry in turn wrote a letter to the two houses of Massachusetts insisting that the Constitution needed amendments, and should not be adopted till they were made. Washington, viewing with alarm the efforts the Virginian opponents were making to influence the action in Massachusetts and to win public opinion in favor of a second convention, wrote to Charles Carter of Virginia, a letter, which was printed in the newspapers.

"Clear I am," said he, "if another federal convention is attempted, that the sentiments of the members will be more discordant or less accommodating than the last. In fine, they will agree on no general plan. General government is now suspended by a thread; I might go further and say it is at an end; and what will be the consequence of a fruitless attempt to amend the one which is offered before it is tried, or of the delay of the attempt, does not in my opinion need the gift of prophecy to predict. The Constitution or disunion is before us to choose from. If the first is our election, when the defects of it are experienced, a constitutional door is open for amendments, and may be adopted in a peaceable manner without tumult or disorder."[1] This advice of Washington was printed in the "Boston Centinel," and so emphasized the perils with which the scheme for a second convention was fraught that the advocates of the Constitution stirred themselves to the utmost to avert this disaster.

The main support of Samuel Adams had ever been his constituents of the industrial classes. By the secret agency of the friends of the Constitution, a meeting of these was now convened at the Green Dragon, the former headquarters of the Sons of Liberty. Resolutions were passed that the rejection of the Constitution would cause navigation to languish and skilful mechanics to emigrate, and that " any vote of a delegate from Boston against adopting it would be contrary to the interests, feelings, and wishes of the tradesmen of the town." A committee headed by Paul Revere was appointed to meet the Boston delegates, and Revere himself put these resolutions into the hands of Samuel Adams. The account of the interview between Revere and Adams sounds a little apocryphal, even as told years afterward by Webster to the people of Pittsburgh. Yet as by this interview Samuel Adams was won to the support of the Constitution, and as the action of Massachusetts proved decisive, it is by no means improbable that "the fate of a nation"

[1] Washington to Charles Carter, December 14, 1787; Pennsylvania Packet, January 11, 1788; Boston Centinel, January 23, 1788.

went with Revere in this interview with Samuel Adams, as much as in his "midnight ride" on the 18th of April, 1775.

The next step was to hold a secret caucus, at which Hancock, Adams, Parsons, Gorham, Bowdoin, Sullivan, and a very few other resolute and trusty men were present, and a plan of action was matured. Hancock was now quite ready to attend this caucus. In his seclusion, due to gout and perhaps even more to his uncertainty as to the state of the popular pulse, he had begun to fear that the Constitution might be carried in opposition to his opinion, and the idea was dreadful to one whose love of popularity was so great. He desired to have its success, if it must be carried, attributed to him. He was ambitious to be thought the pivot on which great events turned. The advocates of the Constitution were entirely willing to gratify Hancock's desire to play the rôle of the great pacificator. To satisfy the honest objections of Adams, to win the necessary votes, and to stifle, if possible, the movement for a second constitutional convention, it was resolved to combine with ratification a recommendation of amendments. Hancock was assured that he alone by his popularity could be the saviour of his country.

At the fitting time Parsons moved the adoption of the Constitution by the Convention. Hancock then left the chair and presented the nine amendments which had been drawn up in the terse and fitting words of Parsons, though they were probably in the handwriting of James Sullivan, Hancock's confidential adviser.[1] Adams then moved to consider the proposals made in the paper of his Excellency. Their success depended mainly on the popular supposition that the governor had presented his own views. Hancock had been careful to nourish this supposition. "With a confidence astonishing to all who were in the secret, he called them his own, and said they were the result of his own reflection on the subject in the short intervals of ease which he had enjoyed during a most painful disorder."[2]

In Adams's speech nothing is more noticeable than his persistent assumption that the amendments were Hancock's own. So much stress does he lay on Hancock's agency in the matter, that we cannot but feel, as we read, that the "great commoner" "doth protest too much."

Before putting the question to vote, Hancock said: "I give my assent to the Constitution in full confidence that the amendments proposed will soon become a part of the system."[3] With this the Constitution was ratified by the slender majority of nineteen, and amendments recommended. By her careful and dexterous manage-

[1] Life of Theophilus Parsons, p. 78; Amory's Sullivan, i. p. 223.
[2] Life of Theophilus Parsons, p. 71.
[3] Elliot's Debates, ii. 175.

ment Massachusetts had made her ratification valid whatever might be the fate of her amendments, had transformed a hostile majority into a loyal minority, and, by devising a plan which might unite all true Federalists, had made futile all further efforts for a second constitutional convention. This, however, could not be at the time distinctly seen. Massachusetts was but the sixth ratifying state. Three more were needed.

Ratification in New Hampshire would have followed soon after that of Massachusetts, had not some of the favoring delegates been fettered by instructions from their towns. Adjournment till June, 1788, was carried, that these delegates might consult with their constituents, and that New Hampshire might also prudently see what the other states should decide.

The convention of Maryland did not meet till two months after a decision had been reached in Massachusetts. The Anti-federalists were busy with efforts to secure Maryland's vote against adoption. Richard Henry Lee was as zealous as ever for a second convention, and Patrick Henry had been the whole winter of 1787–1788 putting forth propositions for a southern confederacy. In a letter to Madison, January 18, 1788, Carrington said this was Henry's attitude: "The other states cannot do without Virginia, and we can dictate to them what terms we please. Should they be weak enough to stand out, we alone may enter into foreign alliances." [1] But the sentiments and words of Washington and Madison proved more than a match for the intrigues of the Virginian Anti-federalists, and on April 26, 1788, Maryland unanimously ratified. A little later, South Carolina, following the Massachusetts plan, became the eighth ratifying state, and by her fidelity crushed the plan for a southern confederacy.

Even Richard Henry Lee now faltered in his opposition, but Patrick Henry was unmoved. Was this the same Patrick Henry who in 1774 had declared, "The distinctions between Virginians, Pennsylvanians, New Yorkers, and New Englanders are no more: I am no longer a Virginian, but an American"? [2] In 1776 he had incurred reproach by his anxiety to defer independence until a basis for general government should be established, lest the several states, in separating from England, should lapse into separation from one another. From 1776 to 1779, as Governor of Virginia, his correspondence with the president of Congress, with the Board of War, and with the general of the army had been pervaded by proofs of respect for the supreme authority of the general government. From 1780 to 1784, as leader of the Virginia House of Delegates, he had been in the main a supporter of a policy giving greater strength and dignity to the general government.

[1] Bancroft, Hist. Const., ii. 456, 457.
[2] Tyler's Patrick Henry, 271.

In 1784 Madison wrote to Jefferson that Henry was strenuous for invigorating the Congress, and as late as 1786 had said that Henry had "been hitherto the champion of the federal cause."[1] Not far from that date Henry became its most formidable antagonist, and so remained till some time during Washington's first term, when he gave the Constitution his firm and lasting support.

What is the clew to Henry's conduct from August, 1786, till December, 1791? Was he unpatriotic, short-sighted, or narrow-minded? Or did there come into his life for those five years some influence powerful enough entirely to reverse the habitual direction of his political thought and action? Wirt fails to find any sufficient motive for Henry's actions during this period other than his honest conviction that the Constitution as it came from the hands of its framers was dangerous to the liberties of the people, and menaced the integrity of the state governments.

The best defence yet made of Henry's conduct is that by Professor Tyler. He considers it not an example of gross political inconsistency and fickleness, but a most logical proceeding, in perfect harmony with the principles underlying his whole public career. He believes that Henry ceased to champion the federal cause because of

[1] Rives's Madison, ii. 142; Madison Letters, etc., i. 264.

the danger in August, 1786, that Congress would for twenty-five years forego the rights of navigation of the Mississippi as the price of a treaty of reciprocity with Spain. To Henry this seemed a cool proposal to sacrifice Southern interests for a quarter of a century in order to build up Northern interests in that time. In November, 1786, the next legislature of Virginia resolved: " that nature had given the Mississippi to the United States; that the sacrifice would violate justice and contravene the end of the federal government, and would destroy confidence in the federal councils necessary to a proper enlargement of their authority."[1] The day following the passage of this resolve Henry's term as governor expired, and five days later he was chosen one of seven delegates to attend the Philadelphia Convention. He declined to serve, as did also Richard Henry Lee, who was appointed in his stead. They were little inclined to strengthen a confederation ready, as they believed, to sacrifice Southern interests.

In December, 1786, Madison wrote Washington : " Henry has become a cold advocate, and in the event of a sacrifice (of the Mississippi) would unquestionably go over to the opposite side."[2] March 18, 1787, he writes again to Washington: "I hear with much concern that Mr. Henry has positively declined his mission to Philadelphia.

---

[1] Bancroft, Hist. Const., ii. 297.
[2] Rives's Madison, ii. 142; Letters, Madison, etc., i. 264.

Besides the loss of his services on that theatre, there is danger, I fear, that this step has proceeded from a wish to leave his conduct unfettered on another theatre, where the result of the Convention will receive its destiny from his omnipotence."[1] In the same strain he wrote to Jefferson the next day: "Although the intended sacrifice of the Mississippi will not be made, the consequences of the intention and the attempt are likely to be serious. Mr. Henry's disgust exceeds all measure, and I am not singular in ascribing his refusal to attend the Convention to the policy of keeping himself free to combat or espouse the result, according to the result of the Mississippi business among other circumstances."[2]

It would appear from Madison's letters that the Mississippi question to a large extent influenced Henry's action, yet it does not fully explain it. Henry's place, both for his own good and his country's welfare, was in the Federal Convention. The refusal of Henry and Lee to join in the task of revising the Articles of Confederation was ominous. To us at this distance the part that Henry and Lee took with respect to the ratification of the Constitution does not seem either noble or useful. Still, justly to view the motives and the efforts of those who favored and of those who opposed a second constitutional convention, we need

---

[1] Letters, Madison, etc., i. 283, 284; Sparks's Corr. Rev., iv. 168.
[2] Madison Papers, ii. 623.

to divest ourselves of the knowledge of the working of the Constitution for a hundred years, and to carry ourselves back to the time when all that is now familiar to us was as yet untested theory. Had we listened to the deep and eager discussions that then took place, we should doubtless have been much puzzled to determine on which side the weight of argument lay. We might have undertaken to place the preponderance upon one side, but we could not have denied the vast gravity of opposing considerations. Now it is not easy for us to make the comparison fairly. It is not alone the subsequent facts that we cannot obliterate. The entire atmosphere of political thought and feeling in which we have been bred is impregnated with elements that a century ago were but in the process of introduction. Even if we could destroy the intervening historical facts, we could not think and feel as Patrick Henry and James Madison thought and felt.

If Jefferson, with his calm nature, aloof from the actual conflict, could write so strongly as he did from Paris, was it strange that Henry, who never did anything by halves, should, with a passion as hot as it was comprehensive, break forth in the Virginia Convention, " Give me leave to inquire what right the members of the Convention had to say, We, the People, instead of We, the States?" " The Constitution is a severance of the Confederacy."[1] Henry's pride and power

[1] Elliot's Debates, iii. 23.

were concentrated in state sovereignty. Membership in the Union seemed a poor exchange for Virginia's commanding position of sovereignty. He was unable or unwilling to see the distinction between a federal and a consolidated republic. Though the decision of Maryland and South Carolina had quenched the hope of a Southern Confederacy, Henry said: " Compared with the consolidation of one power to reign with a strong hand over so extensive a country as this is, small confederacies are little evils. Virginia and North Carolina could exist separated from the rest of America." [1] Henry had the courage of his convictions, for he declared that " if twelve and one half states adopted it, I would with manly firmness, and in spite of an erring world, reject it." [2] " You are not to inquire how your trade may be increased, or how you are to become a great and prosperous people, but how your liberties may be secured." [3]

Such expressions, urged with all the eloquence of which Henry was master, had great power over the Convention. While in every other state the conservative, the educated, and the wealthy ranged themselves on the side of ratification, in Virginia as many of these classes were against it as for it. In no other state convention was the debate more nearly equal, more able, or more

[1] Elliot's Debates, iii. 161.
[2] Wirt's Patrick Henry, 272.
[3] Ibid.

protracted. Against all the array of learning, genius, character, and logical acumen, Henry held the field for twenty-three days.[1] There were but five days when he did not take the floor. On each of several days he made three speeches; one day, five; another, eight. In one speech alone he was on his feet seven hours. Every argument, every motive he could bring to bear against adoption, every fear or prejudice he could appeal to in favor of its rejection, was urged with all the force of his passionate oratory. To the poor, to the Southerners, to the Kentuckians in fear of losing the navigation of the Mississippi, to those owing British creditors, to slaveholders, to lovers of personal liberty, he in turn addressed his pleas for rejection of the Constitution till amendments were made by a second constitutional convention.

However, from the moment on the fourteenth of June when the Convention entered upon the consideration of the Constitution clause by clause, Henry and his fellow-opponents had to descend from the airy regions of declamation and fancy, and grapple with the advocates of the Constitution on the solid ground of a written text. Madison, the only member of the Federal Convention present who had signed the Constitution, was constantly appealed to for explanation and defence of its provisions. Finding he could not meet the

---

[1] Tyler's Patrick Henry, 285.

solid reasoning of Madison, or the careful statement of Marshall, Henry introduced Jefferson's name. "I might, not from public authority, but from good information, tell you that his opinion is that you reject this government till it be amended. His sentiments coincide entirely with ours. His attachment to, and services done for, this country, are well known. At a great distance from us, he remembers and studies our happiness. Living in splendor and dissipation, he yet thinks of bills of rights, thinks of those little, despised things called *maxims*. Let us follow this sage advice of this friend of our happiness."[1]

To this reply was made that, if the opinions of important men not in the Convention were to govern its deliberations, a name equally great could be adduced in its favor.

Yet Henry's use of Jefferson's name carried great weight, and served the purpose for which he had introduced it. It gave him the opportunity to quote Jefferson still further. "You say," replied he, "you are certain New Hampshire will adopt the Constitution; then she will be the ninth state, and if Mr. Jefferson's opinion is of any value, we ought to reject it till amendments be obtained."[2] The very day that Massachusetts adopted the Constitution, Jefferson wrote Madison: "I sincerely wish that the first nine conven-

---

[1] Elliot's Debates, iii. 142.
[2] Ibid., iii. 200.

tions may receive and the last four reject it."[1] This was the last influential word heard from Jefferson prior to the Virginia Convention. So soon as Jefferson heard of the action of the Massachusetts Convention he declared it far preferable to the scheme for a second constitutional convention,[2] of which he had spoken with favor, but this letter commending the Massachusetts plan arrived too late to influence the result in Virginia.

Henry's plan was not to reject the Constitution outright, but to remit the whole subject to a new general convention. Twenty amendments were proposed and recommended by the Convention. Mason, like Governor Clinton of New York, thought amendments should be exacted previous to ratification, and for that purpose a second national convention should be demanded. In all his powerful advocacy of the Constitution, Randolph had never relinquished the hope that there would be such a convention; but at the opening of the Virginia Convention he declared that the accession of eight states had reduced the question before them to one of Union or no Union; and raising his arm, he cried: "I will assent to the lopping off of this limb before I assent to the dissolution of the Union." He therefore withstood Henry's proposition to make ratification

---

[1] Jefferson to Madison, Bancroft, History of Constitution, ii. 460.
[2] Jefferson's Works, ii. 399.

conditional on the adoption of amendments, believing that these needed amendments could be obtained only in the Union.

Randolph's refusal to sign the Constitution unless it should be submitted to a second convention, and his published criticisms of the new instrument, now handicapped him in his debate with Henry. His course was exposed to the charge of vacillation, and Henry did not scruple to insinuate that Randolph's personal ambition was the reason for this change. There was also in Randolph's possession an ambiguous letter from Governor Clinton in reply to the delayed official letter of the Virginian governor. It was written two months after the delayed letter was received, and about a month before the Virginia Convention met. It was doubtless the product of the anxious consultations of the Federal Republican Club in New York. It was in Clinton's most artistic style, and was clearly intended to reach and influence the action of the Virginia Convention. Had it been laid before that body, it is probable that it might have reversed its action. But it was not addressed to Henry or Mason, under cover to "Mr. George Flemins, Merchant, Richmond," as had been other communications from the Anti-federalist Club in New York. Clinton apparently desired to utilize Randolph's official weight in getting his letter before the Virginia Convention, while leaving himself free to explain that he never dreamed that his personal communication to the Virginia governor would be thus used.

This letter, at once official and unofficial, Randolph laid before his Executive Council, and on the first day of its legal meeting in special session, Governor Randolph sent to the legislature Clinton's letter with this message: "Richmond, June 23, 1788.—The enclosed letter from Governor Clinton of New York is in answer to a short circular letter which I wrote to the executives of the different states transmitting the acts of the last session concerning the Convention. I laid it before the Board immediately on receiving it, and requested their opinion, whether it was of a public or private nature. They conceived it to be of the former description, and therefore it is now forwarded." [1]

This was but two days before Virginia's ratification, and so intense was the desire to hear Patrick Henry in the Convention that the legislature could obtain no quorum till after the decisive vote against Henry's proposition not to ratify before amendments were obtained. In support of this plan Henry put forth all his powers, and invoked the terrors of a passing thunderstorm in aid of his rhetoric.[2] "And all the time," says Mr. Conway, "the voice which might have

---

[1] Conway's Edmund Randolph, p. 112.
[2] Wirt's Patrick Henry, 296, 297.

saved Henry's cause was not in the heavens, or the tempest, nor in his own flame, but lay small and still on the table of a neighboring room made vacant by his eloquence."[1]

The Convention knew nothing of Clinton's letter till the day after it had unconditionally ratified the Constitution, when it was read to the reassembled legislature. That Clinton's manœuvre to compel Governor Randolph to lay the letter before the convention, and bear any odium that might result, did not succeed, was due to Randolph's clear-sighted honor, and also to the neglect of Clinton's allies in Virginia.

On the plea that a ninth state was needed to ensure the Union, and without any knowledge of the Clinton letter, the Constitution had been carried in Virginia by a majority of ten votes. The discovery that New Hampshire had four days previously become the ninth ratifying state, and the too late knowledge of New York's proffer of aid, made Henry and his followers very sore over their defeat. Still one great hope was left, — that a second constitutional convention might be summoned. Henry's closing words in the Convention were: "My head, my hand, and my heart shall be at liberty to remove the defects of the system in a constitutional way."[2]

A little more than a fortnight before, Henry had written General Lamb in New York that if

---

[1] Conway's Randolph, p. 113.   [2] Elliot's Debates, iii. 652.

the Constitution were adopted and previous amendments precluded, it would be necessary to form the society which Lamb had proposed, — a Republican club similar to the one in New York. George Mason had agreed to act as chairman of the society, and the plan was for committees of correspondence, as in the days prior to independence. Colonel Oswald was the go-between, who, with Henry's letter, bore a copy of the bill of rights and also of the particular amendments to be proposed in the Virginia Convention.

"To assimilate our views on this great subject," wrote Henry, "is of the last moment, and our opponents expect much from our dissension. As we see the danger, it is easily avoided."[1] To each of the state governors and state legislatures a copy of Virginia's bill of rights and proposed amendments was sent, and fifty more copies were made for the use of each of the counties of Virginia. When Henry, therefore, spoke of being "free to remove the defects of the system in a constitutional way," it must not be supposed that he had relinquished the idea of effort for a new federal convention. If for one moment he allowed the project to slumber, it was speedily awakened by events in New York. Oswald had returned to Richmond, with letters from the Anti-federalists in New York and in Pennsylvania, too late either to admit of the postponement of the decision in

[1] Leake's Life of John Lamb, i. 307, 308.

Virginia, or to concert plans for common action in Virginia and New York.

While the contest was in progress in the New York Convention at Poughkeepsie, the members of the Republican Club at New York held meetings at the custom-house, at which the conduct of the party in the Convention was discussed, and information sent to their sympathizers in the other states. Two thirds of the Convention were opposed to ratification, and Hamilton's efforts, herculean as they were, would probably have been unavailing, had they not been powerfully reënforced by the news of the ratification of New Hampshire and of Virginia. With the failure of the Anti-federalists in Virginia, the situation of the Clintonians became desperate. Even then Clinton kept the Convention from ratifying; fear kept them from rejecting. Madison, from his seat in the Congress, wrote to Randolph: "The opponents in New York cannot come to the point of ratification without yielding a complete victory to the Federalists, which must be a severe sacrifice of their pride."[1]

The Clintonians sought out every possible device by which New York could be admitted without a full and unqualified ratification. They defeated unconditional ratification, but they could not carry rejection. Finally they proposed what they called the *ne plus ultra* of compromise.

[1] Madison to Randolph, Madison Papers, ii. 673.

They would adopt the Constitution either with the express condition that the amendments proposed by them were to be a part of it, or with the reservation of the right to secede if the amendments offered were not acted upon within six years. Against this motion, made by Melancthon Smith, Hamilton spoke with such power that Smith owned himself convinced and withdrew his motion. The next day Lansing renewed the motion. Even Hamilton was in doubt, and for a moment thought the state might be received with this condition. But he wrote in all haste to Madison for his advice. To the Convention Hamilton read Madison's memorable words: "Such conditional ratification would not make New York a member of the Union. The Constitution requires an adoption *in toto* and forever. The idea of reserving a right to withdraw was started at Richmond, and considered a conditional ratification, which was itself abandoned as worse than a rejection."[1]

Lansing's motion was lost, Smith himself voting against the motion he had originally made. At last, on Saturday, July 26, 1788, the New York Convention ratified the Constitution "in full confidence" of the adoption of all needed amendments. But this decision, carried by only three votes, was a Pyrrhic victory. It was purchased at what many of the Federalists thought a shame-

[1] Hamilton's Works, i. 465.

ful and a needless price. This was the unanimous concurrence in a resolution, that a circular letter should be prepared, to be laid before the different legislatures of the United States, recommending a general convention to act upon the proposed amendments of the different legislatures of the United States. This circular letter was made ready with all speed. On Monday, only two days after ratification, it was at hand, prepared and signed by Governor Clinton, as president, by the unanimous order, it was added, of the New York Convention.

This circular of George Clinton was artfully prepared. It declared that several articles of the Constitution appeared so exceptionable to a majority of the Convention " that nothing but the fullest confidence of obtaining a revision of them by a general convention, and an invincible reluctance to separate from their sister states, could have prevailed on a sufficient number to ratify without stipulating for previous amendments." They recommended to the other states to make immediate application to the new Federal Congress presently to meet, that a new constitutional convention might be forthwith authorized under the provision to that effect contained in the Constitution. "We are unanimous in thinking this measure very conducive to national harmony and good government." [1]

[1] Elliot's Debates, ii. 413, 414.

This circular was at once dispatched to the several state governors. The rejoicings which had hailed the accession of New York to the Union were soon clouded by the apprehensions called forth by Clinton's circular. It was the signal of concord and hope to the enemies of the Union everywhere, and it was likely to prove extremely dangerous. Madison, who called it a pestilent proposal, as soon as he heard of it said: "If an early convention cannot be parried, it is seriously to be feared that the system which has resisted so many direct attacks may be at last undermined by its enemies."[1] He wrote Jefferson that this circular letter had rekindled an ardor among the opponents of the Constitution for an immediate revision of it by another general convention. "Mr. Henry and his friends enter with great zeal into the scheme."[2]

No man was better able to estimate the circular letter or judge of its effect than Madison. Less than a month from the date of the circular he wrote Washington from Congress: "The circular letter from this state is certainly a matter of as much regret as the unanimity with which it passed is a surprise. I find it everywhere, and particularly in Virginia, laid hold of as a signal for the united exertions in pursuit of early amendments. In Pennsylvania, the Anti-federal-

[1] Rives's Madison, ii. 629.
[2] Madison Letters, etc., i. 418.

ist leaders are, I understand, soon to have a meeting at Harrisburg, in order to concert proper arrangements on the part of that state. I begin now to accede to the opinion which has been avowed for some time by many, that the circumstances involved in the ratification of the State of New York will prove more injurious than a rejection would have done. The latter would rather have alarmed the well-meaning Federalists elsewhere, would have had no ill effect on the other party, would have excited the indignation of the neighbor states, and would necessarily have been followed by a speedy reconsideration of the subject."[1]

Much complaint was made that the Federalists in New York, in their excessive desire for the accession of that state, had seriously imperilled the success of the new government to be established. The expiring Congress of the Confederation had to provide the measures for putting the Constitution in operation. These, and the measures of the new Congress to be chosen under this new agitation, might be very seriously modified by the sentiments Clinton's circular called forth. But Hamilton and Jay had to choose between the dangers resulting from a mere call for a second constitutional convention and those resulting from a rejection by New York. They believed the latter the greater, and acted accordingly.

[1] Madison Letters, 412, 413.

Washington wrote Jay afterward: "Considering the great majority that appeared to cling together in the Convention, and the decided temper of the leaders, I did not, I confess, see how it could be avoided."[1]

How definite in some quarters was the expectation of another general convention is shown by the action of North Carolina. The Convention of that state had known that the new government would be organized. It assembled five days before New York had ratified the Constitution, but that event was not known to them at the time of their adjournment, August 2, 1788. They determined not to enter the Union until amendments were obtained. Under the lead of Willie Jones they followed the ideas of the Virginians who favored a second general convention. They decided that, previous to ratification by the State of North Carolina, a bill of rights and certain amendments ought to be laid before Congress, and the Convention that might be called for amending the Constitution.[2] They assumed that the Congress of the Confederation would not provide for the organization of the new government till another general convention had been held, or, should Congress make such provision, they believed such a convention would be called by the the new Congress. Great was their surprise, then, to find, when their amendments reached

---

[1] Washington's Works, ix. 408. [2] Elliot's Debates, iv. 242.

New York, that Congress had already done everything necessary to put the new government in operation.

Washington's letters betray great anxiety about the effect of Clinton's circular. He wrote Benjamin Lincoln a month after the circular was issued: "I apprehend that the New York circular is intended to bring on a general convention at too early a period, and by referring the subject to the legislatures *to set everything afloat again*."[1] The circular was the standard to which all disaffected toward the new Constitution repaired. New and most serious difficulties would arise if they, by combinations among themselves, or by injudicious state action, should succeed in putting quickly into effect the objects of Clinton's circular.

The first open attempt to follow Clinton's lead was made by the restless Anti-federalists of Pennsylvania. On the 3d of September, 1788, less than forty days after the circular was issued, a conference of thirty-three members assembled at Harrisburg. Among them was Albert Gallatin. The proceedings of the conference bear the stamp of his hand. After "free discussion and mature deliberation," a report or declaration of opinion was adopted. Among Gallatin's papers are two drafts of this document, both in his own handwriting, one of them much amended and inter-

[1] Rives's Madison, ii. 630.

lined, obviously a first sketch, used probably in committee as a groundwork of the adopted instrument. The natural inference is, that Gallatin was the one who drew up this interlined document. This rough draft is therefore of special interest as showing how far he was disposed to carry his opposition to the Constitution.[1]

Speedy revision, the draft says, is necessary to prevent the dissolution of the Union and to secure our liberties.[2] The safest manner of doing this is, in conformity with the request of New York, using our endeavors to have a general convention called as soon as possible. Therefore the state assembly should make an application at the earliest opportunity for that purpose to the new Congress. Committees of correspondence between the friends of amendments in the different states is recommended. A general conference of the friends of amendments is advised, to devise the most needed amendments and the most likely way to carry them into effect. The place and the time of the proposed conference were left in blank.

If Gallatin went to the Harrisburg conference having in mind the objects indicated by this draft, he must have met in the conference persons who greatly modified his views before the conference adjourned. This first draft is significant as revealing the precise nature and details of the plan

[1] Adams's Gallatin, 78, 79.
[2] Writings of Gallatin, Adams, p. 2.

for securing a second general convention. Instead of saying that only speedy revision of the Constitution can prevent a dissolution of the Union, the revised draft begins with a recommendation to the people of the state of acquiescence in the organization of the new government. Not losing sight of the grand object of obtaining very considerable amendments, it declares necessary a speedy revision by a general convention, and petitions the legislature to apply to Congress for this purpose.[1] The changes in tone and contents from the other draft in Gallatin's handwriting are marked. How far he resisted or led this policy is unknown. Like Jefferson he had no fondness for energetic government. Madison wrote Washington that the friends of the meeting at Harrisburg represented it as conducted with much harmony and moderation.[2] All their actions were kept within the bounds of legality.

But in Virginia, the state that had taken the lead in the great and arduous work of reconstruction, all the mischief apprehended from Clinton's circular letter was realized. The Anti-federalists, encouraged by the action of the Harrisburg conference, laid hold of Clinton's recommendation as the sure harbinger of that second constitutional convention on which they had been so insistent. Washington feared that, by this attempt to ob-

---

[1] Adams's Gallatin, 78, 79; Elliot's Debates, ii. 544.
[2] Madison Letters, etc., i. 410.

tain amendments before trial of the new Constitution, more was meant than met the ear; that an intention was concealed to accomplish slyly what could not be done openly, to undo all that had been done.[1] He was disposed to put the worst construction on Henry's conduct.

His apprehensions were most painful from the fact that in the Virginia assembly, whose members had been chosen prior to the meeting of the Virginia Convention, Henry would have most favorable materials for accomplishing his hostile designs.[2] This assembly was to choose the senators, and to district the state for the choice of representatives to the first Congress under the Constitution. It might do much to cross or cripple the new government, and from the complexion of the assembly there was much to be feared. Corbin was the only member of the assembly who in the Convention had taken part in the debates in favor of the Constitution. Henry's sway over the assembly was apparent from the moment they met, October 30, 1788. He seemed determined to avenge his defeat in the Convention by as decisive a course of action against the Constitution as it was possible for him to adopt. Washington wrote Madison, November 17, 1788: "The edicts of Mr. Henry are registered with less opposition in the Virginia assembly than those of

---

[1] Rives's Madison, ii. 631.
[2] Washington, ix. 433.

the Grand Monarch by his parliaments. He has only to say, Let this be law, and it is law."[1]

Before such an assembly Clinton's circular letter was laid, and Virginia was the first state to take it into consideration. Four state conventions which had recommended amendments had favored amendment by the direct action of Congress. New York alone called for a second constitutional convention to act upon the amendments desired. Within ten days after meeting, resolutions were adopted whose purport was to ask Congress to call immediately a national convention for proposing to the states the required amendments. In the debate upon this subject, Henry is said to have declared that he should "oppose every measure tending to the organization of the government, unless accompanied with measures for the amendment of the Constitution."[2]

Mr. Tyler thinks that in all his action Patrick Henry was consistent throughout. He and his friends had fought hard for amendments before adoption. They had failed, and now must fight for amendments after adoption. By a popular agitation widespread, determined, vehement, and even alarming, those hostile to amendments must be convinced that till amendments were made there would be neither peace nor content. The

---

[1] Bancroft, Hist. Const., ii. 483.
[2] Corr. Rev., iv. 240, 241.

Virginia assembly was the conspicuous stage where this violent agitation in favor of Clinton's scheme for a second convention should begin. Yet Henry's violence lessened his influence in the assembly. His resolution to ask Congress to call a second convention passed by a vote of eighty-five to thirty-nine. The actual application to Congress, the circular letter to the other states, and the reply to Clinton's circular, passed by a vote of seventy-two to fifty only. A majority of forty-six had been reduced to twenty-two. Possibly the tone of these communications led to this result. Their language bespeaks Henry as their author.

After stating that the Virginia legislature had been obedient to the voice of its constituents, and that, so far as depended on them, the plan of government would be carried into operation, the letter contains among other statements these significant sentences: "Though they dreaded that operation, they had consolation from a full expectation of its imperfections being speedily amended. This confidence will support them while they have reason to believe they have not calculated upon it in vain. . . . Objections not founded upon speculative theory, but upon established principles, will never be removed until the cause itself shall cease to exist. . . . The anxiety with which our countrymen press for this will ill admit of delay. . . . The slow forms of congressional discussions and recommendations, if indeed they should ever agree to any change, would be less certain of success. The Constitution happily presents an alternative. To this we resort as a source of relief. We do, therefore, in behalf of our constituents, in the most earnest and solemn manner, make this application to Congress, that a convention be immediately called of deputies from the several states, with full power to take into their consideration the defects of this Constitution that have been suggested by the state conventions, and report such amendments as they shall find best entitled to promote common interests, and the great and inalienable rights of mankind." [1]

A copy of this application was transmitted to each of the states, and hearty concurrence in sentiment and action invoked. Clinton was informed that his circular had been laid before the Virginia assembly, and that between that body and the New York Convention there was an entire agreement in feeling and purpose. Clinton was requested to lay before the New York assembly Virginia's application to Congress for a second constitutional convention. The most earnest wish was expressed for the approbation by New York and all the other sister states of Virginia's application.

As soon as these measures were carried, Henry turned his attention to the choice of senators, and

[1] Journal Virginia House of Delegates, 42, 43.

the districting of the state in such a way that representatives animated by his own spirit might be chosen. It was desirable to have such members of the new Congress as would favor Virginia's application for a general convention. In ordinary fairness, as the state, in its popular convention, had so recently accepted the Constitution, the Federalists were entitled to at least one of the senators. But Henry took what Wirt mildly terms "the unusual liberty"[1] of nominating both candidates, Richard Henry Lee and William Grayson, from the party opposed to the Constitution, and he was able to command votes enough to elect them. Henry went out of his way to denounce Madison as against, or as unfriendly to, amendments,[2] though Madison had repeatedly said in the Convention that such amendments as seemed in his judgment to be without danger he would readily admit. Madison was unquestionably the fittest man in Virginia to be in the United States Senate. His friends stood by him nobly, and a change of five votes would have elected him. Residence in the representative district was made a requisite for the candidate, and Henry took pains to have Orange County, in which Madison resided, associated with seven other counties thought to be unfriendly to federalism, so that Henry believed Madison's elec-

[1] Wirt's Patrick Henry, 299.
[2] Journal Virginia House of Delegates, 32.

tion impossible.[1] To make assurance doubly sure, Monroe, a popular candidate, was to run against Madison. But Madison boldly took the field, had several discussions with his competitor before the people, and in spite of Henry's gerrymandering was triumphantly elected.

Meanwhile the association in New York city, which had so strenuously battled for previous amendments, had, on October 30, 1788, met at Frannces' Tavern, and again organized, under the designation of Federal Republicans, for the purpose of procuring a second federal convention.[2] A committee consisting of Melancthon Smith, John Lamb, and James M. Hughes were appointed to open correspondence with certain persons in the several states, and in the counties of New York, for the purpose of explaining the reasons which induced the adoption of the Constitution by the New York Convention, and for requesting their assistance to procure the requisite amendments by having a general convention called as soon as Congress should assemble.[3]

The letters to the counties had special reference to the election of members to the next state assembly, and urged the choice of those favoring amendments, the uniting of all diverse sentiments to this end, and the formation of societies like the

---

[1] Tobias Lear to John Langdon, Bancroft, Hist. Const., ii. 488, 489.

[2] Leake's Life of John Lamb, 320.   [3] Ibid. 321.

one in New York city. The letters to persons in other states advised the same care in the choice of Congressmen, and the formation of committees of correspondence. This renewed activity of the Clintonians in New York was the result of Pennsylvania's and especially of Virginia's response to Clinton's circular. Their labors in relation to calling a new convention were superseded by Governor Clinton's calling an extra session of the New York assembly. Before they separated, however, correspondence was opened in relation to the candidate for the Vice-Presidency, and it was determined to cast their votes for Clinton.[1] New York's disorganizing policy recoiled upon herself. Rival factions and obstinate contentions between the two branches of her legislature left her without senators at the opening of the first Congress that met in her own metropolis, and without electors in the choice of the first President.

Deluded by the proceedings of New York, North Carolina continued to pursue the phantom of a second constitutional convention for nearly a year and a half before she ratified. Fear of increased taxation, dissension in the state, the baneful influence of paper money, and the opinion that they were able to come into the Union when they liked, made it easy for Willie Jones, a Jeffersonian admirer and a politician of great

[1] Leake's Life of John Lamb, 325, 326.

skill, to delay ratification and to confuse the public mind, so that men did not think of themselves as outside of and independent of the Union, but spoke of themselves as still in the Union, and made no remonstrance against the establishment of the new government before their consent.

Rhode Island, too, was encouraged in her opposition and distrust by the New York circular, and all the efforts to which it gave birth. She adopted the extraordinary course of demanding a second constitutional convention to revise the Constitution, before she had even condescended to deliberate upon it at all in the manner required both by the Constitution and by the solemn resolves of Congress. Her course in the whole matter of the formation and establishment of a new government was such that even the opposition in other states, in all their arguments against the Constitution, never ventured to defend the people of Rhode Island. The project of a new convention, favored by New York and Virginia, received, of course, a very strong support from North Carolina and Rhode Island, and their sentiments had still greater weight from their refusal to come into the Union in their desire to compel a second general convention.

All these movements of the Anti-federalists might have seemed to indicate that the current of the popular sentiment was steadily setting toward a second constitutional convention. Nevertheless the deep undertow was flowing powerfully in the opposite direction. The moderate of all classes, who constitute the majority in every nation, were surfeited with conventions. They admired and honored Henry, Gallatin, and Clinton, but they trusted and followed Washington, and Madison, and Hamilton. Their faith in the new Constitution deepened when such Anti-federal Titans as Henry and Clinton failed to overthrow it. They knew Washington had attended and presided over the Federal Convention, and had been intensely anxious for the adoption of the Constitution. He who concentrated the confidence and affections of all Americans was sure to be chosen to preside over the inauguration of the new government. With him the interests of the nation would be safe. Monroe wrote Jefferson the truth: "Be assured Washington's influence carried this government."[1]

The response of the ratifying states to Clinton's circular showed that the decision in favor of the Constitution was not to be revoked by any appeals, however artful or urgent, for a second convention.

In the Connecticut legislature the circular letter of Clinton had a reading among other publications, but, as Trumbull wrote to Washington, "No Anti-federalist had the hardiness to call it up

[1] Monroe to Jefferson, July 12, 1788.

for consideration, or to speak one word of its subject." [1]

In Massachusetts the legislature concurred with Governor Hancock that an immediate second federal convention might endanger the Union.[2] The sentiments of the ratifying states were voiced by the legislature of Pennsylvania : " The House do not perceive this Constitution wanting in any of those fundamental principles which are calculated to ensure the liberties of their country. The happiness of America and the harmony of the Union depend upon suffering it to proceed undisturbed in its operation by premature amendments. The House cannot, consistently with their duty to the good people of this state, or with affection to the citizens of the United States at large, concur with Virginia in their application to Congress for a convention of the states." Early in March, 1789, Governor Mifflin communicated this vote to the governor of Virginia,[3] and in the state legislatures the scheme for a second federal convention was heard of no more.

Before the House of Representatives Theodoric Bland in May, 1789, laid the Virginia resolutions proposing a new general convention.[4] Pursuant to pledges of the Federal leaders in many states,

---

[1] Letters to Washington, iv. 238.
[2] New York Daily Gazette. February 17, 1789.
[3] Pennsylvania Archives, xi. 557, 558.
[4] Gale's Debates, i. 258–261.

and in compliance with the general voice, Madison called up the subject of proposing new amendments to the states.[1] It may well be doubted whether, in the four great states of Massachusetts, New York, Pennsylvania, or Virginia, in all of which the agricultural interest was very powerful, there was actually any Federal majority. Only in Connecticut, New Jersey, Delaware, and Maryland, all of which in the Convention had supported at first the state rights view and had opposed the formation of a national government, did the Constitution, now that it was adopted, seem certain of steady support. With such a prospect before them, the proposal for a new convention excited in the minds of the Federalists the liveliest alarm. The Federal Convention nominally called to amend the Articles of Confederation had ended in producing a system entirely new. Who could tell that a second convention would not reverse the action of the first?

In ample season for discussion and action before the adjournment of the first session of the first Congress, Madison presented a selection of the most desirable amendments suggested by the ratifying states.[2] The changes most widely called for sacrificed nothing vital to the success of the new instrument. They rendered the Constitution its own expounder; they concentrated all

---

[1] Rives's Madison, iii. 38.
[2] June 8, 1789.

the tenets of liberty in Magna Charta, the Petition of Right, and the Bill of Rights. The prompt action of the states in ratifying ten out of the twelve amendments submitted by Congress proved that these amendments were needed, and that the efforts of the Anti-federalists for a second constitutional convention were not fruitless or unreasonable.[1]

At first thought it might seem that it was a misfortune that Samuel Adams, Patrick Henry, and George Clinton were not members of the Convention that framed the Constitution. Had they participated in those debates they might have been changed from critics to champions. Had they seen the Constitution in the same light as did those who signed it, they would have saved their friends and the cause they sustained many embarrassments, and would have deprived the adversaries of the Constitution of weapons which they used with damaging effect; their states would have been as zealous and unanimous as they were divided.

Yet it is by no means improbable that their presence would have strengthened the discordant elements in the Philadelphia Convention, and prevented unanimity altogether. Had the states of Massachusetts, Virginia, and New York held their conventions in the first swellings of the tide of opposition to the Constitution and rejected it, it

[1] Tyler's Patrick Henry, 316.

would never have been adopted by the other states. It was fortunate that the honest objections of Samuel Adams were not the same as those which Clinton felt, or as those which troubled Henry most, and of which he said least, in that convention where he objected to the presence of reporters because he wished " to speak the language of his soul." " The articles relating to treaties [involving the payment of debts due to British creditors], to paper money, and to contracts created more enemies than all the errors of the system, positive and negative, put together."[1] It was fortunate, too, that these dissidents could not concert their measures of opposition so well as they could have done in these days of swift communication. Partisan and sectional feeling was perhaps even more violent than now. It was of the utmost advantage that time was given for extremists to grow cool, for the moderate of all classes to assert themselves, and to stifle the movement for a second general convention.

For such a convention, held for the avowed and sole purpose of revising the Constitution, would naturally have considered itself possessed of a greater latitude than a Congress appointed to administer and to maintain as well as to amend the Constitution. Composed of the most violent partisans of both sides, and not made responsible by

[1] Madison to Jefferson, October 17, 1788.

actual administration, it would have been a most heterogeneous body. It is not probable that it could have been in any high degree useful. The sentiments of every fraction would have expected or demanded the complete adoption of their views and principles. The discouraging conviction that the convention had undertaken an impossible task must soon have absorbed all minds. The evils they were seeking to remove would have been increased, and perhaps rendered incurable, by the growing belief that they had no remedy.

Nor was a second convention necessary. The friends of the Constitution were willing to make amendments as the Massachusetts Convention first recommended; some, from the conviction, general in the country, that the Constitution needed guarding by a bill of rights; others, in the spirit of conciliation. Even those federal pilots on board the ship of state who deemed them unnecessary as expositions of the Constitution, soon saw that in these ten amendments the needed tub had been thrown to the spouting whales who were angrily lashing the waves with their fins and threatening to strike with their deadly flukes.

The amendments once ratified, all notes of opposition were lost in the chorus of admiration that resounded from every quarter. In the worship of the Constitution that instantly succeeded, men forgot that " it had been extorted from the grinding necessity of a reluctant people."[1] Even those who had so powerfully contended for a second constitutional convention began during Washington's first administration to pose as preëminently "the friends of the Constitution," and it was almost impossible to believe that an instrument, accepted by all parties as the last word of political wisdom, had been produced in a conflict of opinion, adopted with doubt, ratified with hesitation, and amended with difficulty.

[1] J. Q. Adams.

III.

THE DEVELOPMENT OF THE EXECUTIVE DEPARTMENTS, 1775-1789.

BY JAY CÆSAR GUGGENHEIMER.

THE prevalence of the notion that our Constitution, complete in all its parts, came into existence suddenly and spontaneously, by a marvelous inspiration of the Philadelphia Convention, has long had a depressing effect upon the historical study of American institutions. It has discouraged, or at least offered no incentive to, the thorough investigation of their sources, whether colonial, classical, British, or other. Patriotic Americans, failing to perceive that no meaner grade of statesmanship is required for the successful choice of old principles to be applied to new conditions than for the sudden generation of new principles, have found much satisfaction in maintaining it. It has been fostered by the national pride arising from unique economic achievements, and other experiences common to new countries. And it has also been strengthened by the fact that the period during which our federal institutions received their ultimate form was, in reality, unusually brief.

The birth of American institutions, however, was far from being miraculous, and the object of the present paper is to show that, in one department at least, they came into being in much the same natural and regular way as those of other countries. The executive departments would at first seem to furnish an excellent example for the *inspirationists*. The Secretaries of State, War, and the Treasury still hold their offices by virtue of acts passed by the First Congress in 1789; the Postmaster-General and Secretary of the Navy, under acts of the years 1794 and 1798 respectively. Each of these five acts was the first and only law that the Federal Congress found necessary for the erection of these departments. They (the departments) have since developed and expanded as the increased public business of a growing republic has required, but the laws establishing them have been no more altered than the Constitution itself. How, then, did these seers happen upon a system for the transaction of executive business which, although adopted to meet the demands of an incipient government of four millions of people, has yet automatically expanded so as to serve equally well an established government of sixty millions?

Present institutions are generally a result of negative experiences. Yet, if on the one hand we know that a given thing will *not* do, on the other, we have no previous guarantee that what we substitute in its place will better serve our purpose. Under normal conditions, if this suits we retain it; if not, we continue experimenting. Institutional evolution grows out of this succession of discoveries that certain established forms will *not* suit, and the conscious or unconscious substitution of others to fill their places. The framers of the Constitution had at least the knowledge that the tacit agreement of 1774, and the more formal if not much more effective union of 1781, had *not* proved successes. So, also, when our legislators proceeded to the establishment of executive departments in 1789, they enjoyed the benefit of an abundance of experience with failures, in addition to some little, but very valuable, acquaintance with successes. Consequently their choice was not a difficult task.

The necessity of delegating its executive power was realized by Congress very soon after it convened. The devices first resorted to for this purpose were, in nearly every instance, those crude and imperfect contrivances which our Revolutionary statesmen had been accustomed to see amply serve similar ends in their respective colonies. And from these simple beginnings our present departments sprang by direct lineal descent.

The battle of Lexington was a quite sufficient excuse for making war the most prominent idea in the minds of the Congressmen who slowly gathered at Philadelphia in May, 1775. When a quorum had at length appeared, they resolved to put the colonies in a state of defence,[1] and preparatory thereto appointed a committee to consider ways and means to secure ammunition and military stores. Early in June[2] a committee was appointed to devise a method for introducing the manufacture of saltpetre into the colonies; a few days later another followed, by whom an elaborate set of rules for the government of the army was submitted; and on June 24th still another sprang up, whose task was no less than to discover "ways and means for putting the militia of America in a proper state for the defence of the colonies." In this way the management of the war was begun. Particular business was parcelled out to numerous committees, varying in size from three to thirteen members, the latter number being usually selected for the more important ones, so that each colony might be represented.

As the war waxed warmer and details increased correspondingly, the first change was noticed in the diminished specialization of the work, and the organization of grand committees with more general duties. Of these latter, perhaps the most important was the "Secret Committee," authorized by resolution of September 18, 1775, to contract for the importation of gunpowder, or, if necessary, to manufacture it, and also to purchase

---

[1] Journals of Congress, May 26, 1775.
[2] Ibid., June 10, 1775.

arms and ammunition. Next in importance was the "Cannon Committee," established in January, 1776,[1] and authorized to contract for any cannon necessary for the defence of the colonies. And still another was the "Medical Committee," whose name is a sufficient indication of its duties.

The impossibility of conducting a great war through these committees, and others of less importance, of which mention has been omitted, soon became painfully apparent. The management of military affairs had been entrusted to a legion of small boards, who neither took pains to render mutual assistance to each other, nor to preserve peace within their own ranks. That something must be done to concentrate the military energy of Congress, and effect some degree of harmony between the distracted offices to which authority had been dealt out, was soon plainly evident.

For the management of their own military affairs, the separate colonies had already found a device in the Councils of Safety and Committees of Observation. Crude as they were, springing up hastily as the invention of an excited people, and promptly disappearing with the cause for their existence, they nevertheless served admirably the purposes for which they were designed. They were nothing more than committees or boards, usually composed of the most substantial

[1] Journals of Congress, January 15, 1776.

citizens, and appointed by the colonial assemblies to assume the control and direction of any military preparations in their respective colonies. In some cases they subsequently ceased to be strictly military boards;[1] and in New York the duties became so varied that a sub-committee, known as the Committee of War, was found necessary for the original work of the main body. The principle, however, was everywhere the same. The assembly remained always the ultimate authority, delegating to a board the direction of military affairs, and granting it considerable latitude in its direct dealings with the militia.

In January, 1776, the Continental Congress, after having been spurred on by an appeal from Washington,[2] determined to establish a war office for its own military business. The matter was placed in the hands of a committee for consideration, and on June 12th it was resolved to establish a Board of War and Ordnance. In name and outward form this body resembled the contemporary English Ordnance Department, but in function it was hardly more than a national Council of Safety, with the necessary modifications. The Secretary at War had long been the recognized War Minister of England, while the Board of Ordnance under him was a subordinate

---

[1] American Archives, Fourth Series, vol. ii. p. 1551.
[2] Bancroft, vol. iv. p. 425.

body, corresponding rather to the "Secret" or "Cannon" committees above described. The board authorized by Congress in June, 1776, embraced the functions of the Secretary at War as well as his Ordnance Department, and was much broader in its sphere of action than the latter. It was to consist of five members of Congress, who, with the assistance of a secretary and a few clerks, were to keep a record of the officers of the army and disposition of troops, take charge of supplies, superintend the raising of troops, forward money to the army, preserve the papers of the department, and perform other similar duties. The members being themselves members of Congress, it was not considered necessary to emphasize their responsibility to that body, but this was distinctly understood.

On the day following the passage of the resolution the members were selected, and John Adams was made chairman. The preliminary work on the Declaration of Independence was at this time fanning patriotism into its brightest flame, and the labors of the new board were consequently burdensome from the outset. Congress, always glad to relieve itself of details, at once emptied all letters, petitions, reports, and documents that contained the slightest odor of powder, into the lap of its Board of War, whose activity was in a very short while manifested through its reports, recommendations, appointments, and answers to the countless questions ingeniously devised by the already inquisitive Congressman.

Naturally most of the work fell to the chairman, and John Adams, always irritable, appears really to have had good cause for complaint on this occasion. Nevertheless, he stood manfully at his work from the time of his appointment until his departure from Congress in 1777. Mornings and evenings were taken up with the monotonous work of the board, and the chairman must always be on hand, whether the other members saw fit to appear or not. When the reports reached Congress it again fell to Adams to explain and justify them, and defend his colleagues against attack; all of which he did with as much grace as his disposition permitted.

For a time the board was assisted in a slight degree by the " Secret," " Cannon," and " Medical" committees already mentioned; but not caring to be held directly responsible, and yet leave the custody of supplies in other hands, it eventually assumed the functions of all of them. Its duties also increased as the country became more deeply enveloped in war, and the struggle, on each side, grew more intense. By the beginning of 1777 Congress seemed to have developed into a permanent council of war. Little else was discussed besides reports from the Board of War and the commander-in-chief. In March, 1777, an additional member was appointed to the board; but it was already manifest to close observers that it was a sheer impossibility for a committee of members of Congress to attend to their duties as delegates, and at the same time take upon themselves the management of the details of a great war.

As early as December, 1776, a committee had been appointed to devise an improved plan, and Gates had been asked[1] for his ideas. The first Board of War, with its indefatigable chairman, was, perhaps, as efficient a one as could have been organized; yet its work was not accomplished smoothly and satisfactorily. At this distance from the scene we can easily discern the cause. There is now no question but that the direction of the war could have been conducted with far more skill and dispatch by a single qualified executive officer than by a board of two, three, or twenty members. Our Revolutionary patriots, however, overlooking the difference between the work required of the colonial Councils of Safety and of the corresponding Continental body, were not a little perplexed that like effects did not follow from what seemed to them like causes. They were, notwithstanding, certain that the board was not fulfilling the anticipations of its inventors, and accordingly sent it to a committee for repairs.

[1] American Archives, Fifth Series, vol. ii. p. 412.

DEVELOPMENT OF EXECUTIVE DEPARTMENTS. 125

After considerable deliberation, Congress, by a resolution of October 17, 1777, resolved upon the establishment of a new Board of War, to be composed of three members, not delegates in Congress.[1] A little later this number was increased to five, in order that one of them might, from time to time, visit the armies;[2] and after the usual delay, General Mifflin, General Gates, Colonel Timothy Pickering, Joseph Trumbull, and Richard Peters were selected as members. General Gates was made president, and allowed to remain in the field or take his place at the head of the board, as he might elect, his friends in the "Conway Cabal" having secured for him these privileges.

The duties of this body did not differ materially from those of the board to whose place it succeeded, save that they were made more comprehensive through the operation of one or two general clauses. It was known simply as the Board of War, and thus distinguished from its predecessor, the Board of War and Ordnance. The assumption of control by the new officials in the latter part of 1778 was not, however, a signal for the retirement of those already in office. Work was still found for both. Properly enough, the ordinary routine work was left to the Board

---

[1] A resolution providing for a similar board had been passed on July 18. 1777, but was allowed to lapse.
[2] Journals of Congress, November 24, 1777.

of War; while the Board of War and Ordnance, whose members had seats in Congress, served as a superintending committee,[1] transmitted messages from Congress to its commissioners and back again, and sometimes acted as the mouthpiece of the latter in the legislative body.

Under this form of organization the department continued until 1781. Its disadvantages are too patent to require more than the briefest notice. The entire absence of any responsible party in the whole system was alone a sufficient excuse for its abolition. The constant changes in the membership of the boards, due either to the retirement of members from Congress, or their refusal to be further taxed with arduous labors of the department, were also fatal defects. The substitution of single executive officers for the clumsy and irresponsible boards was the only method for securing responsibility and permanency. Congress hesitated long before venturing upon this step. In spite of the most incontestable evidence of continually increasing disorders, there were many who feared even more dire results from placing any great power in the hands of one man. It was only after a prolonged struggle, and when the combined influence of the ablest men in the colonies had been brought to bear, that the change was accomplished. On February 7, 1781, it was resolved to appoint a Secretary at War.

[1] Hamilton's Republic, vol. i. p. 375.

Before treating of the full significance of this change, however, it may be well to follow the course of the other departments through the same period. We shall presently see that at least three of them were subjected to a similar metamorphosis about the same time, and the Treasury and Navy by the identical resolution. Retracing our steps, then, to the beginning of the war, we find that, having once begun to fight, the next matter to engage the attention of Congress was the means of paying for this expensive occupation. The month of June, 1775, was largely given to the consideration of the financial condition of the country, and the first act was naturally an order on the printer for $2,000,000 in bills of credit. Another million soon followed, and Congress began to look about for some official to take charge of the treasure.

In that most difficult branch of government, the administration of finance, the colonies had had only the most primitive experience. With the possibly single exception of the levies for the French and Indian War, the colonial dealings in money matters had never required the employment of many figures, and even then they were not large. To the uses of the various intricate and treacherous devices for the management of public debts they were almost total strangers. In fact, more than once during the anxious days of the Revolution it seemed as likely that their hopes would be shattered by the unfortunate condition of their monetary affairs as by the cannon and muskets of the British.

The simple expenditures of the colonies had never required the services of more than a single official, or sometimes two, who bore the modest title of Treasurer. Occasionally he was more pretentiously called Treasurer and Receiver-General, but his duties and importance were not increased by this high-sounding addition. These officers were generally respected citizens who accepted their posts in the spirit in which they were offered, as honorary trusts; their duties being merely to receive, keep, and pay out the funds of the colonies as ordered. Further than this they exercised no executive or ministerial prerogatives, and consequently there was no one trained to fill such an office; but withal, matters were conducted as well as could be desired.

And now, when in 1775 Congress found itself with $3,000,000 in promises to pay, a vast sum for those days, its reception, safe-keeping, and payment were provided for by the adoption of the system so long in vogue, and two treasurers were appointed for the purpose.[1] They were ordered to give bond to a committee of Congress, and take up their residence in Philadelphia. By the same resolution it was recommended that the various colonial assemblies choose treasurers also,

[1] Journals of Congress, July 29, 1775.

DEVELOPMENT OF EXECUTIVE DEPARTMENTS. 129

one to be stationed in each colony, to receive and pay out, on orders from the Continental treasurers, the quotas due from the colonies by which they were respectively elected.

Congress soon learned, as its accounts began to multiply and its creditors to become impatient, that there was other work to be done besides that of its treasurers. The next step was the appointment of a Committee of Claims, in September, 1775,[1] consisting of thirteen members, all delegates in Congress, whose business was to examine any claims against the United Colonies, and report upon the same. This was followed on February 17, 1776, by the formation of the germ of the Treasury Department. The shape it assumed was that of a standing committee of five members of Congress. The chief object of its establishment was to secure a superintending body with control over minor officials, and with the further duties of attending to future emissions of bills of credit. To these were added the functions of the modern Congressional Committee of Ways and Means. These duties it performed under the same difficulties attending the Board of War and Ordnance. The members, being also members of Congress, found the double work beyond the capacity of ordinary men, and therefore it was not a matter of surprise that by the first of April Congress was again obliged to make further

---

[1] Journals of Congress, September 23, 1775.

additions to its rapidly-expanding Treasury Department.

The office now established was known as the Treasury Office of Accounts. It was placed under the direction of the standing committee for superintending the Treasury, which was henceforth styled the Treasury Board. At the head of the new office was placed an Auditor-General, and under him such clerks and assistants as were necessary to keep the government accounts. Their business was to examine and audit accounts and report to Congress through the Treasury Board, but disputed accounts were still settled by the Committee of Claims until July,[1] when their work was turned over to the board.

When Congress began to borrow, additional machinery was again required. On October 3d a loan office was opened in each of the colonies, the superintendent of each office being appointed by the colony in which the office was situated. They received subscriptions to loans; disbursed the money on drafts from the treasurers; and paid interest on the sums borrowed to the creditors in their respective colonies. Thus it will be seen that up to this time the policy pursued by Congress with reference to the management of its financial affairs had been the establishment of separate and semi-independent offices for the administration of each tolerably

[1] Journals of Congress, July 30, 1776.

important class of business. Frequent demands for a simpler and more compact system [1] now began to be heard, but for the present nothing was done. The Treasury Board soon tired of the work of the Committee of Claims, and in March, 1777, secured the appointment of a new committee, to consist of three Commissioners of Claims, who were to adjust accounts and hand them over to the Auditor-General. Special committees were continually being appointed to assist the treasury officials, usually to devise plans for raising money. There were also special officers appointed for auditing special accounts in the different armies or different colonies, and for other purposes, until by degrees the work of the Treasury had enlisted the services of an army of officials, boards, and committees.

Save the usual changes in the Treasury Board, which were always being made, either through additions to its membership or changes in its *personnel*, there was no important event in the history of the department in 1777. In July [2] of the following year a Continental Treasurer of Loans was appointed, whose services had now become necessary through the extensive credit operations upon which Congress had entered. He was to sign all loan-office certificates and bills of exchange for the payment of interest thereon, and put them to any use ordered by Congress or

---

[1] Journals of Congress, October 17, 1776.
[2] Ibid., July 15 and 28, 1778.

the Treasury Board. A month later the appointment of a committee of five was ordered, to consider the state of the finances of the United States and report from time to time to Congress. This body, subsequently known as the Standing Committee of Finance, had Robert Morris for its chairman, and submitted frequent reports on matters proposed in Congress.

By far the most important resolution of the year 1778, however, was that of September 26, remodelling the entire establishment. It provided, first of all, for giving some degree of unity to the Treasury by authorizing Congress to secure a house for the various offices of the department. Provision was then made for the annual appointment of a comptroller, auditor, treasurer, and two chambers of accounts to consist of three members each, besides the clerks necessary to assist them. Under this system accounts were first examined and adjusted by the auditor, and sent to one of the chambers of accounts, where the commissioners made whatever corrections or reductions they saw fit. They were then returned and examined a second time by the auditor, who heard any objections to the decisions of the chamber, and from his ruling there was no appeal except to Congress. The account, having been finally endorsed by the auditors, was forwarded to the comptroller, by whom drafts were issued on the treasurer for the amount involved. By this organization the Treasury Office of Accounts was entirely superseded, but the Treasury Board, that is, the original standing committee of Congressmen appointed early in 1776, was still retained as an intermediary between Congress and its treasury officials. It is worthy of note, in passing, that the system of checks and balances here for the first time instituted among the officers of the Treasury Department, and even the titles of the officials, have not, with a temporary exception, been since materially changed.

At the time, however, Congress was not over-sanguine as to the result. In October, an invitation was extended to Dr. Price,[1] the English economist, to consider himself a citizen of the United States, and assist in regulating their finances; but the learned financier declined to accept. The new arrangement was in working order by the beginning of 1779, and was allowed to remain undisturbed for several months. But on July 30th we find the inevitable treasury resolution again at work. This time it carried away the old Treasury Board, which for nearly four years had withstood the continued attacks to which almost every other branch of the department had yielded. In its place there was provided a new board to be composed of three commissioners, not delegates in Congress, and two members of that body. The commissioners were

[1] Dipl. Corr. of the Rev., vol. iii. p. 64.

to be annually elected by Congress and continued in office until a new election; but no member of Congress was to serve for more than six months by virtue of one election. In addition to the board there were to be an Auditor-General, a Treasurer, two Chambers of Accounts, and six auditors for settling claims and accounts arising in the army. The new Board of Treasury was " to have general superintendence of the finances of the United States, and of all officers entrusted with the receipt and expenditures" of public funds. The members of the board were, further, to inspect the Treasury; lay before Congress estimates of public expenses and necessary supplies; call on public officers for information; and carry into effect all acts and resolutions of Congress relating to financial affairs. Accounts were now to pass through the hands of the Auditor-General, then to a Chamber of Accounts, and then back to the Auditor-General, much as under the previous organization, except that appeals now lay to the Board of Treasury and not to Congress. The new auditors were to reside in whatever detachment of the army they might be assigned to by the board; to adjust all accounts; and to submit their reports to the Auditor-General.

With the exception of a few minor changes, the treasury establishment under this arrangement continued for two years — a somewhat extended period for this chameleon-like department. It was allowed so long a life, doubtless, because Congress had grown weary of constant change, and probably for the better reason that the supply of artificial remedies had by this time been almost exhausted. The courage to apply the proper remedy, which in the case of the Treasury seemed to be surrounded by greater dangers than in the other departments, was still lacking. And, in fact, Congress was driven to it finally only by the most pressing force of circumstances. Previously to this, much care and diligence had been exercised in detecting the first signs of disorder and friction. By continual watchfulness and timely action, dangerous accidents had been averted. This latest experiment, however, was permitted to remain undisturbed until tragic disaster was almost imminent.

During the first year there were comparatively few complaints urged against the new management. But as the summer of 1780 approached and sped along, murmurs began to rise on many sides which bore no complimentary allusions to those in charge of the national purse-strings. At first indifferent, Congress allowed them to develop into a loud wail before it saw fit to take action. The matter was at length placed in the hands of the usual investigating committee, and the report submitted in August presented no pleasing picture of unselfish patriotism. After a series of damaging charges of a general character, it was alleged that the members could only be seen between the hours of nine and twelve in the morning, and the unfortunate Treasurer of Loans complained that when he had, on one urgent occasion, sought information at an hour other than those specified, the door had been unceremoniously slammed in his face. This was followed by other specific charges, apparently well founded, which led the committee to recommend the dismissal of two members of the board for "disgusting conduct."

In addition to these internal disorders, which it required a committee to discover, there began to crop out on the surface little irregularities that all the world might see. There was, it is true, no startling exposure of fraud or defalcation, but when, at intervals, a committee of Congress happened to encounter the Treasury Board, instead of that willing courtesy with which scrupulous public servants meet their superiors, we find the members of the Board of Treasury standing upon hollow formalities, engaging in senseless quibbles, and throwing whatever obstacles were possible in the way of the investigating committees.[1] To say the least, such conduct leaves unpleasant suspicions in the minds of the critical.

The report of a second committee in November[2]

[1] MSS. in State Department, No. 26, p. 165.
[2] Ibid., No. 19, vol. iii. p. 179.

was no less damaging than the one of August. Perhaps Congress was influenced also by a final exhibition of carelessness on the part of the board, which led to the seizure of the Treasury buildings in December for unpaid rent.[1] At any rate, on February 7, 1781, the appointment of a Superintendent of Finance was ordered, and by the same resolution which had authorized the office of Secretary at War.

Returning again to our starting-point, and taking up the development of the Navy Department, we find that for the beginnings of the naval history of the United States we must turn to the very humble fleets of the colonies. At the outbreak of the Revolution, nearly all of them had one or two vessels in fighting trim, and, until the close of the war, moderate naval forces were maintained by Massachusetts, Rhode Island, Connecticut, Pennsylvania, Virginia, and North Carolina.[2]

In some of these states the conduct of naval as well as military affairs was entrusted to the Councils of Safety; while in others it was early considered best to establish separate boards. Virginia was one of the latter number. Here too, however, naval affairs had at first been placed under the supervision of the Council of Safety, and it was not until June, 1776, that a Board of

[1] MSS. in State Department, No. 136, vol. iv. p. 773.
[2] Winsor, Narrative and Critical History of America, vol. vi. p. 568.

Commissioners[1] was organized to "superintend and direct all the naval affairs of the colony." This is particularly interesting for the reason that it was as near an approach as is to be found in any of the colonies to the later Continental idea of an executive department. The ordinance of the assembly establishing the board was a carefully drawn document providing for the appointment of five commissioners, the president to be known as the First Commissioner of the Navy. And so satisfactory were the operations of the commissioners that South Carolina followed the example of her sister state, a few months later, and established a similar institution.[2]

The origin of the Continental navy proper is to be found in a resolve of Congress of October 13, 1775, to fit out two armed vessels to intercept transports bringing supplies to the enemy. To do the work connected therewith, a committee of seven was appointed.[3] They were, in the course of a few days, given power to engage seamen and officers; and in a little while almost any matter pertaining to naval affairs was transferred to them immediately upon reaching Congress. In consequence of this they soon came to be known as the Naval Committee, and served as a miniature

---

[1] American State Papers, vol. vi. p. 1598.

[2] The model used in this case was doubtless the English Admiralty Board, with the presiding officer patterned after the First Lord of the Admiralty.

[3] Journals of Congress, October 30, 1776.

DEVELOPMENT OF EXECUTIVE DEPARTMENTS. 139

Admiralty Board. On December 11th, a committee consisting of one member from each colony was appointed to report a plan for furnishing the colonies with a naval armament, and within two days Congress had ordered the construction of thirteen vessels. For the management of this enterprise a new committee of thirteen[1] was appointed, who, on account of the magnitude of their work, were not long in overshadowing the the less important Naval Committee. The latter completed its work and sank into insignificance, while the general conduct of naval affairs was transferred to the later committee of thirteen, now known as the "Marine Committee." It was allowed considerable independence of action, and was soon in entire control of the navy. For naval affairs, it corresponded exactly with the Board of War in its relation to military matters;[2] was the custodian of naval supplies; recommended officers and seamen; superintended the construction of vessels; and performed other duties of a like nature.

These duties became more arduous during 1776, as the navy increased in size, and in October[3] Congress authorized the committee to employ such assistants as were necessary for the proper execution of its business. This led, a little

---

[1] Journals of Congress, December 14, 1775.
[2] Ibid., December 22, 1775; April 16 and June 6, 1776.
[3] Ibid., October 28, 1776.

later,[1] to the appointment of a board of three commissioners who were to perform the work of the Marine Committee under its direction. This was precisely what was done afterwards, as we have already seen, when the Board of War was appointed and placed under the supervision of the old Board of War and Ordnance. On the recommendation of the Marine Committee, Congress appointed Colonel John Nixon, John Wharton, and Francis Hopkinson to be the commissioners, and the duties of their office were promptly assumed. They at once became known as the Navy Board, and were soon the recognized heads of the department.

After a few months, a similar board was established for the Eastern States and located at Boston.[2] It was also composed of three members, and was directly responsible to the Marine Committee. This was followed shortly by another at Philadelphia for the Middle States.[3] These assistant boards relieved the Continental Navy Board of all matters purely local in their bearing, and were even given power, on occasion, to suspend insubordinate officers within their respective departments.[4] The central board reserved for itself jurisdiction in all matters of a general character, and the superintendence of any naval

[1] Journals of Congress, November 6, 1776.
[2] Ibid., April 19, 1777.
[3] Wells's Life of Samuel Adams, vol. iii. p. 18.
[4] Journals of Congress, December 30, 1777.

business in those colonies not provided with subordinate boards.

As might have been expected, the clumsy and numerous Marine Committee could not always continue the management of the department. In October, 1779, it was instructed to prepare a plan for its own supersedure, and promptly complied with the order. Here, again, we find Congress unable to improve upon the work already done in the colonies. The form of organization long before adopted by Virginia and South Carolina was now put into practice on a broader scale, and on October 28th a resolution was passed vesting the superintendence of all naval and marine affairs in a Board of Admiralty. It was to consist of two members of Congress, and three others, " to be in all cases subject to the control of Congress," although specific duties were also assigned by the resolution itself.

Though marking no definite stage in the development of the departments, this method of constituting the executive boards, partly of members of Congress and partly of outsiders, at least indicates a tendency of thought that influenced the legislative body in 1779. An attempt had been made in the previous year[1] to apply this form to the Board of War, but did not receive the necessary support. It was, however, adopted in the succeeding July, in the case of the Treasury Department, as we have already seen, and was now, again, applied to the navy. This method

[1] Journals of Congress, October 29, 1778.

of organization, while possessing no special advantages, was yet no worse than others, and the new Admiralty Board was not disturbed until February 7, 1781. Then, by the resolution already mentioned as providing a Secretary at War and Superintendent of Finance, the Navy Department was placed in charge of a Secretary of Marine.

Turning now to the State Department, it will be well to remember that, of the functions of sovereignty imposed upon a newly formed state, the management of its diplomatic relations is certainly not the least difficult. When the United Colonies emerged from submission to aggressive independence, they were in this particular most delicately situated. With no previous experience in international dealings, their sturdy patriots were thrown without warning among a set of wily diplomatists trained in a school not over-sensitive to questions of casuistry. Yet they proved themselves worthy foes for these hardened warriors, and some of the greatest victories of the Revolution were those won on diplomatic battle-fields.

It was then, as it still is, the policy of England to relieve her dependencies of the arduous tasks incident to diplomatic negotiations. Each of the colonies was allowed an agent in the mother country, the same person frequently representing several of them, but they partook chiefly of the nature of business agents, and were principally occupied in looking after the interests of individual citizens. They were in no sense diplomatic officials, save that they presented any petitions forwarded by the colonies to the home government.

It was early recognized that communication must be opened with foreign countries, and it was in the achievement of this that we may best notice the simple, and in this case purely indigenous, origin of the departments. On November 29, 1775, it was resolved by Congress that a committee of five be appointed "for the sole purpose of corresponding with our friends in Great Britain, Ireland, and other parts of the world." This committee immediately received the title of "Committee of Secret Correspondence," and one need not look far to find its prototype. One of the most powerful pieces of Revolutionary machinery was that little contrivance of Sam Adams which, in very homely language, he called a "Committee of Correspondence." At first embracing only a narrow circuit of Massachusetts towns, it soon spread to every colony, then to their principal towns, and in a twinkling the colonies were bound together by an electric chain, which, with a deft manipulator at the Boston end, carried fiery currents into every corner of the land.

What, then, could have been more natural than the formation of a Committee of Correspondence on a larger scale, for foreign communication? It answered the further purpose, moreover, of being only a *committee* and not a *foreign office*. For although hostilities had already begun, there were, nevertheless, many who still hoped for a bloodless reconciliation, and who would not have sanctioned the hanging out, at this time, of a bolder sign of sovereignty.[1]

This was the simple beginning of the diplomatic history of the Revolution. The committee soon threw aside its mask and appeared as the Foreign Office of the government, although as yet its work was only clerical. Franklin, Jay, Dickinson, Harrison, and Johnson were the original members, but, as in the case of all the other committee departments, the membership was subject to continual change. They had charge of all foreign correspondence; prepared commissions and instructions for ministers going abroad; and communicated with the ministers and agents of the colonies at foreign courts.[2]

In April, 1777, the style of the committee was changed to the "Committee of Foreign Affairs," but no change whatever was made with regard to its duties. For more than five years, by virtue of the simple resolution of November, 1775, which limited its duties to "corresponding" with the friends of the colonies abroad, this committee

---

[1] Morse's John Adams, pp. 111, 112.
[2] Journals of Congress, March 13, 1777.

conducted the business of the department. At the same time it must be borne in mind that it was not a diplomatic office in the modern sense. It was rarely entrusted with the determination of weighty questions of policy, such matters being usually left with special committees. The consideration of proposed treaties was nearly always disposed of in this way; applications from foreigners for commissions in the army were heard by the standing Committee on Foreign Application; and a fair share of the foreign correspondence was, during this period, attended to by the Treasury officials, since the American ministers and agents abroad were principally engaged in trying to raise funds. So that, after all, the Committee of Foreign Affairs was left with little more on its hands than writing letters.

It did not, however, escape the criticism which fell upon those in charge of the War, Treasury, and Navy Departments. Its correspondence was attended to with such regularity only as the time and inclination of the members admitted. They alternated in filling the position of secretary, and then left it vacant again during long intervals. They were sufficiently taxed by attendance upon Congress, and the multitude of minor committees that were continually being appointed. Delay in disposing of the heavy correspondence of the department was unavoidable. At the same time, the representatives abroad were not to be blamed for lodging complaint on the score of receiving no replies to their letters, and very meagre intelligence of any sort from America.

Already, in 1779, complaints against the committee's tardy work had begun to reach Congress. Nearly every representative of the government in Europe had some grievance to urge, either because he received no letters at all, or only very brief and unsatisfactory notes. This continued throughout 1780, and at length, in December, Arthur Lee wrote in a most desperate strain that, unless the department were reorganized on a different basis, and more regular communication with ministers assured, it was useless to expect anything to be accomplished. This pressure for a change, coming as it did from those immediately concerned, led to the establishment of the office of Secretary for Foreign Affairs a month in advance of the others. The office was authorized by a resolution of January 10, 1781.

These radical changes in the departments in the early part of 1781 are attributable to causes both general and special in their nature. The specific disorders in each having been sufficiently considered, it may not be inappropriate at this point to survey their general progress during the period already covered. We have seen that in their origin they were all characterized by the entire absence of any exotic elements. The Committee of Secret Correspondence, afterwards the Committee of Foreign Affairs, maintained its native purity throughout. The War, Treasury, and Navy Departments yielded to the attacks of foreign influences. That which predominated was undoubtedly English. The evidences of this are apparent not only in the forms borrowed, but also in the titles applied to them, several of which were appropriated, either unaltered or with very slight verbal change. There were, nevertheless, other agencies also at work. It is quite certain, for example, that the Chambers of Accounts established in 1778 were fashioned after the French " Chambres des Comptes;"[1] it is more than probable that the Comptroller's office was modelled after that of the " Controleur-Général," since the English Comptroller-General is of a subsequent date;[2] and it is also possible that there were still other influences brought to bear.

It is to the British influence, however, that the adoption of the system of board management may unhesitatingly be ascribed. Differences in the prevailing conditions of the two governments will account for differences in detail; but there can be no question that the general conception of the Board of War, the Admiralty Board, and the several Treasury Boards, was determined by the forms of the corresponding contemporary English bodies. Both England and America have since

[1] Chéruel, Dictionnaire des Institutions Françaises.
[2] 4 Wm. IV. c. 15; Todd, Parl. Govt. in Eng.

discovered the principle which should have been applied. The more timely recognition of it on this side of the Atlantic was due only to the peculiar circumstances under which we first found departments necessary at all, and the crucial tests to which they were subjected before time was had for crystallization.

Our own experience with boards, if brief, was none the less bitter. It is positively pathetic to follow Congress through its aimless wanderings in search of a system for the satisfactory management of its executive departments. At no period between 1774 and 1781 can we find it pursuing any consistent line of action with reference to them. A humble committee served as the common origin of all. With the exception of the Committee of Foreign Affairs, they developed independently into boards, and afterwards each was tossed about and tinkered at different times and under different circumstances. They were variously composed of members of Congress, of civilians, or of both, but always with the same unhappy results. Some were kept well under the control of Congress; others were allowed considerable independence of action. The membership of all was continually fluctuating, and nearly every member of Congress served at one time or another on one of the War or Treasury boards. Being usually appointed for no definite time, members would serve for a few months and then resign on the plea of other pressing business. Where salaries were attached to the offices, they were subject to continual change, and varied with the market value of the currency. There was, in short, no element of permanency to be found anywhere in the entire system. Worse than all, petty jealousies and local prejudices frequently distracted the otherwise peaceable councils of the boards, and any wise and patriotic intentions on the part of some were sure to be neutralized by the selfish and personal biases of others. The result was, that where peremptory and decisive action was most essential, there was only childish hesitancy and delay.

It was impossible that such a condition should reach a climax without attracting attention. Congress endeavored to correct the earlier disorders by patching and mending its boards. This proving of no avail, it began to remodel and reorganize; but farther than that it refused to move. As the abuses became more flagrant, and rumors were carried outside the halls of Congress, inquiries began to be made as to why more radical remedies were not applied. With them came suggestions and recommendations, and not a few early advised the appointment of single executive officers. These propositions met with little favor when they first reached Congress. The legislative body jealously guarded the limited executive prerogatives vested in it, and shrank from entrusting them to individuals who might therewith set themselves up as an independent power.

The clamor for the adoption of improved methods eventually grew so loud that it could no longer be ignored. In January, 1779,[1] the Committee of Foreign Affairs was instructed to secure, through the ministers and agents abroad, copies of the arrangements and forms of conducting the executive departments of the various governments to which they were respectively accredited. But this having been done, Congress manifested no further intention to act.

The matter was then taken up outside, and a vigorous crusade against the boards was begun. To Hamilton the greatest credit is due for urging on this opposition with the energy that characterized him in all undertakings. He had given the whole subject careful attention, and acquainted himself thoroughly with the forms of other governments. Having mastered the situation, he proceeded to impress his views on members of Congress, as well as on other men of influence throughout the colonies. Writing to Morris in 1780, he thus expressed his reasons for preferring single ministers of War, Foreign Affairs, Finance, and Marine: "There is always more decision, more dispatch, more responsibility, where single men than where bodies are concerned,"[2] and he

---

[1] Secret Journals of Congress, vol. ii. p. 130.
[2] Hamilton's Works, vol. i. p. 129.

then takes occasion to remark that "men will only devote their lives and attention to the mastering a profession on which they can build reputation and consequence which they do not share with others." A little later he repeats these arguments to Duane, and now goes so far as to suggest General Schuyler as a fitting person for Minister of War, and selects McDougal and Robert Morris for the Navy and Finance Departments respectively.[1] He wrote to Sears in the same strain, and also to others,[2] and undoubtedly influenced some of them to see the situation from his point of view.

Washington also assisted by direct appeals to Congress,[3] and others of less prominence lent their aid in numerous ways. The contagion even spread to the colonial assemblies and conventions, and in August, 1780, the Boston Convention passed a resolution recommending the adoption of "a permanent system for the several departments." There were also pamphleteers in the struggle; and only a few weeks before the office of Superintendent of Finance was established, Pelatiah Webster published a paper on the "Nature, Authority, etc., of a Financier-General," in which he heartily urged the appointment of such an official.[4]

---

[1] Hamilton's Works, vol. i. pp. 155-159.
[2] Ibid., p. 189; Lodge's Hamilton, pp. 28-30.
[3] Washington's Writings, vol. iii. p. 420.
[4] Pelatiah Webster's Essays, ed. 1791, p. 171, note.

In spite of all this there were still some who clung to their predilection for boards. They made no attempt to deny that abuses had arisen under their favorite system, but only endeavored to diminish the force of this objection by pointing out the evil consequences which might follow from allowing improper persons to secure control under the new plan. Samuel Adams placed himself at the head of those who opposed the innovation,[1] and presented a vigorous opposition. Nevertheless, a majority finally consented to make the experiment, and the resolutions necessary were accordingly passed.

There is nothing to indicate which one of the Continental systems was most resorted to for models by those who championed the reform. Of the English and French departments, on which particular stress had been laid when, two years before, the Committee of Foreign Affairs was ordered to secure copies of the various European arrangements, it is likely that the latter played the more prominent part. The principle of one-man rule in the executive offices had at this time developed to a far greater extent in France than in England; but the most that can be said with certainty is, that the stock example used by the Americans to illustrate the advantages of a change was Henry IV.'s great minister, the Duke of Sully.

[1] Wells's Life of Samuel Adams, vol. iii. p. 127; Hosmer's Samuel Adams, pp. 381, 382.

Yet, with all that had been gained, the victory was far from being complete. Resuming the story of the departments *seriatim*, and turning to that of War, we at once discover that the Board of War is not to be immediately destroyed by the mere provision for its successor. Congress had, indeed, provided for the appointment of a Secretary at War. A title for him had been bodily imported from England, including the little preposition *at*. He was granted a liberal amount of authority, and vested with the usual functions of a Minister of War. But when it was proposed to select the secretary, the office proved only a new occasion for reviving the disgraceful brawls between the opposing factions and cliques who represented in Congress the interests of one or the other set of officers then high in command in the Revolutionary army. Many attempts were made to secure an election, but each time a postponement was effected [1] by the faction in the minority In spite of the uneasiness caused by this delay,[2] it was not until late in October, more than eight months after the office was created, that General Benjamin Lincoln was finally chosen to fill the vacancy. It was another month before he entered upon his duties, and only in January, 1782, was the department organized under him, and the new subordinates provided for. Not until then did the Board of War retire from the field.

[1] Washington's Writings, vol. vii. pp. 399, 460.
[2] Ibid., vol. viii. p. 39.

The War Department had naturally declined in importance after the cessation of hostilities, but the work still within its scope was well and faithfully executed by the new secretary.[1] After two years of service General Lincoln resigned, and the business of the department was then conducted by the chief clerk as "Secretary in the War Office." This continued until early in 1785, when an ordinance was passed "for the purpose of ascertaining the powers and duties of the Secretary at War." This had the effect of reorganizing the department, although but few changes were inaugurated. Henry Knox was elected secretary, to preside over the office as now constituted, on March 8, 1785, and entered upon the performance of his duties soon afterwards. Subsequently to this it demanded little attention from the Continental Congress. Under Knox the department developed and was well conducted. He divided the establishment into well-organized bureaus, was economical in his administration, and won the praise of his superiors.[2] The inauguration of the Federal Constitution found him still in charge.

The appointment of a Superintendent of Finance,[3] as required by the resolution of February

[1] Journals of Congress, November 4, 1783.
[2] Ibid., October 2, 1788.
[3] Where the title for the new Finance Minister was found is somewhat doubtful. More than a hundred years before this, there had been a French officer of finance known as the *surintendant*,

7, 1781, was not delayed so long as that of the Secretary at War. When the latter had been once appointed, however, there was an end to the Board of War; but the fight against Treasury boards was more prolonged and bitter. Of the secretarial offices established at this time, that of the Treasury was considered by far the most important. It was only with many qualms that certain Congressmen agreed to place the finances of the country under the management of one man. But having finally summoned courage to take the step, they reserved for themselves no rights which might have tended to interfere with the superintendent in the execution of his trust. He was authorized to examine into the state of the public finances; report plans for improving them; direct the execution of any orders of Congress respecting revenue or expenditure; superintend and control the settlement of the public accounts, and perform other duties relating to his department. The powers granted were all that were necessary for the proper conduct of the affairs of the office, and the friends of the new plan felt more than satisfied with the prospects before them.

Although scarcely twenty-four, Hamilton had

but his office had long been conducted by the *controleur*. Still, they may have gone back a century to borrow his title. The Americans, however, thought it too high-sounding, and called the minister either the Financier-General, or, more frequently, the Financier.

already won sufficient reputation to recommend him for the place,[1] but the successful career of the more mature merchant-prince pointed to the fitness of Robert Morris, and led to his election on February 20th. The choice of Congress met with universal approval.[2] The Board of Treasury continued its work until the Superintendent was able to arrange a plan for the detailed working of his department, and this being completed in September, the board and the offices immediately under it ceased to exist.[3] The office of Treasurer of Loans, having been handed over to the Treasurer in July, also disappeared.

Congress then passed an ordinance providing for the appointment of certain officials in aid of the Superintendent of Finance. These were an assistant, a comptroller, a treasurer, a register, and such auditors and clerks as the Superintendent might consider necessary. The comptroller now assumed the duties of the old auditor-general, and had none of the functions of the comptroller appointed by virtue of the resolution of 1778. The auditing and adjusting of accounts was made less complicated than before, and was mainly the work of the clerks and auditors. The treasurer retained the same functions borne by previous officers with the same title; and the reg-

---

[1] Hamilton's Republic, vol. ii. p. 201.
[2] Bolles, Financial History of the United States, vol. i. p. 268.
[3] Journals of Congress, September 11, 1781; Bolles, vol. i. pp. 306, 307.

ister, now appointed for the first time, was, as he still is, the head book-keeper of the department.

With these assistants under him, Morris took the reins. His driving was more than satisfactory, even to those who at first entertained the gravest fears of recklessness. Instead of any attempts to contract his sphere of action, the tendency was quite the reverse.[1] When it became apparent that he was bringing order into the almost inconceivably chaotic finances of the Revolution, there seemed to be a general desire to assist him in every way possible. But unfortunately this refers to his preliminary work only, and the dreams of those who looked hopefully to the prospects of brighter days were not yet to be realized. The incapacity, and sometimes graver faults, of those who had previously managed the Treasury business, had opened wide the doors to confusion, extravagance, and dishonesty. The numerous officials connected with the department, whose responsibility to any one in particular was uncertain, had made grievous use of their freedom. And, on the whole, the situation could hardly have been worse.

Morris was no ordinary financier, and was not to be easily disheartened. He set to work, and economy and order began to appear. His preliminary labors were well under way, and he

[1] Journals of Congress, July 10, 31, August 1, November 27, 1781.

was just preparing to advance, but the mere announcement was sufficient to make it plain that, for the present, progress was impossible. The first things to be done were, to pay the interest on the foreign and domestic debts, and settle the arrears of the soldiers' pay and the small floating accounts. This required taxation. The states refused to be taxed, and that was the key to the entire situation. The local opposition and apathy at once reacted on Congress, and the encouraging support at first received from this source was immediately withdrawn. However desirous the members themselves might have been to act patriotically, they dared not openly defy the instructions from their states by voting for the measures proposed.[1]

Without funds and without support, there was nothing left for Morris but to resign.[2] Although prevailed upon to remain in office until November, 1784 he tendered his resignation early in 1783. This was a consummation over which those who had opposed the establishment of the office in 1781 chuckled and gloated. They pointed gleefully to the plight as a complete realization of their prophecies, and, to make sure of a return to Treasury Boards, exaggerated the misfortunes of the administration, and invented the most ma-

---

[1] Elliot's Debates, vol. v. p. 29; Dipl. Corr. of the Rev., vol. xii. p. 328.

[2] Bolles, Financial History of the U. S., vol. i. p. 330.

licious charges against it. No sort of dishonesty or corruption was too low for them to attribute to Morris and his agents, and it finally became a matter of self-respect with him to withdraw.

Although he retired in November, 1784, provision for the office had already been made in May. There were many who understood the true causes of his failure, and to these the experience with a Minister of Finance had not been lost. For the present, however, they had to yield to the majority, who now placed the department under the care of a new Board of Treasury, to consist of three commissioners appointed by Congress. They were to have all powers "ever vested in the Superintendent of Finance," which, since 1781, included naval affairs. It was found to be no easy matter to enlist the services of proper persons, and not until a number of gentlemen had been invited and declined, was a complete board secured.[1] It was as late as the summer of 1785 before the board relieved the comptrollers, who, in the interval, had been at the head of the department. When this was once accomplished, however, there was no further attempt made by Congress to regulate the office under the Articles of Confederation. The board managed the finances in much the same way as

[1] Journals of Congress, June 3, November 30, December 10, 1784; January 25, April 1, 1785.

previous boards had done, and continued in power until Hamilton succeeded it.

The consideration of the Navy Department under the Continental Congress, subsequent to 1781, will not detain us long, for as an independent organization it disappeared from view. The duties of the Secretary of Marine and of the Secretary at War differed only in that one had charge of the land and the other of the naval forces of the United States. With rather unusual promptness, General Alexander McDougal was elected Secretary of Marine, but he being excused from serving, the Board of Admiralty was retained in authority. No further attempt appears to have been made to fill the vacancy, and in August a temporary substitute was provided by authorizing the appointment of an Agent of Marine. But when, after a week, Congress found itself unable to select an acceptable incumbent even for this office, the whole Navy Department was summarily turned over to the already overburdened Superintendent of Finance. With this, the Board of Admiralty, the Navy Boards, and all civil offices under them, ceased to exist, and henceforth, until 1789, the Navy and Treasury Departments were under the same management.

Taking up the history of the Foreign Office from the establishment of the secretariat in 1781, one cannot but be impressed with the apparent completeness of the change. After having suffered the department to remain undisturbed for six years under the most primitive form of management, Congress seemed suddenly to have developed, through some source, a fairly modern and comprehensive notion of what the office should have been. The new secretary was to reside wherever Congress might be sitting, and was to have custody of all papers relative to the business of the department, receive applications from foreigners, correspond with the agents and ministers abroad with a view to securing information with regard to affairs in other parts of the world, and forward such instructions to ministers as Congress might order.

It required seven months for Congress to select an incumbent for the position, the choice finally falling to Robert R. Livingston. He settled down right manfully to his work shortly after his appointment, and very soon the beneficial effects of the change were everywhere remarked. A few months after he had been in office, however, he discovered several defects in the ordinance regulating his department, and recommended a number of changes. This led to a reorganization of the department by a resolution of February 22, 1782. The occasion was used first to lengthen the Secretary's title by calling him now the Secretary to the United States for the Department of Foreign Affairs. There were no changes in the duties of the officer as enumerated in the ordinance of the previous year, save that they were catalogued with greater exactness; and it was now carefully prescribed that any correspondence which the Secretary might intend to forward to ministers, either of the United States or of foreign powers, relative to treaties and conventions or "other great national subjects," should first be submitted to Congress and receive its approbation. At the same time the scope of the office was enlarged by making of the Secretary a medium of communication between the states whenever any misunderstanding might arise between them. For, besides being now ordered to correspond with the governors and presidents of the several states to afford them such information concerning his department as might be useful, he was also to inform them of any complaints urged against them by any other states or the subjects thereof. But having once forwarded the communications, his connection with interstate disputes was at an end.

The avidity with which Congress embraced this opportunity to enumerate more carefully the duties of the Secretary, and provide for a closer vigilance over his work, was an intimation that the management of the departments under the new ministers was being closely watched. This supposition was fully justified in the case of the foreign office. Far from being considered as the head of the diplomatic service of the United

States, the Secretary was for several years treated little better than a congressional clerk. He was rarely entrusted with any important business, and then only to be molested by some meddling Congressman. Livingston could not help appreciating the indignities[1] of his situation. To add to his other discomforts, he found the salary wholly inadequate to sustain the dignity of the office.[2] Fortunately for himself he had continued to hold office as Chancellor of the State of New York after accepting the post of Secretary for Foreign Affairs, and at the end of his twelve-month's experience decided to retain his judicial honors and abandon "diplomacy."

He formally tendered his resignation to Congress in December, 1782, but was induced to remain in office until the following June.[3] On the whole, there could not have been much pleasure in presiding over the department. Stowed away on the second floor of a musty little two-story wooden building, "The Secretary to the United States for the Department of Foreign Affairs" conducted the business of his government. Here he received the visits of ministers of foreign powers, while the representatives of "effete despotism," as they climbed the rickety stairs, were obliged to bow their heads lest their

---

[1] Madison's Works, vol. i. p. 142.
[2] Elliot's Debates, vol. v. p. 9.
[3] Journals of Congress, June 4, 1783.

crowns come in forcible contact with the threatening ceilings.[1]

After Livingston's retirement the Secretary of Congress was for a time in charge,[2] and for the vacant office the names of Jefferson, Arthur Lee, George Clymer, and Jonathan Trumbull were submitted by their respective friends.[3] None of them suited, and the office was then placed under the temporary care of the Under Secretary.[4] It was nearly a year before the place left vacant by Livingston was tendered to Jay, and a like period had almost elapsed before he assumed control. At the time of his appointment, in May, 1784, Jay was preparing to return to America after a five years' residence abroad on diplomatic business. He was in many ways admirably fitted for the position. As soon as was possible after his arrival at home, he entered upon the management of the foreign office, and from this time it began to assume the prominence which subsequently made it the first of the departments. This was due wholly to the persistency with which he insisted that Congress should surround the office with that dignity which, as he had learned during his residence at foreign courts, was its peculiar property. He made frequent use of his privilege to appear on the floor of Congress, and embraced

---

[1] Watson's Annals of Philadelphia, vol. i. p. 423.
[2] Journals of Congress, June 4, 1783.
[3] Elliot's Debates, vol. v. p. 91.
[4] Journals of Congress, February 3, 1784.

every favorable opportunity to elevate his office from the petty clerkship toward which it was gravitating to the dignified and honorable ideal that he had set up. When displeased, he did not swallow his anger as his predecessor had done, but openly protested, and usually gained his point. We find him terribly ruffled, for instance, and with good reason, when he discovered that the correspondence pertaining to his office sometimes reached Congress before it had passed under his own scrutiny,[1] and he was not long in having the matter properly arranged. It was consequently not strange that the French Minister should soon be writing home that Jay's influence was very great, and that Congress was frequently guided by his opinions.

Although it had increased in dignity, the department did not grow in outward dimensions. As late as 1788 there were in the office, besides the Secretary and his assistants, only two clerks, or just enough, as may be inferred from a report of this date, for one of them to be in the office while the other went to luncheon.[2] The quarters of the office, the report tells us, consisted of only two rooms, one of them being used as the parlor, and the other for the workshop. Nevertheless, with this little force, Jay continued to give satisfaction, and remained in office until he

[1] Madison's Works, vol. i. p. 142.
[2] MSS. in State Department.

became Chief Justice of the Supreme Court of the United States under the new Constitution.

Up to this point no mention has been made of the Post-Office. The reason for this is, that its development was for the most part different from, and independent of, that of the four departments already considered. To a greater extent than was the case with any of these, however, its early history was directly and intimately connected with colonial institutions, and a word or two historically may therefore be necessary. The American post-office originated in a patent granted to Thomas Neale in 1693 by the Governor of Virginia.[1] At first a private enterprise, it was no sooner discovered that this was a paying institution than it was "established," and by the close of Queen Anne's reign was being conducted as a branch of the general post-office of England.

The post-office in the colonies during the last century was not an institution of imposing proportions. The post-riders started on their circuits only after mail enough had been secured to pay a goodly part of the expenses of the trip; and if letters between points now only a day apart reached their destination within a month, the time was not considered excessive. The riders were generally aged and decrepit citizens, who, we are told, were accustomed to knit their winter hosiery on their journeys, and could, of course,

[1] Hildreth, vol. ii. p. 181.

not be expected to urge on their steeds at a greater pace than was convenient for fine work with the needle.

As the Revolution drew near, the office did not escape the condemnation directed upon all royal institutions. Complaints were frequently heard that the rates of postage were extortionate, but to this the colonists might still have submitted, had not the home government, in 1774, committed an act of bold iconoclasm by removing Franklin from the office of deputy postmaster-general in charge of the colonial post-office. They were now thoroughly incensed, when matters were brought to a climax by the action of the postmaster at Philadelphia. To satisfy some petty spite, he had raised the postage on newspapers to such a rate that it became necessary to discontinue the publication of the paper in that city. William Goddard, the principal sufferer, was an editor of considerable ability, who was not to be thus easily suppressed. He gave some study to the workings of the post-office, and in the winter of 1774 set out for the northern colonies to secure their coöperation in the establishment of an independent route.[1] He called his system the Constitutional Post-Office, and started a test line between Baltimore and Philadelphia, which met with moderate success. He was eminently successful in his visit to the North, and enlisted the interest

[1] American Archives, Fourth Series, vol. i. pp. 500–504.

and support of the assemblies of New Hampshire, Massachusetts, Rhode Island, New Jersey, and New York, and routes were laid out in each of these colonies.[1] It was his desire from the beginning to have Congress undertake the work,[2] and, when that body determined to establish a route in the summer of 1775, it did little more than transfer Goddard's plans to its own management.[3]

After hostilities had once begun, it required no very urgent persuasion to induce Congress to take the matter up. The advantages of a government post-route, from a military point of view alone, were a sufficient consideration for its establishment, and as the preliminaries had all been arranged by Goddard, it was only necessary to put the whole into operation. On July 26, 1775, upon the advice of a committee previously appointed to consider the question, Congress agreed to the establishment of a Post-Office. There was to be a Postmaster-General, a Secretary, and a Comptroller, the latter being the financial officer of the department. The main route extended from Falmouth, Massachusetts (at present Portland, Maine), to Savannah, while the intermediate ramifications, in those states where Goddard had worked at least, were almost identical with

---

[1] American Archives, Fourth Series, vol. ii. pp. 536, 537, 650, 803, 982.

[2] Ibid., vol. ii. p. 1160.

[3] Ibid., vol. iv. p. 184 ; vol. vi. p. 1012.

his plans. The Postmaster-General was authorized to establish cross-roads and appoint postmasters, and in addition had the general supervision of the system.

Franklin was naturally chosen Postmaster-General, because of his experience under the old régime. After the department was once organized under him, it was left entirely to his care,[1] and was rarely the subject of consideration in Congress. When he resigned to leave for France, and the Comptroller, Richard Bache, was promoted to the vacancy, the legislature was compelled to devote more of its attention to the department. The change was soon advertised by the complaints of uncertainty and delay in the delivery of the mails, which early in 1777 began to reach Congress. This led to the appointment of an investigating committee, and during the year several resolutions were passed with a view to correcting the abuses. Another committee was appointed in 1778,[2] and in the following year a standing committee was chosen to which Congress referred all matters pertaining to the post-office.[3]

At intervals these committees would recommend short resolutions, which, in the course of a few years, had become a numerous and scattered

[1] Journals of Congress, December 2, 1775; February 1, 1776.
[2] Ibid., May 29, 1778.
[3] Ibid., April 16, 1779.

series of documents. They were gathered together in October, 1782, and a new ordinance passed for regulating the post-office, containing their general provisions in concise form. Beyond the fact that the ordinance was more carefully prepared, and provided for more effectual work, it differed in no important particular from the one originally passed in 1775. It did, however, fix a punishment for any infringement of " the sole and exclusive right and power of establishing and regulating post-routes throughout all these United States," which, in the preceding year, the Articles of Confederation had vested in Congress. Under this act the Post-Office was conducted until further provision was made by the Federal Government.

This completes the history of the departments under the Continental Congress. It yet remains to consider the several steps preparatory to their arrangement under the new Constitution, and their final establishment by the Federal Congress. The whole question, in connection with the executive branch of the government, was naturally a frequent subject of discussion in the Constitutional Convention of 1787. An examination of the opinions and arguments there brought out cannot but leave the impression that the strength of the old forces, which we have already seen exercising an influence on the development of the departments, had not been seriously impaired.

DEVELOPMENT OF EXECUTIVE DEPARTMENTS. 171

This was particularly true of the respect for types adopted by the states. While the struggle for an effective union had been vainly progressing for a dozen years, the states individually had all succeeded in choosing schemes for their own self-government. They unanimously selected a single executive to preside over this system, and eleven of the thirteen had associated with him various sorts of councils. They differed as to the number of members and manner of appointment, and their duties were either to revise legislation, appoint minor officials, or advise and assist the governor.

It is consequently not difficult to imagine why, when the Convention at length determined that the executive of the United States should be a President, there at once arose a strong sentiment in favor of incorporating in the Constitution a provision for surrounding him with some kind of council. The idea having been once suggested, each member had an opportunity, after arranging the details to meet the broader requirements of the central government, to present that plan with which he had become familiar in his own state, while several occupied themselves with inventing original designs. In the scheme for a constitution submitted by Randolph,[1] there was a proposition to associate a number of members of the national judiciary with the executive as a council

[1] Elliot's Debates, vol. v. p. 128.

of revision. This was held to be open to the fatal objection of being inconsistent with the determination to maintain broad lines between the three branches of government,[1] and was soon abandoned. The plan, nevertheless, received considerable support, and this, as well as the several subsequent attempts to carry out a similar design, met with the hearty approbation of Madison.[2]

Next followed a series of projects for establishing a council to be composed of the heads of the departments. Hamilton, in his outline of a constitution,[3] had vested in the executive the sole power to appoint the "heads or chief officers of the Departments of Finance, War, and Foreign Affairs," but inasmuch as the later plans did not provide for such officers, it would appear that their appointment was preconceived. Pinckney at first suggested that they form a council of revision, but relinquished the idea when it occurred to him that the President would probably consult them whenever he saw fit, whether authorized to do so or not. Gouverneur Morris, with an eye on the English government, thought they would assume such a degree of importance and responsibility that justice would be more directly attained by relieving the President of the liability to impeachment, and imposing it upon the heads of departments.[4]

[1] Elliot's Debates, pp. 164, 165.
[2] Ibid., vol. v. pp. 344, 345, 428, 429.
[3] Ibid., p. 205.   [4] Ibid., vol. v. p. 335.

DEVELOPMENT OF EXECUTIVE DEPARTMENTS. 173

After a brief respite the general subject was revived by Ellsworth, who, in the interval, had devised a hybrid plan for a council,[1] to consist of the President of the Senate, the Chief Justice, and " the Ministers, as they might be established, for the Departments of Foreign and Domestic Affairs, War, Finance, and Marine, who should advise but not conclude the President." Gouverneur Morris came forward two days later[2] with a more elaborate scheme for a " Council of State." It was to consist of the Chief Justice, the Secretary of Domestic Affairs, Secretary of Commerce and Finance, Secretary of Foreign Affairs, Secretary of War, and Secretary of Marine. The functions of these officers were carefully prescribed, but for our present purpose are sufficiently indicated by their titles. The secretaries were to be appointed by the President, and hold office during his pleasure. They were required to submit their opinions, in writing, on any matter which the executive might refer to them, but their advice was not to be binding. Both these plans were handed to a committee, who reported a compromise[3] more complex than anything yet proposed. It was advised that the President be provided with a " Privy Council," of which the members should be the President of the Senate, the Speaker of the House of Repre-

[1] Elliot's Debates, vol. v. p. 442.   [2] Ibid., p. 446.
[3] Ibid., p. 462.

sentatives, the Chief Justice of the Supreme Court, and "the principal officers in the respective Departments of Foreign Affairs, Domestic Affairs, War, Marine, and Finance, as such departments may from time to time be established."

It is unnecessary to refer to the defects of such a council, and its adoption was not seriously considered for a moment. The attention of Congress was soon attracted from it by the novel arrangement proposed by Colonel Mason.[1] He recommended that the Senate appoint a privy council to consist of six members, who should hold office for as many years. Two of them were to be selected from the Southern, two from the Middle, and two from the Eastern States, and they were to retire in rotation, one third every second year. This was the last attempt to encumber the President with a council. The abundant variety of plans for establishing one, most of them involving the destruction of the barriers between the executive, legislative, and judicial branches of the government, had exposed the defects, rather than the merits, of councils in general. After Colonel Mason's scheme had been submitted, Gouverneur Morris abandoned his own, and opposed all other plans; and the opinion finally gained currency that an able council might thwart the executive, while a weak one would

[1] Elliot's Debates, vol. v. p. 522, 523.

either be induced to concur in his wrongful measures, or be used to shelter him from criticism.

The Constitution as finally adopted contained no provision for an established council for the chief magistrate. This omission was the cause of not a little dissatisfaction. Colonel Mason refused to sign the Constitution, because, among other reasons, "the President had no constitutional council (a thing unknown in any safe and regular government)." He expressed the prophetic fear that the clause which authorized the President "to require the opinion, in writing, of the principal officer in each of the executive departments," etc., would result in a council of state growing out of " the principal officers of the great departments." For reasons somewhat obscure, he asserted that a body so constituted contained "the most dangerous of all ingredients for such a council in a free country."

The only opportunity left for him to avert the danger was in the Virginia Convention for ratifying the Constitution. Here he moved an amendment embodying provision for a council more to his taste,[1] but met with little support. In several of the conventions of other states, movements were also instituted to secure the passage of amendments of a similar tenor. In New York it was desired that Congress select a council of ap-

[1] Elliot's Debates, vol. iii. p. 194.

pointment;[1] in Maryland, "a responsible council to the President" was what was wanted;[2] while in North Carolina some one proposed a council of thirteen, to consist of one member from each state.[3] While none of these propositions received the sanction of the state conventions, they elicited sufficient support to demand the respectful attention of those who were working to secure the adoption of the Constitution as it came from the Convention. When Hamilton reached the executive branch of the government in his Federalist papers he did not disdain to reply, at considerable length, to the arguments urged in favor of councils, and point out the evils connected with them ;[4] but the whole matter soon afterwards ceased to occupy public attention.

When the Federal Congress assembled, nothing but the all-important question of finance was allowed precedence over the executive departments. As early as May 19, 1789, the subject was introduced in the House by a motion from Boudinot to proceed to the establishment of a Treasury Department. It being deemed expedient that the number of departments should first be determined, this motion gave way to one framed by Madison, in which it was represented as the opinion of the House, that there ought to be Departments of Foreign Affairs, of War, and

---

[1] Elliot's Debates, vol. ii. p. 408.   [2] Ibid., vol. ii. p. 553.
[3] Ibid., vol. iv. p. 116–118.   [4] Federalist, Nos. 68, 69, 72, 73.

of the Treasury, each presided over by an officer appointed by the President, by and with the advice and consent of the Senate, and removable by the President.

Upon the passage of this motion the Department of Foreign Affairs was at once taken up. All minor questions were quickly disposed of, and attention was concentrated upon the clause vesting the power of removal in the President. The history of the debate that followed is too familiar to require extended notice here.[1] It will suffice to note that the majority eventually concluded that the power in question was confided in the President alone, and it was so decided for all three departments.

The Foreign Affairs and War Offices were then promptly disposed of; but when it was moved to put a Secretary at the head of the Treasury establishment, Gerry at once sprang up with an amendment placing the Treasury in charge of three commissioners. He discoursed at length on the iniquity of the human race; inquired where a man would be found honest and capable enough to fill the office; and reminded his hearers of the ugly rumors that preceded Morris's retirement, and led to the later abolition of the office of Superintendent of Finance. There were a few who silently assented, but on May 21st it was agreed that the three departments should be

[1] Annals of Congress.

established, with a single officer at the head of each.

A committee of eleven was then appointed to prepare bills in accordance with these instructions, and on June 2d Baldwin, as chairman, submitted those for the Departments of Foreign Affairs and War. A fortnight later the bill for the Foreign Affairs Office came up for consideration in committee of the whole, and the fight over the power of removal was at once revived. The great constitutional warriors buckled on their armor for war, and "four days' unceasing speechifying" followed.[1] Benson finally amended the bill by striking out the clause making the Secretary removable by the President, and instead inserted one imposing certain duties on the chief clerk "whenever the principal officer shall be removed from office by the President of the United States, or in any other case of vacancy." This, it was held, did nothing more than "establish a legislative construction of the Constitution," whereas the original clause was equivalent to a direct grant by Congress. Several votes were secured by the alteration, and the bill easily passed the House; but in the Senate the casting vote of the presiding officer was required in its favor.

The bill became a law on July 27th, but only four days later a new one was introduced, entitled "An Act for the safe-keeping of the Acts,

[1] Fisher Ames, Works, vol. i. p. 55.

Records, and Great Seal of the United States," etc., which was finally passed on September 15th. It was by virtue of this act that the title of the Secretary came to be Secretary of State, and he was also now for the first time charged with the duties enumerated in the title of the supplementary act. The change had been precipitated by several abortive attempts on the part of Vining of Delaware to secure the establishment of a fourth department over which a Secretary of Home Affairs was to preside. Congress was not yet prepared to create another department, and satisfied Vining by adding the functions of his Home Secretary to those of the Secretary of Foreign Affairs.

When the bills for the Departments of War and the Treasury came up for consideration, Benson's amendment, with reference, to the power of removal, was in both instances adopted. The one establishing the War Department was passed on August 7th. It was closely modelled after the Foreign Affairs bill, and differed from it only in the duties assigned to the Secretary. The management of naval affairs was now appropriately transferred from the Treasury Board to the Secretary of War, and in addition he had the supervision of bounty lands, Indian affairs, and one or two other matters afterwards placed under the care of the Secretary of the Interior.

The erection of a Treasury Department was

not so simple an affair. The tendency of Congressmen to guard this office more vigilantly than the others had not disappeared. The bill was introduced on June 4th, and the first objection was elicited by the clause authorizing the Secretary to "report" plans for the improvement and management of the revenue. This was no greater license than had been granted to the Superintendent of Finance in 1781, but it was now asked how money-bills could originate in the House of Representatives, as the Constitution required, if it were made lawful, by the bill, for them to originate in the office of the Secretary of the Treasury. Much feeling was displayed in the wrangle that followed, and quiet was only restored by the substitution of "prepare" for "report."

Not yet satisfied, the opponents of the bill made another effort to replace the Secretary by a board. Unsuccessful in this, they proceeded to amend in various ways, until the bill, as finally passed on September 2d, established a radically different department from those of War and State. By its provisions the Secretary of the Treasury was authorized to digest and prepare plans for the management of the public revenue and credit, submit estimates of expenditure, superintend the collection of revenue, etc., etc. The officers who were to assist him, and who were provided for in the same act, were the Comptroller, Auditor, Treasurer, and Register, none of whom differed as to title or function from the corresponding officers under the old Congress.

The differences in the bills establishing the three departments were noticeable even in their titles. The first two were described as acts "to establish an *executive* department to be denominated the Department" of Foreign Affairs, or of War, as the case might be; while the third was merely an "Act to establish a Treasury Department." The distinction implied by the omission of "executive" in the title of the Treasury act was still further carried out in the body of the respective laws. Those for War and Foreign Affairs had made the principal officers entirely subordinate to the President, and had only indicated the general scope of their duties. In the Treasury act, on the contrary, no mention whatever is made of the Secretary's dependence upon the President, at least with regard to the conduct of his office, and specific duties are enumerated and assigned to him. The effect of this was probably not precisely what was anticipated. It set up an independent executive official, who, although at the mercy of the President for the tenure of his office, was nevertheless allowed far more freedom of action than either the Secretary of War or of Foreign Affairs.

In the contemporary speeches in Congress, there is a remarkable absence of any testimony likely to throw light upon the exact intent of those who succeeded in organizing the Treasury Department on a different basis from the others. Nevertheless, it seems clear enough that their only aim was to draw the Secretary of the Treasury into closer relations with the legislature. In practice, the whole matter has been of far less importance than at first promised to result. The only occasion on which the legislature had an opportunity to lay claim to its supposed authority over the Secretary of the Treasury was in 1833, during the discussion that followed the removal of deposits from the United States Bank. Then Jackson promptly put an end to all such pretensions by announcing that he had removed the deposits, because on him " devolved the constitutional duty of superintending the operations of the executive departments," and that view, in the end, prevailed.

The Departments of Foreign Affairs, War, and the Treasury having been provided for, Congress turned its attention to the Post-Office. All the departments, as organized by the Continental Congress, had continued under the new government until otherwise provided for, the Post-Office with the rest. The House was satisfied with this arrangement, and proposed to continue it, at least for a time.[1] The Senate, however, would not concur in this, and a bill for the temporary es-

[1] Annals of Congress, House of Representatives, September 9, 1789.

tablishment of the office was passed. The principle which had been followed during the entire history of the department was still retained, and the general supervision of the office was left to the Postmaster-General. He was now made subordinate to the President, and subject to his direction in several particulars. After one or two subsequent acts had been passed for the purpose of continuing the temporary establishment, the department was permanently organized by the act of May 8, 1794. The Navy Department was not separately established until April 30, 1798.

Although we have followed the departments through checkered careers, there is, after all, a thread constantly present which makes their development continuous. Attention has already been directed to their earlier progress. When the Continental Congress retired in favor of its Federal successor, the thread was in no way severed. Of the various steps in the transformation from committees to boards, and from boards to secretaries, it is to be noticed that the lines of advancement were soon very definitely marked out. The number and scope of the departments necessary for the conduct of the public business was early determined by the Continental Congress. Subsequent progress was entirely confined within the bounds thus fixed. In the Convention of 1787, although that body ultimately saw fit to omit mention in the Constitution of the special departments to be established by Congress, it was noticeable that, whenever suggestions *were* made in favor of such a clause, they were confined to those departments already in existence. An occasional reference to a Home Office was the only exception, but the later refusal of Congress to allow this office to intrude upon the accepted list of necessary departments shows still more conclusively the extent to which opinion had been moulded by the forms that had gradually grown up with the government.

It will also be remarked that in two instances, incidental mention of "heads of departments" is made in the Constitution. Here, again, is demonstrated the existence of a settled conviction that the old boards would not be revived to replace the system adopted in 1781. Were it necessary, by pointing to minor resemblances in the departments as organized before and after the adoption of the Constitution, still further evidence might be adduced; but this will suffice to warrant the acceptance of the general conclusion that the number of departments, and the principles upon which they were established under the Federal Congress, were determined altogether by their previous development. If foreign elements are traceable, they had all crept in before 1789. Experience had indicated the advisability of certain improvements, the achievement of which had produced changes in detail.

The altered relations between the several branches of the government had led to the formation of conflicting views as to the method of bringing preconceived ideas into harmony with the principles of the new Constitution. But in all this there was nothing to sunder the chain of development, which, though composed of many links, was complete in every part. The departments of 1789, which are also the departments of 1889, had evolved by a natural process from the germinal committees of 1775.

IV.

THE PERIOD OF CONSTITUTION-MAKING IN THE AMERICAN CHURCHES.[1]

BY WILLIAM P. TRENT.

WHILE the greater part of the citizens of this country, just after their successful Revolution, would have strenuously affirmed the truth of Bishop Berkeley's famous verse, —

"Westward the course of empire takes its way," —

it may be doubted whether many careful observers would have admitted the realization of that other famous prophecy, of George Herbert's, —

"Religion stands tiptoe in our land,
Ready to pass to the American strand."

We can fancy our supposed careful observers saying that, although Religion might have stood "tiptoe" once, she had long since changed her

[1] I desire here to return my thanks to the following gentlemen for the assistance they have rendered me in my work: to the editor of this volume; to Dr. Herbert B. Adams, of the Johns Hopkins University; to Charles Poindexter, Esq., librarian to the State of Virginia; to the Rev. C. H. Ryland, librarian of Richmond College; to the Rev. Joshua Peterkin, D. D., of Richmond, Va.; to G. M. Nolley, Esq., of Ashland, Va.; and to the Rev. Wm. E. Boggs, D. D., of Memphis, Tenn.

mind, — a verdict which the historical student must confirm with a sadness proportioned to his reading.

And yet it must be remembered that a colony is hardly the place, and the eighteenth century hardly the time, to which to look for any great religious zeal. Bishop Butler had to fight many a deist in England, and his famous "Analogy" might now be forgotten had not Wesley strengthened the church by deserting her. And in an eighteenth century colony it was natural that the philosphy of Franklin should gain more converts than the theology of Edwards. The age was unpoetical, practical, and conceited; the struggling colonists needed common sense and something nearly akin to selfishness.

Already, at the beginning of the century, Puritanism meant little more than formalism for the descendants of the Winthrops and the Bradfords; and after the Great Revival men had sunk into a still deeper sleep. The clerical caste had zeal enough to make full use of all the laws in their favor, and to resist the appointment of an American bishop; but they do not seem to have been especially zealous in looking after the spiritual welfare of their congregations, or why that upcropping of Universalism and Unitarianism? But the Baptists, in spite of stringent laws, had greatly increased since the day when Roger Williams was driven out to found a new state; and the mother church had gained back not a few that had once disowned her, a Johnson and a Cutler among the number. Connecticut, the land of the younger Winthrop and of Hooker, was soon to have a bishop; and Jesse Lee was to preach the principles of the Arminian Wesley where the Calvinistic Edwards had once expounded the cheerful doctrine of eternal reprobation.

In New York we find complications existing between a church favored by law and a church having claims to a distinct nationality and a prior occupation of the territory. Here, too, we find the Presbyterians strong, and their relations with their co-religionists of Pennsylvania important. Nor ought we to overlook the beginnings of Methodism under that old veteran, Captain Thomas Webb, and the equally indefatigable Barbara Heck.

In Pennsylvania we find, as might have been expected, a mixture of religions. There are three different sets of Presbyterians; there are Quakers, and Lutherans, and Moravians, and even the Church of England has four parishes in Philadelphia. Here we may look for great activity in constitution-making for the churches. Philadelphia is as important a point in the history of the American Episcopal Church as she is in the history of the nation at large.

Passing southward we find, at Baltimore, that there are two centres of religious influence in that city, which are to result in two church constitutions peculiar to the two denominations which have ever since been strongest in the city, — the Methodists and the Roman Catholics. Maryland will therefore occupy us nearly as much as Pennsylvania.

In Virginia there was a church established by law; but there was little or no religion among the higher classes, the effect of whose example upon the lower was necessarily bad. So, until just before the Revolution, when the Baptists and Presbyterians gathered strength, religion was by no means as constant a subject of conversation as horse racing and politics. Cock-fighting, card-playing, hard-drinking parsons were so common that we can hardly blame the vestries which gave the Rev. Mr. So-and-So notice " that he need not give himself any further trouble to come and preach in that parish." But the vestries seem to have been by no means eager to have any parsons at all, probably thinking what Mr. (afterwards Sir Lucius) O'Brien was saying about that time before the Irish Parliament, that they wished to be delivered " from the total neglect of those who had nominally the care of their souls and actually a tithe of their property." [1]

Such was, in brief, the religious condition of the colonies just before the Revolution. It does

[1] Lecky, History of England in the Eighteenth Century, iv. 326.

not seem necessary to go farther south than Virginia; for we should simply have to describe the same unpleasant state of things. It is the intention of the following essay, however, to treat mainly of ecclesiastical polity, and to trace the manner in which each of the great churches effected a national organization after our separation from Great Britain.

The ecclesiastical side of our constitutional history in this formative period has been generally overlooked. Yet so great a movement in the affairs of civil government could hardly have gone on without exerting a powerful influence, by attraction, to borrow a phrase from the grammarians, on our ecclesiastical polity. Nor would it be remarkable if the constitutional movements thus begun among the churches should be found to have exerted some appreciable influence upon the similar and contemporary movements in the sphere of national politics. How great these respective influences were can better be estimated when the main facts of the constitutional history of each of the great churches has been stated. And first of that great body known as "the Protestant Episcopal Church in the United States of America."

From the very first landing of Englishmen in America to the successful Revolution of the colonies, the Church of England felt that she had a claim upon the allegiance of Americans fully as great as that which she had upon Englishmen at home. Though Puritanism might intrench itself by laws in New England, the English Church could only recognize it to the same extent that she did in England, and for the same reasons; for from the very nature of her claims the church of the mother country could have no daughter in America unless a bishop and duly ordained priests were in existence to form that daughter church. Now an American bishop was a consummation devoutly wished for but long withheld. Hence in the Southern tier of colonies and in many of the Middle we find for nearly two centuries an anomalous body professing to be the church "by law established," and yet no church after all. For scarcely any of those who called themselves members of the church had ever been confirmed, and thus a main tie of religious fellowship was never knit. People heard the priest exhort parents to bring the newly baptized child to the bishop, and laughed when they thought of the Bishop of London, three thousand miles away. For the Bishop of London had the largest diocese on earth, — his own great city, and all of this great country that belonged to England; but not a single incumbent of the see seems to have set foot upon American soil. Now a bishop who does not visit his see is worse than no bishop at all, and many a good Bishop of London felt this to be true. One suffragan would have solved the difficulty; but when church and state are connected, new bishops are not easily made. The Sir Robert Walpoles and the Latitudinarians have always cast squinting glances at the episcopal office; and when they are in power, it is folly to think that they will turn aside, from purchasing votes and making overtures to dissenters, to furnish struggling souls with a chief shepherd in the shape of a bishop: they will rather say with Seymour, "Souls? Damn your souls! Make tobacco!"

True, commissaries were sent out, good Drs. Bray and Blair, to the latter of whom Sir Edward Seymour made his brutal remark, and the Society for the Propagation of the Gospel did its best to keep parishes supplied with efficient priests; but without a bishop the so-called church was like a plantation without an overseer. There were individual instances of successful pastoral work; but the only bright spot of any magnitude in the American church's early history is the great work done in New England by the Yale Revolters, Cutler and Johnson, and their followers.[1]

It would be useless to recount all the efforts made in this country and in England to procure an American bishop, and it would be painful to enumerate all the lives lost by shipwreck and

[1] For a good account of this interesting episode see Dr. Beardsley's History of the Episcopal Church in Connecticut.

small-pox of those who were brave enough to go to England for ordination. Puritanism, even in dissolution, protested vigorously against a bishop, who would be necessarily connected in its eyes with royalty; and even in the South, as the Revolutionary fever seized upon men, the clergy of one colony, Virginia, refused to join their brethren of other colonies in a petition for a bishop, and were thanked by the House of Burgesses for their patriotic conduct.

But the Revolution came, and the American Church had no longer even a Bishop of London to look up to as a head. Her churches were, in a majority of cases, either destroyed or vacant; her adherents were dropping off into Methodism or Deism; her temporalities were being threatened and curtailed; she was shorn of the little beauty she had had, and was become a scorn to her many enemies: what, then, was she to do?

This question presented itself to many minds, and naturally many diverse answers were given in words as well as in actions. Some young gentlemen immediately embarked for England, and applied to Bishop Lowth for orders, — still cleaving to their patron saint, the Bishop of London. But the Bishop had to require oaths of his candidates inconsistent with new-fledged feelings of independence; and so the young gentlemen were left in a quandary. One of them, a Mr. Weems (plainly Mason L. Weems, afterward the famous

"Parson Weems"), wrote flippant letters to two very distinguished countrymen of his, then in Europe, who he supposed would surely sympathize with his patriotic indignation, and perhaps be able to help him. His letter to Franklin produced an amusing but rather scandalous reply, from which we learn that Franklin had actually asked the Pope's Nuncio whether his young correspondent could not be ordained in the Roman Catholic Church without becoming a member of that communion.[1] Surely this was practicality with a vengeance! The letter to Mr. Adams at the Hague[2] produced an application a little more seasonable than Franklin's had been, for some correspondence was actually entered into with the Danish court relative to the ordination of the young Americans. His Majesty of Denmark, backed by his theological faculty, seems to have been willing to befriend the sufferers from English intolerance in one of two ways: he would either appoint to one of his West Indian islands a bishop who could ordain American candidates, or his bishops at home would ordain such candidates as subscribed to the Thirty-nine Articles, always saving the political parts of the same.[3]

But before any such measures could be taken,

---

[1] Franklin's Works (Sparks), x. 109.
[2] Not at London, as Bishop White says in his Memoirs. 2d ed. N. Y., p. 20.
[3] John Adams's Works, ix. 276; White's Memoirs, etc., 21.

or indeed thought of in America, the vital question of obtaining an episcopal head for the struggling church was being discussed and acted upon in two sections and upon two very different lines.

In Connecticut, which, ever since the days of Samuel Johnson, had given the church a less and less grudging foothold upon her soil, ten of the fourteen remaining priests assembled together at Woodbury, on the 25th of March, 1783, and in "voluntary convention" chose for their bishop Dr. Samuel Seabury, Missionary S. P. G. at Staten Island, New York. This convention came together so quietly, and with so little self-consciousness, that scarcely anything is known of its proceedings, save what the able historiographer of the American Church, the Bishop of Iowa, has been able to gather from fragments of contemporary letters.[1] But to nominate a bishop for Connecticut was not enough: the question still remained who was to consecrate him. Accordingly the convocation instructed Dr. Seabury to apply, first of all, to the English prelates, and, if they refused him consecration, to betake himself to the nonjuring bishops of the Church of Scotland. The English bishops, owing to their connection with the State, were not able to consecrate Dr. Seabury, and so he was driven to seek and obtain consecration at the hands of the Scottish bishops.

[1] The History of the American Episcopal Church, by Bishop Perry (Boston, 1885), ii. 49.

No one now doubts, and few really doubted then, the validity of this consecration; but it was destined to cause some little trouble.

Now, although Bishop Seabury was primarily Bishop of Connecticut, several of the leading clergymen of New York had heartily seconded his nomination; and the scattered clergy of the other New England States, although not bound by the choice of Connecticut, were expected and were willing to receive the new bishop's ministrations. Hence, although the action of Connecticut seems at first sight to exemplify that spirit of autonomy so characteristic of the newly freed states, there are not wanting traces of that spirit of union which was afterwards so powerfully developed both in church and state.

The bishop met his own clergy and others from the neighboring states in convocation at Middletown. Several changes rendered necessary by American independence were made in the prayer book and the offices of the church; and if New England had not done much to provide a constitution which should unite all the members of the Episcopal Church in America, she had at least set the example of obtaining a bishop, and that, too, in spite of Puritan traditions and prejudices.

In the mean time Maryland had been laying the basis of the future constitution of the church. The church having been established by law in that colony, the connection between church and state, of course, came up for settlement after the Revolutionary War. The clergy in consultation determined to draw up a "Declaration of Fundamental Rights and Liberties," stealing a Deist's thunder wherewith to confound Deists. The following is the Bishop of Iowa's excellent summary of this declaration: —

"In this important document we find the first public assumption of the present legal title of the 'Protestant Episcopal Church' by a representative body of that Church. There is also the assertion of the ecclesiastical and spiritual independence of 'the Protestant Episcopal Church in Maryland,' as necessarily following from the civil independence of the state. The right of this Church of Maryland 'to preserve herself as an *entire* Church, agreeably to her ancient usages and profession,' as well as to exercise her 'spiritual power' derived 'from Christ and His Apostles,' independent of 'every foreign or other jurisdiction,' so far as 'consistent with the civil rights of Society,' is claimed. The necessity of Episcopal Ordination and commission, 'to the valid administration of the Sacraments and the due exercise of the Ministerial Functions of the said Church,' is clearly laid down, and the exclusive right of 'the Ministry by regular Episcopal Ordination' to be 'admitted into or enjoy any of the Churches, Chapels, Glebes, or other property formerly belonging to the Church of England,' is emphatically asserted. It is claimed that 'the said Church, when duly organized, constituted, and represented in a Synod or Convention of her ministry and people,' is competent 'to revise her liturgy, Forms of Prayer, and public worship, in order to adapt the same to the late revolution and other local circumstances of America.' Here, also, we have the first authoritative recognition of the right of the laity to admission to the councils of the Church, and this document, it will be borne in mind, was the production of the clergy alone. Deprecating any 'further departure from the venerable order and beautiful form of worship of the Church' of England 'than may be found expedient in the change . . . from a daughter to a sister Church,' these clergymen of Maryland, less than a score in number, laid broad and deep, in this comprehensive and yet conservative document, the foundations of the Ecclesiastical Constitution of the American Church."[1]

So we see church autonomy many miles away from New England, and Maryland gives us our first Declaration of Rights, while New England gives us our first bishop. Truly an anomaly is here. It may be remarked that the Bishop of Iowa's eagerness to point out that the "clergy alone" were willing to give the laity their share in church government was hardly necessary. Whether those clergymen had been grasping of

[1] History of the American Church, ii. 5.

power or not, their action would have been the same. In the mother country the laity had been represented in the government of the church, however imperfectly, by the royal control; it was hardly likely that George the Third's enemies would endure a church organization which George the Third's subjects would not have endured.

In the mean time other workers were afield, the chief of whom was Dr. William White, of Philadelphia, so long and so honorably connected with the American Church. In 1782, before Great Britain had acknowledged our independence, this clergyman had published a pamphlet, now very rare, entitled, "The Case of the Episcopal Churches Considered." From a synopsis of it given by the Bishop of Iowa,[1] it may be gathered that, despairing of obtaining the apostolic succession, the future bishop had advocated a provisional form of government which was to obtain until a duly consecrated bishop should become the head of the church: nor did he stickle for the name "bishop"; a superintendent or an overseer would do. The arguments advanced were very similar to those which Wesley was beginning to cogitate. For the rest, the plan proposed seems to have been wise and comprehensive, including the ideas of church unity, representation of the laity, and a threefold organization, — diocesan, provincial, and continental.[2]

[1] History of the American Church, ii. 8.   [2] Ibid., ii. 9.

The pamphlet attracted much attention, although it was partially suppressed by its author on account of pending negotiations between Great Britain and this country which looked to a recognition of the latter's independence. The convocation that sent Seabury to England gravely criticised its "dangerous tendencies," and many of them doubtless recalled the matter with chagrin when Wesley sent over *his* superintendent.

Although Dr. White has been named as the chief of those who were making this third movement for church organization, the honor of having proposed the first step toward that organization belongs to the Rev. Abraham Beach, of New Brunswick, New Jersey. In a letter to Dr. White, dated January 26, 1784,[1] he proposes that the unsettled affairs of a Society for the Support of Widows and Children of Deceased Clergymen, incorporated in the states of New York, New Jersey, and Pennsylvania, should be made the pretext of gathering together the chief clergy and laity of the three states, who might then consult about the general state of the church. This proposal was carried out, and a meeting was held at New Brunswick on May 11, 1784, ten clergymen and six laymen being present. Committees were formed for discussion and for canvassing the three states, and a special delegation was requested to wait upon the convo-

[1] History of the American Episcopal Church, ii. 16.

cation of Connecticut, and to urge their coöperation in the good work of church organization. This impromptu convention then adjourned to meet at New York in October of the same year. It was destined to be so curiously paralleled in civil affairs by the Annapolis Convention that we find ourselves wondering whether such coincidences are not to be alone explained by the law of cause and effect.

The movement was evidently spreading. Local conventions were held in Pennsylvania, in Maryland, in Massachusetts; and when the New York meeting came, representatives were present from a majority of the thirteen states: from Massachusetts and Rhode Island, from Connecticut, from New York, New Jersey, Delaware, Pennsylvania, and Maryland. Virginia was represented by the Rev. Mr. Griffith, who is described by Bishop White as being "present by permission. The clergy of that state, being restricted by laws yet in force there, were not at liberty to send delegates, or consent to any alterations in the Order, Government, Doctrine, or Worship of the Church."

A committee consisting of four clergymen and four laymen was appointed " to essay the fundamental Principles of a general Constitution" for the church. The report of this committee consisted of seven general articles, of which the import was as follows: —

That there should be a general convention of

the church, consisting of clerical and lay delegates from each state, or from associated congregations in two or more states; that the doctrines of the Gospel held by the Church of England should be maintained, and as much of the liturgy of the said church as would be consistent with the American Revolution; that whenever any bishop was duly settled in a state, he should be considered a member of the convention *ex officio;* that clerical and lay delegates should deliberate in one body but vote separately, the concurrence of both bodies being necessary to legislation; and that the first meeting of the convention should be held at Philadelphia on the Tuesday before the Feast of St. Michael next, to which it was hoped and earnestly desired that the Episcopal Churches in the respective states would send their deputies duly instructed, etc.[1]

The fifth article in this report, relative to the position of bishops in the convention, called forth some severe criticism, especially from the New England churchmen. Connecticut had already given notice that she would soon have a bishop, until which time she could do nothing; but that when that consummation was reached she would come forward with her bishop "for the doing of what the general interests of the church might

---

[1] History American Episcopal Church, ii. 48; White's Memoirs, p. 80.

require;"[1] it was therefore natural that she should be indignant with a constitution which made a duly consecrated bishop merely a member *ex officio* of the proposed convention. Then, too, she was beginning to be sorely tried by the doubts raised on all sides as to the validity of Seabury's consecration.[2] But the whole trouble was destined to be smoothed over in no great time.

The Philadelphia convention met on the twenty-seventh day of September, 1785, and continued in session until October 7th. There were clerical and lay deputies present from New York, New Jersey, Pennsylvania, Delaware, Maryland, Virginia, and South Carolina. New England, with a bishop and organized dioceses, was not represented, although of course invited. The alienation above mentioned, and probably a fear that the Southern delegates would insist on secularizing the church in many other ways, made this action not unreasonable.

Dr. White was chosen president of the convention, which consisted of forty-two delegates. The proceedings of the New York convention were read, and in the main approved, a committee of two delegates from each state being appointed to make the fourth article proposed by

---

[1] White's Memoirs, p. 81, quoted by Perry; History American Episcopal Church, ii. 35.

[2] History American Episcopal Church, ii. 35.

that convention operative by drafting "an ecclesiastical constitution for the Protestant Episcopal Church in the United States of America," and by preparing necessary alterations in the liturgy. This committee was subsequently charged with reporting "a plan for obtaining the consecration of bishops, together with an address to the Most Reverend the Archbishops and the Right Reverend the Bishops of the Church of England for that purpose."

On the 1st of October this committee reported, and on the 4th the draft of the constitution was considered by paragraphs. After the declaration that, "in the course of Divine Providence, the Protestant Episcopal Church in the United States of America is become independent of all foreign authority, civil and ecclesiastical," it was proposed to hold a general convention of the said church in Philadelphia in June, 1786, "and forever after once in three years on the third Thursday of June, in such place as shall be determined by the convention," etc.

The second and third articles of the report ran as follows [1]: —

"There shall be a representation of both Clergy and Laity of the Church in each state, which shall consist of one or more deputies, not exceeding four, of each order; and in all questions the said

[1] I quote from The Journals, etc., of the P. E. Church, published by John Bioren, Philadelphia, 1817.

Church in each state shall have one vote; and a majority of suffrages shall be conclusive.

"In the said Church, in every state represented in this Convention, there shall be a Convention consisting of the Clergy and Lay Deputies of the congregation."

The fifth article did not add to the bishop's dignity; he was still to be a "member of the convention *ex officio*." Article VI. provided for his election according to such rules as should be fixed by the various state conventions, and also laid down the limits of his jurisdiction.

Article VII. was important: —

"A Protestant Episcopal Church, in any of the United States not now represented, may at any time hereafter be admitted on acceding to the articles of this union."

Article VIII. gave the separate state conventions authority to suspend or remove from office every clergyman, whether bishop, presbyter, or deacon.

Article XI. ran: "This General Ecclesiastical Constitution, when ratified by the Church in the different states, shall be considered as fundamental, and shall be unalterable by the convention of the Church in any state."

The next convention was held in Philadelphia from the 20th to the 26th of June, 1786. The same states were represented, but there were only twenty-six delegates. After receiving an address from the English bishops in regard to the consecration of American bishops, the convention took up the Constitution and gave it a second reading. Sundry alterations were made, the major part of which need not occupy us. A bishop was always to preside in the General Convention, if one were present, and the Constitution, "when ratified by the Church in a majority of States assembled in General Convention, with sufficient power for the purpose of such ratification," was to be "unalterable by the Convention of any particular state which" had "been represented at the time of said ratification."

This convention also conducted a correspondence with the English bishops relative to the consecration of bishops for America, and some of the changes in the constitution were due to expostulations on the part of the English prelates. A called meeting of the same convention, held at Wilmington, Delaware, October 10 and 11, 1786, and attended by twenty-one delegates, received another letter from the English bishops and framed a reply to it. The requisite Act of Parliament had been obtained; and before the next General Convention in 1789, Drs. White and Provoost had been consecrated, at Lambeth, Bishops of Pennsylvania and of New York respectively.

The most important of all the early conventions of the American Episcopal Church was held in Philadelphia, July 28 to August 8, 1789. Bishop White, the only representative of the episcopal order present, presided over thirty-three delegates from the same Middle and Southern States. An application for the consecration of the Rev. Edward Bass as their bishop was made by the clergy of Massachusetts and New Hampshire, — an encouraging sign of the fast-approaching union of New England with her sister states; but the convention first appointed a committee to consider the proposed constitution and to suggest amendments. It was evident that a little tact would suffice to bring Seabury and his diocese into the common fold. Accordingly, after long and anxious debate, an amended instrument was prepared and adopted, to which Seabury and his followers subscribed at an adjourned convention held in Philadelphia from September 29th to October 16th of the same year.

The alterations in the constitution, important to our purpose, are as follows: —

Greater strictness was given to the article touching the voting of clerical and lay delegates. The bishops, when there were three or more, were to form a "House of Revision," and when any measure had passed the General Convention it was to receive the sanction of the aforesaid House of Revision. This veto power could be overruled by a "majority of three fifths" of the

General Convention. In all cases the bishops were to signify to the convention "their approbation or disapprobation, the latter with their reasons in writing, within two days after the proposed act" had been reported to them; in failure thereof it was to have the force of law. Article IX. read as follows: "This Constitution shall be unalterable, unless in General Convention, by the Church, in a majority of the states which may have adopted the same; and all alterations shall be first proposed in one General Convention, and made known to the several state conventions, before they shall be finally agreed to or ratified in the ensuing General Convention." The influence of the new Federal Constitution is plainly to be seen in some of these alterations.

The consecration of Dr. Bass, for reasons which need not be dwelt upon, did not take place until 1797; but the convention was not slow in appointing a committee to notify Bishop Seabury, and the churches not contained in the union, of the adjourned session, and to request their attendance in the same.

Accordingly the churches of New England were represented at Philadelphia in October. The good Bishop of Connecticut and his followers were still not satisfied with the episcopal place in the constitution, and accordingly the third article was altered so as to allow the House of Bishops to originate and propose acts for the concurrence of the House of Deputies, and a four fifths majority was made necessary for overriding their veto, which was to be reported in writing in three days instead of two. After these concessions Bishop Seabury and three New England deputies signed the amended constitution. It was also resolved to propose to the separate states that in the next convention the propriety of giving the bishops full veto powers should be discussed.

With reference to this last proposition the delegate from Virginia stated that his church hardly expected any such concession to the advocates of full episcopal powers, and that its passage would probably alienate Virginia from the union. The delegates from New England reluctantly forbore to press the point, and it was not until 1808 that the power of a four fifths majority to overrule the bishops' veto was done away with. By that time the Virginia Church had entered upon a more encouraging phase of its history.[1]

Thus was the Protestant Episcopal Church founded, and upon this basis it has flourished. The conclusions to be drawn from the numerous

[1] My account of the last conventions is taken from the fifth chapter of Bishop Perry's second volume, so often referred to; from Bishop White's Memoirs (pp. 25–30, and notes upon them); and from Bioren's reprint of the Journals.

and often minute facts given are deferred until we have told of the no less interesting struggles and successes of the other great religious bodies. And now, in the natural order of things, we come to speak of Wesley's separation, and of the foundation of the Methodist Episcopal Church.

It will not, of course, be expected that we should here give any account of how Methodism arose in England, of what it did in reviving a sluggish church, or of its disputed relations with that church. Such knowledge is presupposed; for the general reader need not now wade through biographies of Wesley, or histories of Methodism, when he can read such an admirable sketch as that which Mr. Lecky has given us on the subject in his " History of England in the Eighteenth Century." [1]

The first men who preached Wesley's tenets in this country were "irregulars," that is, men neither ordained priests in the English Church, nor sent out by the great founder himself. But very interesting men they were, no matter how irregular their preaching. Philip Embury, Robert Strawbridge, Robert Williams, that old hero Captain Thomas Webb, and the equally heroic Barbara Heck, — all these were more than mere visionary enthusiasts: they were laying fast and

---

[1] For the facts which follow I have relied chiefly upon Stevens and McTyeire.

deep the foundations of a church destined to a growth almost as stupendous in proportion as that achieved by this great republic itself during the century of their common life.

In 1770 a new circuit was reported to the Twenty-Seventh Annual Conference in London; this was no less than the whole continent of America, which ranked as "No. 50."[1] Since the conference of the previous year two missionaries, Boardman and Pilmoor, had been sent thither by Wesley, and had already made a good report. Within six years from this time, six other missionaries were sent over, among whom was the energetic Francis Asbury, perhaps the most typical figure in the American Methodist Church, and one well worthy to be Wesley's "general assistant."

Combining with the irregulars, these men, as a rule, did noble work, and made it possible that, when Great Britain and America had separated, the infant church could stand alone. Indeed, that it stood at all after Wesley plunged into politics with his famous "Calm Address," shows how thoroughly the work was being done. But while Wesley's own work did little harm, the fact that his assistants, with the notable exception of Asbury, hastened back to England to avoid the dangers of the war, contributed in no small de-

---

[1] A History of Methodism, etc., by Holland N. McTyeire, D. D., etc. (Nashville, 1884), page 279.

gree to give a national character to the new church; and this partially explains the wonderful growth of Methodism during the period we are considering.

The first American Conference was held in Philadelphia in 1773. There were ten circuits and sixteen hundred members represented. By 1774 four hundred converts had been added, and there were seventeen preachers on their travels. The road was not smooth for these missionaries, for they found it very hard to enforce Wesley's discipline. In England it was not so difficult to keep the converts within the fold of the mother church, for there they could at least be baptized and confirmed, and take the communion in many a parish church. But in America confirmation was not possible, and few evangelicals cared to receive the communion from hands that were more used to handling cards. Some of the irregulars proposed to extend the influence of Wesleyanism by administering the sacraments, but this the first conference declared to be impracticable.[1] Robert Strawbridge, however, refused to cease a practice which he found so acceptable to his people, and a special exception was made in his case, at the risk, it would seem, of exciting jealousy and rather searching criticism. This question of the ordinances was brought up at all the annual

---

[1] A Compendious History of American Methodism, by Abel Stevens (New York, 1868), pp. 73, 74.

conferences until 1783, but nothing was done except to cool down the rash spirits. In the mean time Methodism had, according to Bishop McTyeire, increased fivefold, in spite of the prevailing want of religion in the country and the excitements of the Revolution. This growth had not been accomplished, however, without the danger of a split in Virginia, which seems to have contained a majority of the American Methodists. Some of the irregulars had ordained one another and had administered the sacraments freely in that state, to the great disgust of their Northern brethren. But the prompt action of Asbury and his friends produced a compromise, and an appeal to Wesley for advice and help. Wesley tried to induce Bishop Lowth to consecrate a young man of his nomination who might administer the sacraments to those Americans who would not receive them at the hands of their dissolute clergy; but the bishop would not grant the request. Whereupon the aged reformer bethought himself of other methods.

It would be useless to enter upon a discussion of Wesley's action in consecrating Coke to be superintendent of his clamoring American flock. To the Episcopalian, nothing can excuse the convert of Lord King; to the Methodist, no excuse seems needed. The present writer has only to record the well-known fact which was Wesley's answer to the appeal above referred to.

With the arrival of the new superintendent, and the presbyters Whatcoat and Vasey, what had before been a mere society became a church needing organization. That organization was effected by the famous Christmas Conference held in Baltimore on the twenty-fourth of December, 1784.

Of the eighty-three traveling preachers, over sixty were present when Coke took the chair. A circular letter from Wesley setting forth his reasons for the ordination of Coke was read, and in accordance with the Revised Liturgy sent at the same time, the conference agreed to form themselves into "an Episcopal Church, and to have superintendents, elders, and deacons."[1] Wesley had appointed Asbury to be joint superintendent with Coke, but that good man refused to be ordained unless his brethren signified their approbation of Wesley's choice by formally electing him to the office. This was done, and seems noteworthy not only as an indication of the man's modesty, but as indicating the growth of a national self-consciousness within the new body. When Asbury was ordained, he requested that his friend, the Rev. William Otterbein, of the German Reformed Church, should assist Dr. Coke. This learned divine was a faithful worker in Baltimore, and subsequently a bishop in a new society, of which he was practically the founder, "The

[1] Asbury, quoted by McTyeire.

United Brethren in Christ." Even at the time of Asbury's ordination, he was endeavoring to perfect some organization among his fellow-clergymen.

The next few days of the conference were spent principally in forming rules of discipline and ordaining regular preachers. Two elders were sent as far as Nova Scotia, and one to Antigua, in the West Indies. These Canadian Methodists remained for many years under the jurisdiction of the American Methodist Church.

Wesley's Abridgment of the Thirty-Nine Articles was adopted, and a new article on Civil Rulers was added by the conference. The English standards of doctrine were received, viz., Wesley's Sermons and his "Notes on the New Testament." No person was " to be ordained a superintendent, elder, or deacon without the consent of a majority of the conference, and the consent and imposition of the hands of a superintendent." The superintendent could be punished and even expelled by the conference. Salaries and other matters of business were discussed and answered in a curious catechism. Slavery was strongly condemned, and directions for emancipation were laid down. There was probably too much special legislation, — as, for example, the rule which forbade men and women sitting together in chapel; but this was to be expected, and produced little harm. Adjournment was made without any provision for a subsequent General Conference, which does not show the highest political training, and was, perhaps, due to over-anxiety for special legislation. Nor was there any regular distribution of the field into annual conferences; the good men only thought of widening that field as much as possible.

It would be out of place to describe the subsequent labors of the itinerants, — how Jesse Lee planted Methodism in New England, talking Dutch whenever his learned opponents spouted Latin; or how Asbury rode from state to state, now in Delaware with his friend Bassett, one of the members of the Convention of 1787, now in Charleston, whose inhabitants were "vain and wicked to a proverb."[1] The success they had may be measured by the fact that in 1788 eight annual conferences, five of them new, were held.

In the mean time an event of some significance happened which must be briefly noted. Freeborn Garrettson had been sent as a missionary to Nova Scotia, and had acquitted himself so well that Wesley sent over a request to the Conference of 1787 that he should be made a superintendent for the British Dominions in America. The Christmas Conference had previously entered into an "engagement clause" to the following effect: "During the life of the Rev. Mr. Wesley, we acknowledge ourselves his sons in the gospel,

[1] Asbury, quoted by McTyeire.

ready, in matters belonging to church government, to obey his commands. And we do engage after his death to do everything that we judge consistent with the cause of religion in America, and the political interests of these states, to preserve and promote our union with the Methodists in Europe." In the face of this the conference, not caring to lose Garrettson, refused compliance; nor would they ordain Whatcoat joint superintendent with Asbury, as Wesley advised. They also annulled the "engagement clause" from the next minutes, so that Wesley's name did not appear therein. The word "bishop" was also used instead of Wesley's "superintendent." All this grieved Wesley, and distracted the new church; but in the following year some reparation was made by an acknowledgment of Wesley's episcopal function in the curious catechism already mentioned. The whole incident has been mentioned here as a proof of a growing self-consciousness on the part of the American Methodists, doubtless prompted by the movements for autonomy going on in the various churches that surrounded them.[1]

But a want of union between the annual conferences was being felt, and so in 1789, a year as important to many of the churches as to the general government, a council met according to a plan previously approved by a majority of the

[1] See McTyeire, chapter xxviii.

preachers. This body was made to consist of the bishops and presiding elders, and was never to be less than nine in number. Their powers were general, and in reality small. Besides securing unity in the form of worship and doctrine, they were to mature " recommendatory propositions " for the general good of the church. But all power was taken away from this council by the necessity of unanimity among its members, and the fact that their decisions were binding on no district unless agreed to by a majority of the conference for that district.[1]

The first council was pleased with its work, and called another at Baltimore in 1790. But certain forced constructions were put upon its acts, and the experiment was evidently a failure. A General Conference was therefore called to meet at Baltimore in 1792. This was the first that had been held for eight years, and a curious proof of how little parliamentary training its members had got is found in the fact that no official record of its proceedings exists.

Here James O'Kelley, of Virginia, moved to allow an appeal to the conference by any one who thought himself injured by his appointment to any particular circuit by the bishop. This motion being defeated, the O'Kelley schism followed.

The conference then applied itself to shaping

---

[1] See McTyeire, pp. 402, 403.

the polity of the church. The office of presiding elder was defined, each elder presiding over a district consisting of from three to twelve circuits, and a conference being allowed each district. Four years later, annual conferences including several districts were mapped out. With the other provisions of this conference we need not concern ourselves, except to remark that it did not adjourn without providing for the assembling of another body like itself.

This met in 1796 and at once remedied the inconvenient number of yearly conferences by dividing the church into six conferences "independent of each other, with defined boundaries and limited powers."

Still our itinerants seem to have been behind the other religious bodies in their constitution-making. The General Conferences were attended with inconvenience and irregularity, and they had too much power. In 1800 they were limited to the elders; but these, having absolute power, could easily change the doctrines of the church.[1] Then, again, their meeting in Baltimore threw too much power into the hands of the preachers of the Central States. A proposition for delegated attendance was negatived in 1800, and also in 1804, the last time with the understanding that it should be matured by the various annual conferences and brought up again in 1808.

[1] McTyeire, p. 405.

There was also another question pressing for solution,—Was the vigorous church to do forever without a constitution? The previous conferences had had the powers of conventions, and could have changed the discipline at their pleasure; a delegated General Conference working under a constitution was a crying necessity. So in 1808, after much discussion and some ill-feeling, a plan for a delegated General Conference with limited powers was adopted. Space will not permit us to enter into a description of this plan, and we have already gone far beyond our period.[1] But it was necessary to follow the fortunes of this great religious body until we saw it safely provided with a constitution, and we cannot better take our leave of it than at the time when William McKendree was made one of its bishops.

After the establishment of the English Church in Maryland in 1692, and the passage of rigorous laws against a previously tolerant religion, the Roman Catholics led but a precarious existence. In 1774, when Father John Carroll returned from abroad, there was no "public Catholic Church in the Province of Maryland."[2] There were private chapels, of course, and a few priests travelled about, holding services in out-of-the-way houses;

---

[1] For details see McTyeire, p. 513.
[2] Shea, History of the Catholic Church, etc., ii. 48.

but their ministrations were hampered in every way, especially by the fact that no confirmations could be held. For the Roman Catholics were in this respect as much tried as the Episcopalians; since all of America lay under the jurisdiction of the Vicar Apostolic of London, and bishop there was none.

All the priests in the colonies seem to have been Jesuits. They attended their regular missions in Maryland and Pennsylvania, the only states where they were tolerated, and also assisted some of their faith in Virginia and New Jersey. The few faithful who found themselves in New York had to come as far as Philadelphia to meet a priest. Under all these circumstances the presence of a bishop was a necessity.

But the Jesuits, as Mr. Shea shows, were not anxious to have one who would too probably be nominated by their sworn foe, the Cardinal of York, and they paralleled the action of the Virginia clergy in petitioning against the appointment of a bishop. The parallel is completed by the fact that the Vicar Apostolic of London, Bishop Challoner, was himself extremely anxious to have his authority transferred to another.[1]

All his endeavors having failed, Bishop Challoner turned to the Bishop of Quebec for aid. It seemed easy for that prelate to visit Philadelphia occasionally and administer confirmation; nor did

---

[1] Shea, ii. 58.

the Jesuit missionaries have any objections to the plan. But the English government, which had not dared to establish English bishops in America, could not venture to allow Roman Catholics this privilege, and so the project was interfered with and was finally dropped.

But now, after the French and Spanish settlements east of the Mississippi were, in 1763, brought under English domination, the Roman Catholics were no longer an object of terror to the colonists, and a better era began for them.[1] Then came the suppression of the Jesuits, and the consequent difficulty in supplying their places with fresh recruits, — a difficulty tided over by the zeal of the missionaries, who remained at their posts, using their old property as a means of support and forming a kind of association.[2] As a recompense came also the tolerant feeling which began to pervade society now that liberty and the rights of man began to be talked about. Such was the condition of affairs when the Rev. John Carroll, the chief figure in the history of the Roman Catholic Church in this country, returned to his native land.

John Carroll, cousin to Charles Carroll of Revolutionary fame, was born on the 8th of January, 1735. He was educated first at a Jesuit school in Maryland, and afterwards at the famous English Jesuit College of St. Omer in French Flan-

---

[1] Shea, ii. 61.   [2] Ibid., ii. 85.

ders. Pious from his early youth, he entered the novitiate of the Society of Jesus in 1753, and became a professed father in 1771. After the suppression of the society in 1773, he took refuge in England with Lord Arundel, but on the eve of the crisis between the colonies and the mother country he thought it his duty to return home. Upon his arrival in Maryland he was invited to join the association of priests above mentioned, but declined, on account of its lack of formal sanction by the Vicar Apostolic. He therefore began private work upon the borders of Virginia and Maryland.

In the mean time the Revolution was looming up apace; and the Roman Catholic Church furnished further occasion for the prevalent bad feeling. The Quebec Act had established that church in Canada and in the Northwest Territory; this drew protests from many zealous Protestants, and even from the Continental Congress. But graver matters came along, and as men saw Roman Catholic priests hastening back from Europe to stand with their native land, and Roman Catholic laymen foremost in all patriotic undertakings, they ceased to remember John Jay's address, and received their allies with open arms.[1] But there seemed small hope for the patriotic church. Mr. Shea says: "The Catholic bodies were widely separated; in those of French

[1] Shea, ii., chapter iii.

and Spanish origin, the royal aid was withdrawn and the people were discouraged. The suppression of the Society of Jesus cut off all hope of further missionary supply from that order, and the prospect for the future was bleak enough, as no provision for the maintenance of a clergy and divine worship was made."[1]

The patriotism of the Roman Catholics during the war which followed was disinterested and notorious.[2] It cannot be dwelt on here, but the mission of the two Carrolls along with Franklin and Chase to Canada, and the names of Moylan and Barry, must at least be mentioned. In the rank and file of the army the same zeal and patriotism were displayed, deserving, it would seem, better recognition than was shown in most of the new state constitutions. For in many of the states none but Protestants were admitted to office, — a provision which was more favorable to Deists than to Roman Catholics, for the former had the benefit of presumption in their favor.[3]

The Revolution being over, the question of obtaining a bishop and securing an organization confronted the lately freed church. The new Vicar Apostolic of London disclaimed all jurisdiction over the United States, and refused faculties

---

[1] Shea, ii. 142.

[2] For a correction of Bancroft on this point see Shea, ii. 186.

[3] On the restriction imposed by these constitutions see Shea, ii. 155–161.

to two Maryland Jesuits, thereby giving a parallel to the Weems incident mentioned before. These priests then wrote to the Propaganda for faculties, and brought to their attention the condition of the church in America.[1] The Maryland priests desired no negotiations with England, for fear of exciting prejudices; but their ranks had been frightfully thinned, and they had little means of obtaining a hearing at Rome. They determined therefore, in the interim, to call a meeting of consultation, over which the Rev. John Lewis, who still continued to act as Vicar General for the Vicar Apostolic of London (an office, it would seem, analogous to the commissaryship held by Messrs. Bray and Blair), was asked to preside.

This meeting was held at Whitemarsh, Maryland, on the 27th of June, 1783. It was attended by six priests, one of whom represented three who were unable to attend.[2] Views were interchanged and a plan of government submitted to the priests of Maryland and Pennsylvania, who were for convenience formed into deputizing districts. Later in the year, seven clergymen of the Southern district met and suggested amendments to the plan.

The delegates from the districts met at Whitemarsh on the 6th of November of the same year. They were five in number, and their work was

---

[1] Shea, ii. 205.   [2] Ibid., ii. 207.

directed to revising the previously drafted plan of government, the final adoption of which was referred to a future meeting. A committee was also appointed to petition the Pope to constitute the Rev. John Lewis, Superior, "with power to administer confirmation, bless chalices, and impart faculties to the priests in the mission."

Meanwhile efforts were making by certain visionaries in France to attach the Roman Catholics in this country to a French Vicariate Apostolic.[1] Franklin was drawn into it, much to Mr. Shea's surprise, but hardly to ours, who have seen his remarkable action in the Weems case. A communication on the matter was actually made to the Continental Congress, but that body, of course, declared that such affairs were not intrusted to it by the states. Franklin, shortly before, had been enlightened as to the true nature of the scheme, and in reparation he proceeded to press the claims of Father Carroll, whom he had learned to know during the Canada mission, as a proper person for the office of Superior. In the mean time the priests in America were ignorant of the insult that had been offered them; but the only result of the whole affair seems to have been that the honor destined for Father Lewis fell upon the fittest man to receive it, — the Rev. John Carroll. "The decree organizing the Catholic Church in the United

---

[1] For a good account of this see Shea, ii. 213.

States as a distinct body, and appointing the Very Rev. John Carroll Prefect Apostolic, was issued by Cardinal Antonelli, Prefect of the Sacred Congregation de Propaganda Fide, on the 9th of June, 1784."[1] As Mr. Shea points out, it was probably overlooked that the Bishops of Quebec and of Santiago de Cuba had jurisdiction over parts of Father Carroll's territory.

Although informed privately of his promotion, the official notification did not come until after the meeting of deputies for consulting on a plan of government was held. Father Carroll therefore attended the meeting as a simple delegate. A form of government for the clergy of Maryland and Pennsylvania was adopted. The priests were to form a body corporate until the restoration of the Society of Jesus; the affairs of the corporation were to be managed by a delegated chapter of priests. This chapter was to meet every three years, and rules were laid down for its conduct. Considerable jealousy was shown towards the Superior *in spiritualibus*, for fear he might cast longing eyes upon the temporalities.

When the official notice of Father Carroll's appointment as Prefect came, the worthy man was much troubled by apprehensions lest his dependence upon the Sacred Congregation might give umbrage to ultra-Americans. He would also be much hampered in securing missionaries. But

[1] Shea, ii. 223.

after due consideration he accepted the inevitable and entered upon the duties of his office.

In an unused draft of his first circular letter Dr. Carroll alludes to this dependence upon the Sacred Congregation, and declares that in a few years the American church must have a diocesan bishop, whose appointment must come neither from his Holiness nor from the assemblies or different executives, but from the Catholic clergy themselves.[1] But six long, weary years elapsed before this consummation was realized in the person of Dr. Carroll himself. The same thoughts form the tenor of his letter of acceptance to Cardinal Antonelli; he is especially urgent that no Vicar Apostolic dependent on the pleasure of the Sacred Congregation shall ever be appointed for republican America. He also calls attention to the action of the Episcopal Church, and the fact that their proposed bishops had excited no scandal because the selection of such bishops was to remain with the churchmen of the different states.

But we soon find the chapter proposing a memorial to the Pope on the appointment of a diocesan bishop. This memorial was distasteful to the clergy of the Southern district; indeed, there seems from the first to have been decided jealousy toward the project among some of the priests. Dr. Carroll, though firm in his purpose,

[1] Shea, ii. 251.

felt it necessary to temporize, especially as he was troubled with the management of a recalcitrant priest in New York. This very trouble it was which did away with all opposition to the memorial for a bishop, for it became evident to all that the powers of a prefect were not ample enough. A petition was accordingly drawn up and transmitted to Rome through the Spanish envoy, Don Diego de Gardoqui. On July 12, 1788, Cardinal Antonelli replied that Pius VI. had signified his gracious assent to the petition. He adds further: "By you, therefore, it is first to be examined in what city this episcopal see ought to be erected, and whether the title of the bishopric is to be taken from the place of the see, or whether a titular bishop only should be established. This having been done, his Holiness, as a special favor and for this first time, permits the priests, who at the present time duly exercise the ministry of the Catholic religion and have care of souls, to elect as bishop a person eminent in piety, prudence, and zeal for the faith, from the said clergy, and present him to the Apostolic See to obtain consecration." [1]

Whereupon a meeting was held at Whitemarsh, and twenty-four out of twenty-six votes were given for the Rev. John Carroll as their choice for bishop. Baltimore was fixed upon as the site for the see. The choice of Dr. Carroll was natu-

[1] Shea, ii. 393.

rally satisfactory at Rome, and a bull creating the new see of Baltimore was made out on the 6th of November, 1789.

Meanwhile the Constitutional Convention had been held, and the United States had entered upon the first century of her greatness. Two Roman Catholics had attended the Convention, and the eyes of all their coreligionists were, of course, fixed upon the treatment religious liberty was to receive at the hands of the deliberating statesmen. The provisions of the sixth article were satisfactory, and the Constitution received the support of Roman Catholics in the only two states where they were strong, — Maryland and Pennsylvania. No small part of the opposition in some of the states was due to the abolition of test oaths and to anti-Catholic feeling. The First Amendment completed the security given to freedom of conscience. Mr. Shea discredits the report that Roman Catholics petitioned Congress to add this amendment. The usual address to General Washington followed, and the cautious, perfunctory reply. Then Bishop Carroll sailed for England, and was consecrated in the chapel at Lulworth Castle on the 15th of August, 1790.[1]

Before his return to America the new bishop was confronted with the difficulty of supplying his growing flock with properly trained priests.

---

[1] Shea, ii. 348. For a strange proposal to establish a bishopric among the Oneida Indians, see Shea, ii. 373, 374.

CONSTITUTION-MAKING IN THE CHURCHES. 231

But by a fortunate arrangement with the Superior of St. Sulpice, a band of trained Sulpitians was secured, and St. Mary's Theological Seminary was opened in Baltimore in 1792. The Carmelite nuns of Antwerp, also, soon formed a convent at Port Tobacco, Maryland. In the mean time the ambiguity about Bishop Carroll's jurisdiction had been cleared up, and he had the whole of the United States as his field.

On the 7th of November, 1791, Bishop Carroll opened his first synod in Baltimore. The young church was represented by a bishop, four vicars-general, the superior of the seminary, and seventeen priests. Its organization was then completed.

The first presbytery, or meeting of presbyters, held in America, was that of Philadelphia, which was organized by Francis Makemie about 1706.[1] It was, as Dr. Briggs clearly shows, a missionary presbytery connected with energetic London ministers who were working side by side with the Society for the Propagation of the Gospel in Foreign Parts. "It was not organized by a higher body. It did not seek authority from the General Assembly of the Church of Scotland, or from the Synod of Ulster. It organized itself by a voluntary association of ministers. It seems

---

[1] American Presbyterianism, by Charles Augustus Briggs, D. D. New York, 1885, p. 140.

to have taken the Presbytery of Dublin as a model."[1]

This newly organized body, of course, had many things in common with the New England Congregationalists. Several Presbyterian churches in New York and New Jersey were of New England origin and type; and the friendly relations between the two bodies led, as we shall presently see, to *quasi* unions between them. But, as in the case of the Episcopal Church, we shall find the Middle States more active in constitution-making, and Philadelphia will still hold its central position.

After the formation of the Presbytery the growth of the body it represented was remarkable. In ten years there were four presbyteries instead of one, forming a synod of fifteen members. In 1729 there were thirty members, and delegation had been introduced, to favor pastors dwelling at a distance. So far, no one suspected his brother's Calvinism, but in the last-mentioned year the suspicion of certain Arian heresies, imported from Ireland, led to the first great leg-

---

[1] Dr. Baird in his Digest (revised edition, page 276), says that this body "ordinarily assumed the title of ' *The Presbytery*,' never that of ' The Presbytery of Philadelphia,' " and hence he draws the conclusion that the General Assembly to be mentioned hereafter was not the creature of the voluntarily uniting presbyteries and synods, but itself created them. Analogous to this was the origin of the General Assembly of Scotland, and this view of the case would seem to hold, à *priori*, from the nature of Presbyterianism, — government by Presbyters.

islative measure of the American Presbyterian Church, viz., the Adopting Act, which required all presbyters to agree in and approve the Confession of Faith and the Larger and Shorter Westminster Catechisms.[1]

This was by no means a narrow platform for the church, and we find the number of her ministers rapidly increasing. But the unfortunate division between the Old and the New Lights in 1741 — the result of Whitefield's preaching — checked the progress of the church, and gave the world another example of Christian disparateness, until the Union in 1758. In the mean time a Synod of New York had been formed in the interests of the New Light party, and its members had increased to seventy in thirteen years (1745–1758). The united Synod of New York and Philadelphia numbered at the time of the Union ninety-four ministers, of whom forty-two met in Philadelphia. With these, fourteen elders took their seats. This represented a vast increase in the influence of Presbyterianism throughout the Middle and Southern colonies. It was the period of the founding of Princeton, of the work of Samuel Davies, — him who prophesied Washington's future greatness, — and of the formation

[1] History of the Presbyterian Church in the United States of America, by the Rev. E. H. Gillett, D. D., etc., revised edition, Philadelphia, vol. i. p. 55.

of the Hanover Presbytery, so active for religious reform in Virginia.[1]

A period of prosperity naturally develops social feelings in men, and it need not surprise us to find the United Synod in 1766 devising a plan for closer intimacy with the Consociated Churches of Connecticut. This state, by the Saybrook Platform of 1708, was the only one in New England that had permanent councils, — formed usually by the consociation of the pastors and churches of a county, and also of the whole state in a General Association.[2] With such an organization holding similar doctrines union was practicable, easy, and Christian-like. For nearly ten years conventions attended by delegates from both churches were held annually: they were discontinued in 1776 on account of the disturbances produced by the Revolution. The object of these conventions was, according to Dr. Gillett, "simply Christian and patriotic." The establishment of episcopacy in America was vehemently fought by them, — with what effect we have already seen.[3]

Nor was this the only union proposed. Shortly after the arrival in this country of that distin-

[1] See for this period Briggs's American Presbyterianism, chap. viii.

[2] Such associations were formed in Massachusetts in 1803, in Vermont in 1796, and in New Hampshire in 1809, succeeding in the latter state a pastoral convention formed in 1747.

[3] Gillett, i. 165.

guished man, Dr. Witherspoon, efforts were made to bring the Associate Presbytery of Pennsylvania into the Synod of the main church. These efforts failed in 1774, but they give us an opportunity to say something about some of the minor Presbyterian organizations of which Pennsylvania was the nursery.

The Associate Presbytery of Pennsylvania was a daughter of the Associate Presbytery of Scotland, which had been formed after the Secession of 1733. That secession had taken place on account of enforced patronage and other grievances; but the seceders had speedily quarrelled among themselves, becoming Burghers and Anti-Burghers, according as they were willing or not to take the oath prescribed to the burghers, or freemen of towns. The Associate Presbytery of Pennsylvania was Anti-Burgher. It was formed in 1754, and by the time of the Revolution had thirteen ministers. In 1776 a new Presbytery of New York was formed.

Now there was in Pennsylvania another body of dissenters from the Church of Scotland, viz. the Reformed Presbyterians. These were descendants of the true-blue Covenanters, who disdained to acknowledge that William the Third had any rights over the church. Their first Presbytery in this country was formed in 1776. With these good men the Associate Presbyterians endeavored to effect a union, a project which was accomplished in 1782 by the formation at Philadelphia of the "Associated Reformed Church." This synod consisted of three presbyteries and fourteen ministers. But the union had not been entire. Instead of one body, three came out; for some of the ministers and people of the two joining churches preferred to cling to their own organizations; and so Pennsylvania is as much the Mother of Synods as Virginia is the Mother of States.[1]

We now come to the proudest day in the history of American Presbyterianism, when the Synod of 1775 addressed its patriotic pastoral letter to a nation girding itself for the fray. Lexington was fresh in all men's minds, and the American Congress was sitting in the same city with them. What wonder, then, that these men, inheriting Puritan traditions, espoused the cause of the Revolution with heart and soul? They gave to Congress their most conspicuous member, Dr. Witherspoon; they uttered themselves in a letter which nerved the shrinking hearts of thousands. Many a political sermon did they preach, and heavily did they pay for every sermon. The Presbyterian minister was one of the first objects a British raider sought.[2]

[1] The above is taken from a laborious compilation, An Original History of the Religious Denominations, . . . in the United States, . . . compiled by I. Daniel Rupp, Phil. 1844. See, also, Briggs's American Presbyterianism, p. 276.

[2] See Gillett, i. 173, for an excellent account of this period; also the ninth chapter of Dr. Briggs's monograph.

During the troublous times of the Revolution the synods were sparsely attended. In 1780 only fifteen ministers and four elders were present. But soon the face of things brightened, and plans were even laid to bring about some union with the Dutch Reformed and the Associate Presbyterian Churches. These failed, but the efforts are worthy of notice.

And now, in view of the increasing power of the church and of the changed relations with Great Britain, it was thought necessary to map out the future policy of American Presbyterianism. One synod would not do; a General Assembly must be had. So in 1785 the Synod appointed a committee to draft a constitution for the church, and to submit the same to the succeeding synod. Their report was referred to another committee, who had powers " to digest a constitution for the Presbyterian Church, print it, and send copies of it to each of the presbyteries," who were in turn to report their written judgment of the same to the Synod of 1787. Acting upon these reports the Synod issued another pamphlet to the presbyteries. This formed the basis of the discussions held by the Synod of 1788, which promulgated the Constitution of the Church, — a constitution unalterable " unless two thirds of the presbyteries under the care of the General Assembly shall propose alterations or amendments, and such alterations and amendments shall be agreed to and enacted by the General Assembly." [1]

There was some question whether the supreme judicatory should be called a General Council or a General Assembly, the point being decided in favor of the latter. In the Confession of Faith no alteration was made except with reference to the civil government and magistrates. The latter of course could not have the power, accorded them in Scotland, of calling and supervising synods; they were therefore exhorted not to show preference to any denomination of Christians, and to protect all ecclesiastical persons while discharging their sacred functions.[2]

At the same time the presbyteries were distributed into four synods, — those of New York and New Jersey, Philadelphia, Virginia, and the Carolinas. From these sixteen presbyteries the General Assembly was to be recruited by delegation. Every presbytery of not more than six members might send one minister and one elder, this proportion of six to two being kept up indefinitely.[3]

The first General Assembly met in Philadelphia in 1789. In 1790 measures were taken to reëstablish the intercourse which had existed before the Revolution between the Synod and the New England churches. The result was that in

---

[1] Band's Collection, etc. (revised edition), p. 36.
[2] Gillett, i. 204, 205. [3] Ibid., i. 268-270.

1793 delegates from New England took their seats in the General Assembly. These mutual delegates were accorded full privileges of voting in 1794.[1]

Although most of the events to be recorded in connection with the Dutch Reformed Church happened before the period we are discussing, it seems proper to give a short account of how this historic church gained its independence. With the founding of the colony of New Netherland came missionaries to plant a branch of the Church of Holland. This branch grew and flourished, being the object of the especial care of the Classis of Amsterdam, which occupied practically the same relation to it that the Bishop of London did to the Episcopal Church. Even when New Netherland became New York, this prosperity continued; for the spiritual rights of the church had been secured by understanding and by treaty. But when Governor Fletcher came into power, the face of things changed. He was bent upon advancing the interests of the Church of England; and at last, overcoming the remonstrances of the Assembly, he had Episcopacy established in New York and the surrounding counties. Thus from 1693 to 1776 the Dutch Church, and indeed all the bodies of Christians outside of the Established Church, were bound by law to pay

[1] Gillett, i. 288-290.

taxes for the support of a comparatively small number of Episcopal churches. This was felt as a particularly galling yoke by the Dutch Church, for she was now treated as an alien upon soil that had once been her own.

Meanwhile, however, internal troubles vexed the church far more than the mild persecutions alluded to. It was early felt that too close a dependence upon the Classis of Amsterdam checked the growth of the daughter church. All cases of ecclesiastical controversy had to be decided in Holland, where neither party could be on hand to plead his cause; and the risk and expense undergone by candidates for orders in crossing the ocean limited the supply of available native ministers. But these facts, obvious as they now seem, did not appeal strongly to the conservative ministers who had been educated in Holland, and who realized all that the Classis of Amsterdam had undoubtedly done for the infant church in America. Nor was this Conservative or Conferentie Party, as it was called, weak in numbers or in character. Many of the oldest and most scholarly of the Dutch divines and some of the principal elders enrolled themselves in it.

In opposition to these we find five prominent ministers proposing in 1737 to form an assembly, or Coetus, for counsel and intercourse, and such ecclesiastical business as was not really inconsistent with the dependence on Holland. This was the germ of the so-called Coetus Party.

A plan for such a coetus having been adopted, it was sent to the various churches for their concurrence. At a convention of ministers and elders held in 1738 the reports of the various churches were received, and the plan was adopted and sent to Holland for ratification. It was nearly ten years before this ratification was received, the first coetus being held in 1747. Even with the consent of the Classis of Amsterdam to the formation of the coetus, many of its members were found opposed to its taking any powers upon itself; and when it was discovered that a total separation from Holland was mooted, violent animosities arose. Inflammatory letters were sent to Amsterdam denouncing the new movement, and pulpits rang with denunciatory sermons; while, to add the finishing touch to the misery of these good old conservatives, English began to supplant Dutch in service and sermon.

But in 1770 a personage appeared upon the scene destined to restore unity to the distracted church. Dr. Livingston, one of the most interesting figures in the religious history of this country, came home from his ministerial studies in Holland. His influence with the Classis of Amsterdam, and his winning, commanding character, pointed him out as the man to heal the schism and obtain the consent of the mother church to her daughter's independence. In 1771 he succeeded in having a convention of the church called. In October, twenty-two ministers and twenty-five elders met in New York city. A committee of twelve was appointed to mature a plan for union and church government. Four of this committee were of the Conferentie Party, four of the Coetus, and four represented the churches of New York city and Albany, which had been neutral. To these men Dr. Livingston submitted a scheme matured by him while yet in Holland. It provided for the establishment of a separate classis, for correspondence with the Church of Holland, and for measures calculated to overcome existing animosities. It was kindly received, for both parties now wished for peace, and, after amendments had been made, was referred to the convention, and there adopted by an almost unanimous vote. The consent of the parent church was now the only thing necessary, and this was obtained in 1772.

Thus the Dutch Reformed Church entered upon entire independence. At the beginning of the Revolution she numbered eighty churches in New York and forty in New Jersey. These were divided respectively into three and two particular assemblies or classes, meeting twice a year. Each classis delegated two ministers and two elders to a "particular synod" which met annually. In 1784 this body took the name of

General Assembly. But it was soon thought necessary to form a higher body, and in 1792 the first "General Synod" met. It consisted of all the ministers and an elder from each congregation, and met every third year. Delegation from the ministers was afterwards introduced, and annual meetings instituted.

As Baptist churches maintain their independence of state associations and of each other, we need not look to them for any important attempt at constitution-making. Yet there are reasons, which will appear as we go on, for sketching the condition of the Baptist body in a typical state during the period we are considering, and for choosing Virginia as that state.

In 1768 the Baptists numbered, in the thirteen colonies and in Nova Scotia, 137 churches. They had made a good fight in New England, and had been relieved from tithes in Massachusetts and New Hampshire for forty years. From New England they came into North Carolina under Shubal Stearns in 1755, and from thence they passed into Virginia.

Other branches of Baptists had previously settled there, but these New England worthies were the chief cause of a revival of religion in Virginia, and of the foundation of a church made strong by persecution. How that church flourished, not only in Virginia, but elsewhere through the country, may be seen by contrasting the figures given for 1768 with the fact that in 1790 the Baptists numbered 872 churches, 1,171 ministers, and nearly 65,000 members. Of these last, Virginia contained about 20,000.

The story of the rise of the Baptist Church in Virginia has been ably told by a minister of that denomination, the Rev. Robert B. Semple, of King and Queen County. His book was printed in Richmond in 1810, and is now quite rare. It is delightful reading, its strong, pure style showing that the author knew his Bible well. From this I have drawn materials for my sketch.

The first "separate"[1] Baptist Church in Virginia was opened in 1760. Five years afterward Samuel Harriss preached at Culpeper, but whips being brought out, he removed to Orange County. A revival set in both of religion and of persecution, — the former flaming with zeal and success; the latter, with some zeal but no success. Persecution began with whipping and stoning, but in 1768 three Baptists were imprisoned in Spottsylvania for preaching without a license. Two of these men were kept in jail for ten weeks; another case was still more brutal from the disgusting condition of the prison. Unremitting efforts were made to stop this persecution, and Patrick Henry was found an efficient helper; but the safest way was soon seen to lie in obtaining licenses to preach.

[1] That is, of the followers of Stearns.

If ever persecution failed of its object, it did in Virginia. In 1770 there were six churches; in 1774, fifty-four. So favorable, says Semple, did their prospects appear, that they actually began to entertain hope not only of gaining liberty of conscience, but also of overturning the establishment. Then came the Revolution, for which the Baptists were zealous. Emerging from the struggle less crippled than the Established Church, they joined with Presbyterians and Deists in powerful attacks upon her privileges, and after a series of victories succeeded in 1798 in taking away her last remaining privilege and possession, — her glebe lands.

In the mean time associations of churches had been formed, that is, councils composed of delegates from each church, which were to consider the welfare of the churches, and to assist them by counsel in the preservation of order and discipline among them.[1] The acts of these councils were, of course, not authoritative. At first the Virginia churches were represented in a North Carolina association; but in 1771 a separate association was held in Orange County, at which twelve churches were represented by thirty-one delegates. The total number of church members represented was 1.335. The delegates agreed upon nine rules of business, which were in fact a constitution for the association. Only one

[1] Semple, p. 41.

point need be dwelt on: quite a pretty question for casuistry was left open by the juxtaposition of an article disclaiming all power over the churches and an article declaring a "right in the association to withdraw from delinquent churches in certain cases." For this was evidently a claim to judge of the doctrines and conduct of particular churches. Thus we see that these good ministers were no wiser than certain other constitution-makers of whom the world has heard a good deal.

In 1774 the association was divided into two, — a Northern and a Southern. Such questions as the eternity of hell-fire and marriage with a deceased wife's sister were largely discussed. There was also a rather curious experiment made in appointing an "apostle," after Ephesians iv. 11-13, on which Semple judiciously observes that this was only the old plan of bishops under a new name. In a year it was agreed "that the office of apostles, like that of prophets, was the effect of miraculous inspiration, and did not belong to ordinary times." Semple attributes the failure of the experiment either to the spirit of free government among the churches, or to the displeasure of God. In 1775 the two associations united in a General Association, in order better to oppose the Established Church. In 1776 an abortive attempt at division into local associations was made, which was finally carried into effect in 1783.

In the minutes of these associations we find that political affairs receive considerable attention; indeed, one resolution expressly declares that associations afford "opportunity to consult respecting the best modes of counteracting national grievances." Nor did they shrink from appointing delegates to memorialize the legislature.

At the last meeting of the General Association in 1783 it was resolved that a General Committee should be instituted, to be composed of not more than four delegates from each district association, and to meet annually. This association also adopted the Philadelphia Confession of Faith.

The General Committee held its first meeting in 1784, with delegates present from four associations. A plan of government was adopted, and one of its most striking features was a concentration of all political action in its hands; no local association was to petition the legislature for anything. One extract from the minutes of 1786 may well be given in this connection. "Reuben Ford, who was appointed to wait upon the assembly with a memorial and petition against the bill for a general assessment,[1] *Reported*, that he waited on the house of assembly according to

---

[1] This was a bill proposing state aid for ministers of all denominations; it was the last struggle of the Episcopalians, and fell under the denunciations of Mr. Madison.

appointment; that the law for assessment did not pass; but, on the contrary, an act passed explaining the nature of religious liberty."[1]

But meanwhile (1787) a union took place between the separate Baptists, whose history we have been giving, and the other Baptists, who had preceded the followers of Stearns, and were known as Regular Baptists, — the resulting church taking the name of the "United Baptist Churches of Christ in Virginia." At a meeting of the General Committee for this strengthened body, held in 1788, the following minute was made : " Whether the new Federal Constitution, which had now made its appearance in public, made sufficient provision for the secure enjoyment of religious liberty ; on which it was agreed unanimously that, in the opinion of the General Committee, it did not."[2]

In 1791 the Committee got into a quandary as to whether it had not exceeded its original powers. It was resolved, in face of a very clear article, that they had deviated from their original plan, which was only to consider religious political differences and to seek for redress, and that those words should be struck out of the obnoxious article which gave them the right to consider "all references from the district associations respecting matters that may concern the whole body." That the discussion of political questions had been the chief business of the Committee was

[1] Semple, p. 72.   [2] Ibid., p. 76.

true; but it is hard to account for their timidity in the other respect, except on the supposition that it was due to a reaction in favor of extreme free government caused by the late consolidation in the government both of the country at large and of the other religious bodies. Be this as it may, Semple could find no reason for it, and the power of the Committee began so steadily to decline that it was dissolved in 1799. It is true that in 1792 the Committee contradicted itself, and reverted to the wider view of its powers; but the false step once taken, no business of any importance was transacted except continued remonstrances against the possession of glebes by the Established Church. After the fall of the Committee a General Meeting of Correspondence was instituted in 1800, into whose history we need go no further than to remark that on Jefferson's retiring from the Presidency an address of admiration was offered to him, — a proof that the old alliance against the Episcopalians had not been forgotten. The significance of the facts we have given concerning the Baptist Church in Virginia is apparent, — the Baptists are our religious Anti-Federalists.

The Free-Will Baptists, founded by Benjamin Randall in 1780, soon gained ground in New England, and several quarterly meetings were formed. These meetings were distinct, but were connected by correspondence. In 1792 a yearly meeting was formed, composed of delegates from all the quarterly meetings. As the body spread, several yearly meetings were instituted, which were finally gathered into a General Conference in 1827.

The Lutheran Church during this period was divided into "five or six different, distant, and unconnected synods."[1] These were not combined into a General Synod until 1820, and therefore we need not consider the history of this church.

The Universalists owe their origin in this country practically to John Murray, who had been converted from Methodism. By 1780 there were several societies in New England. Legal persecution and controversial attacks induced them in 1785 to unite in a Confession of Faith. For this purpose delegates from nine or ten societies assembled at Oxford, Massachusetts, in 1785. They took the name of "Independent Christian Universalists," and recommended a "General Convention of the New England States and others," which met in Boston in 1786 and continued to hold annual meetings.

There seems to be little of constitutional interest in the history of the Friends during this period. It is worth mentioning, however, that at the London Yearly Meeting of 1784, just three

---

[1] S. S. Schmucker's Retrospect, etc., p. 16, quoted by himself in an article in Rupp's History of all the Religions Denominations, etc.

years after the close of the Revolution, ten members were present from America, and that the powers of the Woman's Yearly Meeting were enlarged in accordance with the ideas prevailing in America. These facts tend to show how thoroughly the Friends carried their peace principles into practice. The period was not marked by any significant changes in the polity of the Congregational churches.

And now what conclusions are to be drawn from the numerous facts recorded in the foregoing pages? Do any relations subsist between the Constitution of the Republic and the constitutions of the churches? On a survey of the material we have collected, it is obvious that such relations, of a general kind at least, do exist.

In the first place, the contemporaneousness of the two movements for ecclesiastical and civil government is a clear sign of a relation between them. Both movements have their origin in our separation from Great Britain, and our consequent need of civil and religious autonomy; both practically end in 1789 with constitutions that are destined to stand the test of time. If some of the religious bodies did not complete their constitutions until after this period, neither did two of the states recognize at once the advantages of constitutional union. And while during the life of the Confederation the individual states were practically supreme, so during the same period the churches in the various states were supreme, or else were joined by loose and uncertain bonds. While Madison and Hamilton were casting about for some deliverance from the impending anarchy, White and Witherspoon, and Asbury and Carroll, were laboring to bring about unions that would prevent anarchical subdivisions of the great religious bodies. In both spheres we find the same objects pursued at the same time with almost the same means. If the states frame new constitutions or make the necessary modifications in preëxisting charters, will not the advocates of religious union make use of the weapons thus forged to their hands? And do not the advocates of civil union find example and encouragement in the efforts making around them for religious union? Certainly here is no mere coincidence; in both spheres, and in matters particular as well as general, we can see the relation of cause and effect.

In the next place, is it not likely that the tendency to state autonomy was checked by such facts as these: that the Episcopalians of the South and East had been maturing measures for union; that the Presbyterians formed one church which was being strengthened by efforts for closer union; that these same Presbyterians had fraternal relations with New England Congregationalists; that the Methodists were one body and zealously extending their influence throughout the country; that the Roman Catholics were banding together with all the strength that new-born hopes can give? These different religious unions, these conventions, — what meant they but that men felt drawn toward their co-religionists, no matter what their state, — that they saw how good a thing it is for brethren to dwell together in unity? And was the inference a rash one that, if religious unions were good and practicable, political union might be practicable, too, in a measure? The churches had united after the reverses of the Revolution, when there seemed no hope but in union; might not the states in their disorder apply the same principle? And there was one church, not numerous, it is true, but very important, which presented the opponents of state autonomy with striking arguments. The Episcopal Church was made up of dioceses, local units corresponding to the various states. These were to be united under a general government, and yet the individual and rather jealous units were to retain certain powers. Nay, had not this church even shown a way by which subsequent religious units might put themselves under the general government, and would not this same plan apply to recusant but finally repentant states, and to territories yet to be settled? We can hardly believe that such thoughts did not occur to reflecting churchmen; we can hardly think that even Deists like Mr. Madison failed to watch these movements for religious union, and to draw such inferences as we have suggested from them. Now, if the various religious unions were at variance with obstinate state autonomy, they were assuredly factors in the great movement for political union under a constitution.

But there seem to be further analogies between the actions of the Episcopalians and those of the promoters of Federalism. Just as the Episcopal clergy made use of the New Brunswick meeting to discuss affairs and call the New York convention, so the meeting of the commissioners at Annapolis led to the Philadelphia convention. After an examination of Madison's correspondence and other papers of the time, I have not been able to find any proof that this action of the Episcopal clergy suggested the scheme of utilizing the Annapolis commission; but it is altogether likely that such was the case. That Madison was deeply interested in the condition of the Episcopal Church at that time, is evidenced by his speech in opposition to the bill for a general assessment in favor of the Virginia clergy, and by the constant references to the subject in his letters to Jefferson and others. That he received copies of the proceedings of the various conventions may be inferred from the letter of July 26, 1785, in which he thanks Edmund Randolph for a copy "of the ecclesiastical Journal," which in all probability refers to the minutes of the Virginia Convention of that year. When John Page of Rosewell, a member of the Episcopalian Convention of 1785, took the trouble to send this same " ecclesiastical journal" to Jefferson, at Paris,[1] we may be sure that Madison must have heard much about Episcopalian affairs. Whether he consciously followed the New Brunswick experiment is, of course, another question.

That the other church constitutions affected the Federal Constitution to an appreciable degree can hardly be maintained; but, as we have already said, the efforts necessary for obtaining these constitutions militated against the spirit of state autonomy and so aided the Federalists. The first amendment was largely due to the influence of the various churches, especially the Baptist. We have already seen how the Baptists in Virginia decided that the new constitution did not provide sufficiently for religious liberty, and it is highly probable that they were influential backers of Patrick Henry, with whom they had always been in league, when he made his famous attack upon the new instrument in the Virginia Convention. Indeed, it would hardly seem an unwarrantable assumption to affirm that the individual principles of Baptist polity made this church naturally suspicious of any projects for union.

[1] See the letter given in Bancroft's History of the Constitution, vol. i. 450.

We have looked at one side of the question, let us now consider the other. Did the various churches adapt their constitutions to the new instrument which was to unite the states politically? It would seem that the Federal Constitution had some influence upon the church constitutions, but not a great deal. Upon the Presbyterians, Methodists, and Roman Catholics I should say that its influence was small. The action of the Roman Catholics in obtaining a bishop of their own election was due to a fear that foreign dependence might alienate their fellow-citizens from them, and this fear affected Carroll before the Constitution was framed. The synods held by Bishop Carroll represented priestly government, and concerned themselves chiefly with matters of faith; the new Constitution could not in the nature of things affect them to an appreciable degree. The Roman Catholics saw in the Constitution a guarantee to their political liberty, and therefore they espoused its cause; they were not prepared to extend its principles to the government of their church.

That the Methodists were not greatly affected by the Constitution needs hardly be stated when we remember that not until 1808 did they have a constitution at all. They were finally driven to form one by the fear that their ministers might play fast and loose with Wesleyan principles, though, of course, the sight of the general government and the various churches working smoothly under constitutions must have quickened their self-consciousness in the direction of constitutional government. We have already noticed how lacking the early Methodists were in parliamentary training. Their dependence upon Wesley, their social status, their enthusiasm looking only at the heavenly side of things, fully explain their loose method of general church government.

With regard to Presbyterianism we cannot do better than to quote Dr. Briggs: "The American Presbyterian Church continued to grow with great rapidity after the Revolution. It was spread over a large territory, from New York to Georgia; and it was simply impossible for all the ministers, or even a majority of them, to meet together in the Annual Synod. A system of representation was rendered necessary. This might have been accomplished by changing the Synod into a representative body; but it was preferred to use the Synod as a larger Presbytery, in which all the ministers residing in a section of the country might assemble, and to organize a representative General Assembly. The American Presbyterian Church, under the influence of Dr. Witherspoon, was tending strongly towards the methods of government and discipline of the Presbyterian Church of Scotland."[1] In the last sentence I think we have the gist of the matter.

[1] American Presbyterianism, p. 362.

But there was not wanting in this ecclesiastical attempt at union the same feeling which characterized the future anti-Federalists, for Jacob Green and his followers seceded and organized an Associated Presbytery, which increased rapidly for some years. Green had also objected to the Synod's action on many other matters, and these objections were shared by some who went along with the attempts at union. It was, therefore, necessary to adopt a harmonizing constitution which might at the same time "appease the jealousies of foreign influence in the government of the Church."[1] From our account of this movement it will be seen that the Presbyterian constitution was being discussed a little before and during the period of the discussion of the national instrument.

A harmonizing constitution at such a time, however, could not have been wholly Scotch, and so the power given to the General Assembly of altering the constitution would seem to be of American growth. The retention, also, of the synods between the smaller Presbyteries and the General Assembly, is strikingly analogous to the position of the states between the local and general governments.[2] The breadth and tolerance

---

[1] American Presbyterianism, p. 364.

[2] According to Dr. Baird, these synods and presbyteries did not grow but were made, which would make the process just the reverse of that in the political sphere.

claimed by Professor Briggs for the Synod of 1788, which adopted the constitution, and the measures taken to secure the opinions and advice of the presbyteries and the laity, are probably to be ascribed to the causes which produced similar results in the sphere of federal affairs. This is as much influence as the movements in civil affairs could be expected to exert on presbyters[1] whose assemblies were like ecclesiastical courts, and whose constitution was akin to a code.

It will hardly be asserted that the Baptists were much affected by the constitution-making going on around them, but plainly the Episcopalians were. Not that we can draw a full parallel between the evolution of one house containing bishops and deputies into two, — one of bishops and one of deputies, — and the evolution of the Senate and House of Representatives from the single house of the Continental Congress. Such a full parallel would only be illusory, for the House of Bishops evidently had its *raison d'être* in the upper house of the English Convocation, although the institution of two houses in the Federal Congress might have reconciled some of the Southern delegates to this extension of the episcopal powers. But we do see a strong influence flow-

[1] The lay element was, of course, not wanting; but the proportion of ministers to elders in the committee of 1786 for drafting the "Book of Government and Discipline" was nine to three. Baird's Collection (revised ed.), p. 34.

ing from the national Constitution to this church when we find this future House of Bishops called a "House of Revision," and its powers very analogous to those of the new President. For it will be remembered that this house was not to originate measures, and that its veto could be overruled by a three-fifths majority in the lower house. Indeed, it seems as though the enemies of episcopal powers were determined to outdo all the checks against presidential tyranny by making a smaller majority necessary to a veto. The provision that the disapprobation of the bishops must be sent to the lower house in writing within a certain number of days, failing which the act should have the force of law, reminds us strikingly of the similar requirement made of the President; and it may have been the analogous spectacle of the Senate originating legislation that subsequently made the Southern delegates willing to grant the House of Bishops a similar power. Nor does the influence of political environment appear less strong when we remember that, while the plan of having bishops, and priests, and laymen sitting in one body was in force, the unicameral Continental Congress was dragging its weary length along; and our belief in this influence is also strengthened when we find the church in each state having one vote, just as in the Continental Congress and the Philadelphia Convention of '87.

We see a further instance of the influence radiating from the political sphere in the various provisions made for altering the different constitutions of this church. The Constitution of 1785 provided that when ratified by the church in the different states, it should be itself " unalterable by the convention of the church in any state." From this it might be inferred that alterations by the General Convention were possible, but nothing was said on the subject. The Constitution of 1786 makes matters worse by adding to the clause just quoted the following words: "which hath been represented at the time of such ratification." How the convention of a particular state, even though not represented, could alter the constitution and remain in the union, is hard to conceive, and yet I am at a loss for any other inference to be drawn from the clause. But in 1789, the new national constitution with its amendment safety-valve being in full operation, we find this intelligible article concluding the constitution: " This constitution shall be unalterable, unless in General Convention by the church in a majority of the states which may have adopted the same; and all alterations shall be first proposed in one General Convention, and made known to the several state conventions, before they shall be finally agreed to or ratified in the ensuing General Convention." The details of this scheme for amendment strongly resemble those of the national Constitution; they coincide still more completely with those of the Presbyterian constitution adopted the year before.

The main facts of our ecclesiastical polity during the formative period have now been given and their relation to our civil polity has been discussed. A reciprocal influence between the two spheres of thought might have been inferred both from the history of other nations and from the nature of the human mind; but such *à priori* proof cannot take the place of detailed conclusions based upon minute research. The writer is fully aware of the imperfect character of his own work; but he feels certain that the influences he has attempted to define were real and formative. They are, too, precisely such influences as the more ambitious historians, secular and religious, are apt to overlook. To the student of our national Constitution, Mr. Madison is of more moment than the whole Methodist Church; to the historian of Methodism, Francis Asbury is of more moment than all the worthies who formed the Convention of 1787. But the careful reader perceives that either historian would profit by a short and peaceful incursion into the province of the other.

V.

THE STATUS OF THE SLAVE, 1775-1789.[1]

BY JEFFREY R. BRACKETT.

THERE were in the thirteen American colonies, at the time of separation from Great Britain, some half a million slaves. The purpose of this study is to note any changes of moment in the status of the slaves during the period in which the states, become "free and independent," adopted new constitutions, and in which the Federal government was formed. Alike in some ways in all the colonies, the position of the slaves yet varied in many important respects. It may be well, in order to understand these differences, to digress briefly, to glance at the growth of slavery in the colonies.

The use of negroes as slaves was little thought of in Western Europe, when the colonies were founded; but custom still tolerated the enslavement of heathen captured in war, and the founders of the colonies received as slaves the captive Africans who were imported, and also freely en-

[1] The principal sources of the following essay have been the acts and resolves of the legislatures of the several states, and the journals of their proceedings.

slaved the Indians whom they themselves captured in war. For years the number of slaves grew but slowly; they were scattered among the whites from Massachusetts to Carolina, and little mention was made of them. But within a century, came radical changes in some of the colonies. Tobacco had become the staple of Maryland and Virginia, and the few grains of rice planted in a back garden in Charleston, about 1683, had multiplied to thousands of barrels yearly. The slave-trade to the Southern colonies was pushed with all the power of British merchants and British officials. Nor were the colonists averse to it, for a time. The old-fashioned preambles of some of the laws of these colonies tell us of the need of goodly numbers of negroes for the development of the lands. These Africans, accustomed to heat and exposure, were first settled in the low and rich but malarious coast regions. Then the lines of settlement were pushed inland. Cities and towns were exceptional, the colonies, in the main, being aggregates of many little plantation communities, often separated from each other by miles of woods and water.

If we find these Southern colonies, on the one hand, with large black populations, we find New England, on the other hand, with comparatively few blacks. New England, perhaps, was little suited to slave labor, in its soil, climate, and industries. Here, the number of slaves grew slowly.

On the farms, in the country, they could be counted on the fingers; the larger part of them were servants and lived in the towns. Over half the negroes in Massachusetts, in 1740, were in Boston.

By the time of the Revolution there were in round numbers, — for the early estimates cannot be called more than approximate, — in New Hampshire, a hundred whites to one slave; in Massachusetts, sixty to one; in Rhode Island, twenty to one: while in North Carolina there were half as many slaves as whites; in Maryland there were three slaves to five whites; in Virginia and Georgia the numbers were about equal; in South Carolina, one would meet two slaves to one white person. The number of slaves in Pennsylvania does not seem to have been large, but in New York and New Jersey there was one slave to seven or eight whites, and in Delaware the proportion was greater. Here, more than in New England, they were used for agriculture, though large numbers were in the cities.

It was as natural for the English colonists to follow largely the usages and traditions of England, their old home, as it was for Rip Van Winkle, on awaking from his long sleep, to toast King George. Thus, in the early laws for the administration of justice, it was the rule that English law and custom should be followed, unless modified by statute law of the colony or held by the courts to be inapplicable to colonial life. But negroes were practically unknown in England, and the colonist brought no more precedent for any special treatment of them than he did cut-and-dried rules to guide his relations with the Indians. In looking over the old collections of laws, we find — just what we should expect — that there is little mention of slaves in the colonies in which the slaves were few. In 1775 slavery existed in all the colonies, but in some of them there was, properly speaking, no slave code.

Everywhere, North and South, there were what we may call police regulations for the slaves, — regulations which were usually directed also against white indentured servants, and often, later, against free blacks. Thus, slaves were not allowed to be abroad after certain hours at night without leave, and all persons were forbidden to sell liquor to them, or to trade with them, without leave from the master. For instance, in Connecticut, an Indian or colored servant or slave, taken up after nine o'clock without permission to be out, could be taken before a justice, who might order not over ten lashes on the bare back, with costs, unless the master should choose to redeem his servant by paying a fine of not over ten shillings. Any strange Indian or negro might be taken up to be sent home, unless found to have a pass or to be free. For the better government of Indian and colored servants and slaves in the town of Newport, an act of Rhode Island of 1770 empowered the town to erect a cage for the imprisonment overnight of servants and slaves found abroad, and unable to give good account of themselves. The masters, if they chose, could save them a whipping next morning by payment of a few shillings. This act states that the laws in force throughout the plantation had been found insufficient to keep the servants and slaves of Newport in due order.

In Massachusetts and Connecticut, we find also the penalty of a whipping provided for any colored person who should strike a white. In Massachusetts, the punishment for colored persons for improper intercourse with whites was sale out of the province. Also, a fine of fifty pounds was fixed for any one who should join a colored person in marriage with a " Christian," *i. e.* a white, but masters were ordered not to deny unreasonably the desire of the negroes to marry within their own race. An act of New Hampshire of 1715 declared that a master who wilfully killed his Indian or negro servant should be punished with death, and also forbade inhuman severities to " Christian servants" (*i. e.* whites), who, if maimed by the master otherwise than by accident, became free and recovered damages.

The most serious matter in these New England communities, touching the few slaves among them, was the prevention of charges to the public for the support of infirm or idle freedmen. In Massachusetts a master could free his slave by giving security to the town that the freedman should not become a public charge; without this security, the black was not legally free.[1] In Connecticut slaves could be set free at will; but if they afterwards became incapable of self-support, the old master or his heirs became liable to maintain them, and towns could recover expenses. In Rhode Island, an act of 1728 had fixed the necessary security, to give legal freedom, at not less than one hundred pounds. In 1775 this was raised to a thousand pounds.[2]

Such, with one exception, were the important regulations concerning slaves in New England; and that exception brings us to the most interesting topic of our study. An act of Rhode Island of 1718 provided that all negro and Indian slaves who should be found purloining or stealing should be tried and punished by a court consisting of two or more justices of peace or town officers of the town where the offence was committed, instead of in the general courts of trial

---

[1] Here, as elsewhere, no legal contract could be made with a slave any more than with an infant. If a master, for instance, promised freedom to his slave and afterwards changed his mind, the slave had no redress.

[2] In 1770 a special act for Newport secured to the town treasury as much of the estate of a manumittor as would yield twenty pounds a year, and required manumission there to be by instrument duly registered.

and gaol delivery, as before. There was the right of appeal to the higher court only in case the owner of the slave should desire it, and would give bond to prosecute the appeal. With the exception of this act in Rhode Island, there seems to have been no special provision for the trial and punishment of slaves.[1] Thus, when a negro man and woman were found guilty at the assizes at Cambridge, Massachusetts, in 1755, of poisoning their master, the man was drawn to the place of execution, hanged, and his body exposed on the gibbet; and the woman was drawn and burned at the stake, in accordance with the old English law for petty treason, under which a woman was burned in England as late as 1784, for the murder of her husband.[2]

[1] It is interesting to add that a law of Connecticut of 1730 provided that a slave who should speak of any one such words as would be actionable if uttered by a freeman, should be whipped, on due conviction by a magistrate, and be sold to pay expenses, unless these were met by his master. But the slave was not to be debarred from making such pleas and offering such evidences in defence as any person might make use of in an action of defamation, so far as related to the trial before the justice.

[2] A. C. Goodell, Jr., *The Trial of Mark and Phillis, Slaves of Captain John Codman, for Petit Treason.* The legality of slavery, as well as the issues involved in certain suits for freedom, in New England, has been considerably discussed, notably in Massachusetts. Several suits are found, in the years just before the Revolutionary War, in which the slaves obtained not only freedom but certain damages, much smaller than they claimed, from their masters. On the one hand, these suits seem to show, especially among bench and bar, a growing tendency to regard slavery as contrary to the spirit of the times; it seems, on the other hand, as if some of

There were about as many slaves in Massachusetts or Connecticut in 1776 as there were in Virginia a century before. It was not until the close of the seventeenth century, indeed, that the blacks began to increase rapidly at the South, and that the slave code grew up as we know it. There is every reason to believe that, until that time, the slaves of the Southern colonies, as those of the New England colonies, were subject, if accused of serious offences, to the same judicial procedure as freemen were: it is probable that negroes were punished, at first, very much as white servants were.[1]

As the blacks increased, we hear of them more and more in the statutes. In 1690 South Carolina began the use of local magistrates' courts for the trial of slaves for all offences. In Virginia, all criminal cases had been tried before the governors and councils, or the general courts, where met those who were most skilled in law; but after

---

the defendants may not have pushed their claims, willing to be rid of responsibility for unprofitable or dissatisfied servants. It is certain — and this is sufficient here — that the results of these suits did not extend beyond the parties immediately concerned, for slave-holding continued in the same communities. See Dr. Moore's *Notes on Slavery in Massachusetts*.

[1] Slaves were excepted, of course, as Indians were, in the early acts securing to the colonists the rights and liberties of Englishmen. That baptism did not give freedom was, indeed, declared by law, and intermarriage of the races was forbidden; but the other acts touching slaves were in general like those for indentured white servants, and may be called police regulations.

1692, special commissions of jail-delivery were issued for the trial, without jury, of slaves accused of capital crimes. Afterwards, when it had become a journey of many days from the capital of the province to its outlying counties, the justices in each county held general commissions for this purpose. In Maryland, slaves, as freemen, were subject for all petty misdemeanors and offences to the county courts, until 1717, when single magistrates were authorized to try and award limited punishment to slaves for these offences. All persons were tried for capital crimes in the highest courts, until after 1750, when slaves were tried in the county courts.

These examples serve to illustrate the growth of the slave codes; and reasons for it are sometimes given in the laws. Thus, many slave-owners, rather than lose the money and time involved in bringing their slaves long distances to the general or provincial courts, would smother the crimes and keep the offenders at work. Felonies became frequent, and the exportation of felons from England mixed with the fresh Africans, — rude, ignorant, and imitative, — the worst element of English jails. Attempts at insurrection, and the nearness of hostile Indians, increased this legislation. In some respects the slave codes show only that harshness under which white offenders suffered as well, — the severity of English criminal law of that time. In other respects they show that the life of a black man was valued mostly — to the legislators, at least — in pounds and shillings. It is not the growth of the slave codes at that time that is surprising, but the fact that they were allowed afterwards to remain on the statute books so long.

If we turn to the laws still in force in 1775, we find that, in South Carolina and Georgia, a slave found away from his town or plantation without a proper pass, and not in the company of a white man, could be given not over twenty lashes on the spot. If he refused to be examined, he might be moderately corrected; if he assaulted a white, he might be killed. In Georgia, proof of such assault must be made to the satisfaction of any two justices and seven freeholders duly summoned for the purpose; if the assault could not be proven, the white must pay the late slave-owner for the loss of his slave. Male slaves, to the number of over seven, were forbidden to travel together without a white man, in South Carolina and Georgia, under penalty of forty lashes, to be given by any one who might meet them. Slaves going abroad without leave in Virginia might be given ten lashes by the master or overseer of the plantation where found, and more than five blacks were not to meet together except for lawful business or for church. Noisy or suspected meetings were forbidden, — in Maryland the courts could appoint special constables; in Georgia, patrol parties of militiamen were to do duty twice a month. Negroes with guns were liable to lose them and be whipped, unless they were in company of a white man, or had license. In North Carolina, a slave could not hunt with a gun except with a permit from the chairman of the county court, after the master had given security for his good behavior.

A slave, like an infant, not able to enter into a contract, could not legally hold property. In Maryland and North Carolina, slaves were forbidden to own horses, cattle, or hogs. In South Carolina they could not, in addition, keep sheep; in Georgia there was no provision against their having hogs; but in both states they were forbidden to have boats or canoes. These laws were to prevent stealing, and attempts at escape and conspiracy. For the same reason, evidently, it was specially forbidden, in Georgia and South Carolina, to rent in any way a house or plantation to a slave. In Virginia, South Carolina, and North Carolina, masters were forbidden, under fines, to allow any slaves to go at large as freemen, to trade or to hire themselves out — in order, we read, to prevent stealing, drunkenness, and idleness. In the last-named state, if a slave who had been allowed to hire himself out was executed for crime, the master received no recompense from the county. As attempts to poison had not been uncommon, no slave in Virginia, South Carolina, and Georgia could legally give any medicines without the master's leave; and in South Carolina, slaves could not be employed in a drug store. The penalty for teaching slaves to write was one hundred pounds in South Carolina; and twenty pounds, for teaching them to write, or read writing, in Georgia.

In all these states, the county or inferior courts could not try freemen for crimes which might be punished with loss of life or member. In Maryland, slaves were tried and sentenced for capital offences in the county courts. But they were tried, if they wished, by jury; and the council records of the colony go to show that death sentences of slaves as well as freemen were carefully considered by the governor, that pardon might be given when deserved. For stealing and other misdemeanors, for which freemen would be tried by jury in the county court, slaves would be tried by a magistrate, who could not order, however, more than forty lashes. In Virginia the justices of each county held commissions of Oyer and Terminer from the governor, for the trial of slaves for offences punished with life or limb. The trial was without jury, but was held at the court-house, in public. Four justices, at least, must be on the bench, one of them being of the quorum; and sentence of death could not be given unless four, being a majority of those present, should agree therein. Except in cases of conspiracy and rebellion, ten days must elapse between condemnation and execution. A master might defend his slave, except as to formalities in the proceedings on the trial. For minor offences, slaves were evidently tried by magistrates.

In North Carolina, slaves were tried for all crimes and offences by a court consisting of any three justices of the county court, and four freeholders, who were slave-holders in the county. As in Virginia, the trial was public but without jury, and the owner of the slave might make defence as to facts. In South Carolina, the courts were similarly gotten together in the neighborhood of the accused, but the members were not necessarily slave-holders. For offences not punished by loss of life or limb, one justice and two freeholders composed the court, of which the justice and one freeholder must agree in judgment. For more serious crimes, two justices and from three to five freeholders were summoned, and either the justices and one freeholder, or one justice and two freeholders, must agree. The court was to be held within six days after the arrest of the slave, but trial might be postponed, if necessary, to get evidence. The accusation and the slave's defence were to be heard, and judgment given in a summary way. As usual, the freeholders were put under oath.

In Georgia, the special courts consisted of any three justices and a jury of not less than seven freeholders. Trial was to be held within three days, if possible. The slave's defence was to be heard. Punishments not extending to life or limb could be given by two justices, but a majority of the jury must agree with them in a death sentence. If any person, on the slave's behalf, would give security for his further appearance and for all costs, then the execution would be delayed until the case could be reported to the governor, and his pleasure be known. It is interesting to note that free blacks and hostile Indians were tried in Georgia in the same way. The ability to give legal testimony depended on a man's color and not on his status. Negroes, like Indians, could not be witnesses against whites; but, as a rule, could testify against one another, especially against those accused of serious felonies.

There were some penalties provided for slaves only. Thus, in Maryland, slaves who resisted arrest for any crime might be killed. The pursuer might be tried, but if justified in his action would be acquitted, and the county would pay costs. The value of the slave was paid the owner also. In Virginia, if slaves ran away and remained outlying, doing actual mischief, two justices of the county — one being of the quorum — might issue proclamation for the sheriff to seize them; and after this had been read at every church door in the county on two successive Sundays, the slaves, if still outlying, might be killed by any one. If proclamation were issued when the justices were not convinced that actual mischief was being done by the slave, the owner could not claim recompense from the county. In North Carolina this delay of a week was not required after proclamation was issued. In South Carolina the regular patrols could fire on a party of runaways who had been away for a month and resisted capture; and any one might kill a runaway absent for a year, if it were impossible to take him alive. In these cases limited damages were paid the owners by the public.[1]

Usually the exact nature of the punishment was left to the discretion of the court, with the proviso that it be so administered as to deter other slaves from like crimes. In Maryland, a slave guilty of murder or arson might be sentenced, in the discretion of the court, to have the right hand cut off before execution, and the body beheaded and quartered afterwards, when exposed. This had been enacted, as the old preamble of 1729 reads, because the English law was not severe enough for those who, without shame, were kept from crime only by the severity of the penalty. For most offences, the slaves were given the pillory, the whipping-post, the branding-iron,

---

[1] The Virginia act of 1792 still allowed castration in case of slaves convicted of rape, or of attempted rape, on a white woman.

which each county court kept for both whites and blacks. Suffice it to say that the life of a black was not valued as that of a white; the punishment given the black, in the discretion of the court, was often unusually severe.

There were in general much more careful provisions at law for the proper treatment of indentured servants than of slaves. But in North Carolina, if it could be proven that a slave convicted of stealing any goods (from any one other than his owner) had not during the preceding year been properly clothed, and had not received a quart of corn a day regularly, the owner of the stolen goods could recover damages from the slave's master. In South Carolina, a master became liable to be fined five and twenty pounds by a magistrate every time he made a slave work over fourteen hours a days in winter and fifteen hours in summer; for working a slave unnecessarily on Sunday, the fine was five pounds. Any person, on behalf of a slave who was denied sufficient clothing and food, might complain to a justice, who was ordered to summon the master and to fine him not over twenty pounds, for the use of the poor, and to order relief for the slave, unless the master, where positive proof was lacking, should clear himself by oath. Here, too, for dismembering a slave, or punishing otherwise than with a lash, or switch, or irons, or imprisonment, there was a fine of one hundred pounds;

for killing a slave by undue correction or on sudden passion, three hundred and fifty pounds; for wilfully killing a slave, seven hundred pounds, — or labor for seven years in default,— and incapacity to hold office thereafter in the state. In Georgia, killing a second slave was deemed murder. In Virginia, a slave-owner was not liable to prosecution if his slave died during correction or from accident, unless the county court, on examination, was led to believe the killing wilful; and no one indicted for murder of a slave, and found guilty of manslaughter, incurred any punishment "for such offence or misfortune." On injury to another's slave, the important consideration was the master's loss.

On a question of freedom, a negro had to bear the burden of proof. Everywhere, a slave entitled to freedom might apply, in person or by a friend, to the courts. In South Carolina and Georgia, the friend so applying was appointed guardian of the slave, to bring action of trespass in the nature of ravishment of ward. The courts were ordered to give judgment according to the very right, without regard to defects in proceedings. If the plaintiff won, the negro was freed and the defendant had to pay costs and damages assessed by the jury; if he failed, the negro might be given corporal punishment, not to life or limb. Pending trial, the master was obliged to give recognizance, with security, to the plaintiff, that the slave should be produced whenever required, and should not be abused or disposed of. Such safeguards for the slave seem to have been the rule elsewhere, though not always required by law. But it was not evidently the common rule to award damages to a freedman for false imprisonment.

In Maryland, slave-owners could not in any way during their last illness give freedom to slaves. At other times they could free slaves who were able and not over fifty years of age, by instruments properly executed, witnessed, and recorded. In Virginia, no slave could be freed except for some meritorious service, in the judgment and by the license of the governor and council; and slaves set at large illegally could be sold for the benefit of the poor. A similar license had to be obtained in North Carolina from the county courts. Manumission was not regulated by law — it was not recognized evidently — in South Carolina and Georgia. Slaves were personal property, and so were sold at will, and often taken for debts, as other chattels were. Freedom could not be given in prejudice of creditors.[1]

These examples suffice to show the status of the slave in the large slave-holding colonies. If

---

[1] In Virginia, indeed, slaves were deemed real estate, but were treated as such only in particular cases, as in descents, when they could be annexed to the lands and so handed down.

we glance at the colonies to the north of them, which were to become the Middle States, we find many features of the slave code, beside the familiar police regulations. In New York, if four or more slaves were found together without good reason, they could be whipped by a justice's order. Masters were empowered to punish their slaves, saving injury to life or limb. If a slave committed any trespass of which the damage was not over five pounds, the master could be sued therefor, while the slave was tried and given corporal punishment by a justice, and then at once given back to his master's service without other punishment, if the master had paid the usual fee — of not over three shillings — to the whipper. The reason for this summary method, as given in the preamble to the law, which was made in 1730, was that slaves were the property of Christians and Jews, and could not be subject in all criminal cases to the strict rules of the laws of England without great loss or detriment to their masters. For serious offences — which included, for slaves, the burning wilfully of a haystack — a slave was tried by any court of Oyer and Terminer, or by a special court, as follows: —

On complaint of such an offence, any justice of peace might have the slave brought before him, then proceed to examine witnesses, and, if he saw fit, commit the accused for trial. This examination took the place of the customary grand jury. The justice would then summon two other justices, and they in turn would summon five of the principal freeholders of the county. There might be more than three justices, but one must be, in all cases, of the quorum; the freeholders could not be challenged, but were sworn to judge according to the evidence. Of this court of at least eight persons, seven must agree both in conviction and in the punishment. The court, on meeting, appointed a prosecutor, to prefer, in writing, an accusation which should specify the circumstances of the crime as closely as possible with convenience. To this the accused must plead, or have judgment passed as if convicted by verdict or confession. If convicted, capital punishment was to be given immediately, in such way as the court deemed best. If a master was willing to pay the jury expenses, which were limited to not over nine shillings, he might have his slave tried by a jury of twelve men. In this case no challenge was allowed. In no case whatever were slaves received as valid evidence except against other slaves on trial for murder, arson, attempt to run away, or killing their masters' horses or cattle. As to indentured servants in New York, it was specially provided that these were to be treated — in receiving correction as well as in securing relief against unjust masters — as apprentices were treated in England.[1]

In New Jersey, slaves were tried in the ordinary courts, as freemen were, for all serious offences. Special courts like those in New York had been used, but given up in 1768, having been found inconvenient, so the new act reads.[2] A sheriff was entitled to five pounds for executing a slave, and this and other regular fees incident were paid by the county, but were afterwards assessed on all the slave-owners of the county in proportion to the number of their able-bodied slaves. In connection with this it is interesting to note that a largely increased tax was put, about the same time, on every slave purchased who had not been in New Jersey for a year; because, we read, other colonies had found duties beneficial in promoting industry and the introduction of sober, industrious foreigners, and in order that those who chose to purchase slaves might bear some equitable portion of the public charges.

[1] In New York, a slave who got drunk, or cursed, or talked impudently to any Christian, — as the old law has it, — and who was convicted thereof before a justice, got a sound whipping. A Christian, it is interesting to note, who was drunk or cursed, could be fined three shillings, and in default put in the stocks, by the same tribunal.

[2] To show how the laws varied in different colonies, attempt at rape on a white woman was a capital offence in New York; in New Jersey it was punished by corporal punishment not extending to life or limb.

If a slave in New Jersey could not wander over five miles from home without possible danger of whipping, in Pennsylvania the limit was ten miles; nor could a black meet with three fellows, save on good business, with impunity. Masters were forbidden to allow slaves to go at large, or work at will, under any pretext. All negroes accused of heinous offences, — that they might therefor be given speedy trial and condign punishment, reads the old law dating from 1705, — were tried by a court of two justices, especially commissioned in each county by the governor for that purpose, and of six of the most substantial freeholders of the neighborhood, solemnly sworn to judge according to evidence and full proof. For attempt at rape, and for robbing to the value of over five pounds, the convict, after being whipped and branded on the forehead with R. or T., was to be sent away from the province by the owner, never to return.

In Delaware there were special courts, also, for the trial of slaves for heinous offences, the quorum being the two justices and any four of the six freeholders summoned. Here there was no whipping prescribed for a slave taken up away from home, and a meeting of negroes was not illegal unless there were more than six, belonging to several owners. To secure freedom, the manumittor must give a bond of sixty pounds; and, to prevent colored persons entitled to freedom from being illegally held as slaves, the county courts of common pleas were ordered, on petitions for freedom, to summon the reputed masters of the petitioners, and witnesses, and to give freedom, if deserved. If a master duly summoned did not appear, judgment should be awarded from the statements of the petitioners; and a person duly freed might then maintain an action of false imprisonment against the defendant. The sale out of Delaware of a person entitled to freedom was prohibited under a fine of one hundred pounds. In Pennsylvania, a bond of thirty pounds was required to secure freedom, — as free negroes had been found, so reads the act, to be often idle and bad examples, as well as public charges. In New York and New Jersey, the bond must be for two hundred pounds.

We have reviewed, in general, the laws defining the status of the slaves in all the colonies in 1775. Before turning to see what changes were made in these laws by the men of that day, it is but fair to ask if this tedious recital gives us a true picture of slavery at that time, as seen by the merchants in Boston or New York, and the planter on the James or the Savannah. Nothing is truer to-day than that the majority of us think little of the law and its operation, except where our own interests are concerned. A well-known judge, on coming from a meeting of the American Bar Association, remarked that the customary report of all important laws recently passed was good, but that a statement of how many laws were called for by public opinion, and how many were properly executed, would be much better. We can hardly presume that all men attending country churches in South Carolina in 1774 carried with them muskets or braces of pistols, as ordered to do by an act passed a generation earlier, when there were fears of rebellious slaves within the province, and of Spaniards and Indians from without. It is important to note that most of the few laws touching slaves in New England were made at a time when Indian slaves were being imported from the Carolinas; that the slave code of New York dates from days when rumors of slave insurrections were rife; and that the code of South Carolina, copied largely in Georgia, was passed after the Stono insurrection of 1740.

On the other hand, some parts of the codes were new; and even if some restrictions of the old laws were practically obsolete, if the harsher punishments were not always rigorously given, and if custom allowed the slave many privileges, the distinguishing features of the codes remained in force. Of these, the most significant, perhaps, was the system of impromptu local courts, which was carried to its extreme in South Carolina. These were probably no better then than they were three generations later, when a governor of South Carolina — friendly to the spread of slave-holding — declared to the Assembly that the judgments, owing to lack of humanity and intelligence or to neighborhood prejudice, were rarely in conformity with justice and humanity. "I have felt constrained," he added, "either to modify the sentences or to set them altogether aside, in a majority of the cases brought to my notice."[1]

What changes of moment were made in the status of the slave during the era of independence and of constitution-making?[2] In 1777 the Pennsylvania Council suggested to the Assembly a bill for the abolition of slavery. In the spring of the preceding year, the Assembly had received two petitions on this subject from a considerable number of residents of Philadelphia; one stating that the high security required from manumittors had been a great discouragement to manumission. Of these petitions, referred to the next session, we find no further mention, but the passage of a bill for abolition was urged by the Council in strongest terms in 1779. A bill was introduced in the Assembly accordingly in February, was debated, and ordered to be printed for public consideration. At the August session, there was presented a petition against its passage from a

[1] Governor Adams, Executive Messages.
[2] We confine ourselves strictly to the status of the slaves. It is obvious that this was not affected by legislation against importation of slaves by sea or land, however much this legislation may have been directed against the growth of slavery, or even to ultimate abolition.

number of residents of Chester County, while the Council again urged action. At the November session, this bill seems to have been replaced by another, which was ordered to a third reading and publication by a vote of thirty-eight to eight. In the following January, 1780, four petitions were received from Chester County, and one from Philadelphia, in favor of, and a petition from Bucks County against the bill. It was passed on March 1st. The fifty-five members of Assembly present seem to have agreed that the abolition of slavery was humane, just, and desirable; but twenty-one of them opposed the passage of the bill, as a step imprudent, premature, and not bidden by their constituents. The reasons for this — as elaborated in a remonstrance which was entered in the Assembly journal — were, that the slaves might be roused in the Southern States, which were then the seat of war and could not follow Pennsylvania's example; that freedom, protection, and rights of property only should be given the freedmen at first, and that other privileges given in this bill should be added by future legislation, as the blacks grew fitted to receive them; that more time be given for learning public opinion of the bill.

The preamble to this act of 1780 reads that, when we consider our deliverance from the abhorrent condition to which Great Britain has tried to reduce us, we are called on to manifest the sincerity of our professions of freedom, and to give substantial proof of gratitude, by extending a portion of our freedom to others, who, though of a different color, are the work of the same Almighty hand. By the act, no colored child born thereafter in Pennsylvania, who would have been a slave for years or for life, should serve beyond the age of twenty-eight years, nor should be treated, during the limited term of service, other than indentured servants were treated, — liable to the same correction, entitled to like relief and freedom dues. Such servants, if given up by their masters, would be bound out by the overseers of the poor to the age of twenty-eight. All slaves then owned in the state must be duly registered within fixed times, or they could not be held as slaves for life. Domestic slaves belonging to travellers, foreign officials, and members of Congress from other states, and seamen on vessels owned in other states, could remain temporarily only; and, to prevent fraud by long terms of service, no colored person could be bound out for more than seven years, except infants. All colored persons, bond or free, were thenceforth to be tried for offences as whites were. As before, however, no slave could testify against a freeman.

In 1788 the object of this act was furthered by a supplement providing a penalty of one hundred pounds fine and some months of hard labor for carrying off a slave or servant to be sold or kept as a slave out of Pennsylvania, and a fine of seventy-five pounds for removing such from the state without their consent attested by two justices. And it was added that there should be no separation, under fine of fifty pounds, of husband and wife, or parents and children under four years, beyond a distance of ten miles, without the duly attested consent of the parties, whether slaves or servants.

The history of slavery in Massachusetts has been so thoroughly treated by Dr. George H. Moore that it would be superfluous to do otherwise than summarize his results. For several years previous to 1776, the abolition of slavery had been somewhat vigorously debated in Massachusetts. The Committee of Safety had forbidden the enlistment of slaves, as inconsistent with the principles of liberty. In September, 1776, a resolution was introduced in the legislature, to set free two negroes taken prisoners on the high seas, and declaring the sale and enslavement of human beings to be a violation of natural rights, as well as inconsistent with the avowed principles on which the United States had carried their struggle for liberty to the last appeal. These negroes finally were ordered to be treated as other prisoners of war, but this anti-slavery declaration was cut out from the resolution in its passage through the legislature. In answer to a petition of several slaves, a bill to prohibit slavery was introduced in the House in 1777. Like the previous resolution, this declared slavery unjustifiable at such a time, and provided that all persons over twenty-one years of age should be freed from slavery at some date to be fixed by the legislature, and be entitled to all privileges of the subjects of the state. This bill was referred to the next session, — and no further action on it is to be found. It may have been the proposed equality of blacks and whites which largely defeated this bill, for we find that such an equality was strongly opposed in the constitutional debates of the next year.

In 1783, on considering a repeal of the old law of 1703, which required manumittors to give security for freedmen, the House ordered a committee to bring in a bill declaring that there had never been legal slaves in Massachusetts, and indemnifying masters who held slaves *de facto*. Such a bill passed the House, but did not, for some unknown reason, get beyond a first reading in the Senate. Meanwhile the constitution of the state had been adopted. It is no more probable, as Dr. Moore shows, that the article of the Declaration of Rights stating that all men are born free and equal, and entitled to life, liberty, and happiness, was intended by the Convention to affect the relation of master and slave, than it is that the Virginia Bill of Rights of 1776 was intended to set free at once the quarter of a million of slaves in Virginia — to the great astonishment of unrecompensed masters. But opinion in Massachusetts — if not at once the public opinion, still that of the most influential part of the community — was ready to find freedom for the slave in the constitution, and the decisions of the Supreme Court of the state, in the period with which we deal, practically abolished slavery. Some slaves had been freed, also, to take part in the war. It is said that the blank in the slave column opposite the State of Massachusetts, in the census of 1790, was owing to the fact that each of the few owners of slaves still left, on learning that no others had mentioned their slaves, had the humility not to wish to be "singular," and so made no return.

The little slavery that there was in New Hampshire seems to have died out in the same way. In November, 1779, there was presented to the legislature a petition of nineteen slaves that slavery might be abolished, " that the name of slave may not more be heard in a land gloriously contending for the sweets of freedom." In the following April it was read in the House, and a hearing ordered at the next session, after due public notice. In June, accordingly, the side of the petitioners was argued by counsel, but the House decided that the matter was not ripe for decision, and postponed it to a more convenient opportunity. We hear of no further mention of the subject. The constitution of 1784 began in the same words as that of Massachusetts. The census of 1790 gave one hundred and fifty-eight slaves, — probably those who were born before 1784, and therefore not deemed free.[1] It is interesting to note that the District of Vermont had plainly stated in its constitution of 1777 a prohibition of slavery. It was followed, nine years later, by a law against exporting negroes as slaves.

The Assembly of Rhode Island prefaced an act against importation of slaves, in 1774, by such a declaration as that which the Massachusetts legislature had not passed, — that personal freedom was the great stake in the Revolutionary War, and that those who desire to enjoy liberty should be willing to extend it to others. There is mention in the Assembly journals, the next year, of a bill for freeing slaves, which, after some consideration, was referred to the next session, to be printed meantime in the Newport and Providence papers and laid before the people.

In 1778, in accordance with the advice of General Washington, the Assembly authorized the formation of a battalion of such slaves as might be willing to enlist, and who could be purchased by the state at a reasonable price. These were to be freed at once, and the masters absolved

[1] See article in Magazine of American History for January, 1889, on slavery in New Hampshire.

from any future charges for them. The act states that history affords frequent precedents of the liberation and enlistment of slaves by the wisest, freest, and bravest nations fighting in defence of their country — and also that the British had taken a great part of Rhode Island, and it seemed impossible for the state to furnish sufficient recruits without adopting this measure. A protest to the act was entered by six members, on the grounds that the number of negroes would be small and the expenses great, and that the impression would be given that the state had purchased a band of slaves to fight for its liberties, — which would be inconsistent with the principles of liberty involved in the war. The act was passed in February, and, by act of the May session, expired in June, — it being necessary, we read, that it be temporary, for answering the purposes intended. It is not probable that a large number of slaves were freed under it.

In 1779 an act was passed to forbid the sale of slaves out of Rhode Island without their consent, — a practice, reads the act, against human nature, and tending to aggravate the lot of slavery, which the legislature was disposed to alleviate until a favorable opportunity was offered for abolition. In December, 1783, a bill authorizing manumission was reported by a committee of seven, in reply to a petition from the Society of Friends. It was referred to the next session, and ordered to be printed in the papers meantime. This was probably the bill, or the precursor of the bill, passed in February, 1784, for manumission and gradual abolition of slavery. The preamble declared the holding of mankind as property, which had gradually obtained by unrestrained custom and the permission of law, to be repugnant to the principle that all men are entitled to life, liberty, and the pursuit of happiness, and subversive of the happiness of mankind, the end of all government. The act provided that no person born in Rhode Island after February, 1784, should be a servant for life. And as humanity required that children should remain with their mothers a reasonable time after birth, the towns were ordered to maintain the children of slave mothers, while allowed to bind them out as apprentices until they were of age; and the Assembly expressed the earnest wish that such children be educated. Further, able-bodied slaves between the ages of twenty-one or eighteen and forty might be freed without the need of security given by the manumittors. The next year, as the provisions of this act had been found burdensome, the support of children born to slave mothers was imposed on the owners of the mothers until the children were twenty-one, or the mothers were freed. And the age up to which slaves could be freed without further responsibility to the manumittor was reduced from forty to thirty.

The constitution or declaration of the people of Connecticut of 1776 did not alter the relation of master or slave.[1] In May, 1777, a committee of the Assembly appointed to consider the state of the slaves in the state, and what might be done for their emancipation, recommended that the enlistment be authorized into the Continental service of all slaves who could, by bounties or otherwise, persuade their masters to let them buy themselves. On enlistment they were to be freed, and the masters absolved from all responsibility for them. This plan was afterwards defeated in the Senate; but a number of slaves were freed by their owners to enter the army.[2] In the same year the responsibility of a manumittor for the subsequent maintenance of the freedmen, if disabled and needy, was done away if the master obtained a license from the town officers, the majority of whom must agree that the slave was able and orderly in life and conversation, and would be benefited by freedom.

In 1780 a bill for gradual abolition passed the upper house of the legislature, was continued to another session, and was then apparently set aside. It provided that no Indian or colored child then under seven years, and none whatever born thereafter, should be held in servitude beyond the age of twenty-eight. Finally, in 1784,

---

[1] See Jackson v. Bullock, 12 Conn. 42.
[2] See Livermore's Research, etc.

— as sound policy, we read, requires that the abolition of slavery be effected as soon as possible, consistent with the rights of individuals and the public safety, — it was enacted that no colored child born thereafter should be held in servitude after reaching the age of twenty-five years. And the Superior Court held, the same year, that a slave who had enlisted in the army with his master's consent was thereby absolutely manumitted, and could not be reclaimed.[1] In 1788, the exportation of slaves was forbidden.

In the constituent convention of New York, which ended its work in April, 1777, measures for the abolition of slavery were strongly supported, but were defeated by the members from the Hudson counties.[2] The Declaration of Independence was incorporated into the new constitution, but the relation of master and slave was not changed thereby. In 1781, the legislature voted, in order to raise two regiments for the defence of the state, to give a grant of unappropriated lands to every slave-owner for every able-bodied slave given over for enlistment. The master would be discharged from further responsibility for the black, who would be freed at the end of three years' service, unless regularly discharged before,

---

[1] Arabas v. Ivers, 1 Root, 93. We find mention, also, in the town records, here as elsewhere, of slaves freed on purely moral grounds as well as for military or other services.

[2] Bancroft's Constitution.

or, we are tempted to add, unless he was shot. In 1784, it was ordered that slaves taken from Tory estates duly forfeited, should be maintained by the state commissioners from the rents; and, two years after, all slaves in the hands of the commissioners were declared free, the old or infirm to be supported comfortably at public cost. In 1785, an act for gradual abolition was rejected by the Council of Revision, in accordance with an opinion of Chancellor Livingston, that the bill was unconstitutional, unjust, and unwise, in that it forbade free colored persons to vote. The Senate, still, passed the bill over this negation, by the required two thirds vote, but the House failed to do so.[1]

In 1788, the slave code was revised, with other general laws. There were kept the old prohibitions against harboring, or dealing with slaves, without leave. But a slave who might strike a white person would be tried, not summarily by two justices, but by the courts, — in the same way that any one would be tried for petty larceny, — and not over thirty-nine lashes could be given therefor, in one day. While slave-owners were responsible as before for petty trespasses by their slaves, no punishment was prescribed for the slaves. Most of all, all slaves accused of capital offences were given the privilege of trial by jury, according to the course of common law. They could only testify, however, when other slaves

[1] Street's New York Council of Revision.

were tried for crimes. And instead of becoming responsible, under bond of two hundred pounds, for future needs of a freedman, a master could set free, without further charge, by a license from the majority of the overseers of the poor and from two justices, any slave who was able-bodied and not over fifty. Other slaves could be freed by giving bond, as before; and those illegally set at large should be deemed free, while the previous owners, or their representatives, would be liable for charges. At the same time, the taking of slaves for exportation was forbidden — a measure which had been proposed at least two years before — under penalty of one hundred pounds.

In 1778, the governor of New Jersey asked the Assembly to take action for manumission; but the House deemed the times too critical for the discussion of the matter.[1] Eight years later, the heavy bond required from manumittors was removed, as in New York, when certificates were obtained; but these certificates could be granted only for slaves between twenty-one and thirty-five years. And, we read, as slaves should be protected by law from the wanton cruelty too often practised upon them, the grand juries were empowered to indict persons for inhumanly treating their slaves; and the penalties for such, if convicted, were a fine, for the first offence, of not over five pounds, and for a second, of not over

[1] Bancroft's United States, v. 411.

ten pounds, for benefit of the town. Two years later, in 1788, it was enacted that all colored persons, slaves or free, should be punished, as well as tried, for criminal offences, in the same way that whites were. Every owner of a colored slave or servant born thereafter, was ordered to have the child taught to read, under penalty of five pounds for neglect. And no slave living in New Jersey for a year at any time, could be then removed from the state, to reside elsewhere, without his consent attested by a justice. If he were under twenty-one, the parents' consent must be obtained in addition. Record of the removal was kept by the magistrate, and a copy given the slave. The penalty for illegal removal was twenty pounds; but the act excepted, of course, persons removing with their slaves to reside elsewhere. This bill of 1788 — introduced, evidently, in reply to several petitions, one of them from the Society of Friends — provided, in addition to what we have noted, for the forfeiture of any vessel of New Jersey engaged anywhere in the transport of slaves; and was passed, after some opposition and amendment, by a vote of twenty-four to fourteen. The enlistment of slaves had been prohibited in 1781.

The journals of the Assembly of Delaware tell us that leave was given, in October, 1785, for the introduction of a bill for the gradual abolition of slavery, and that such a bill, presented in the following January, was carefully considered, and then replaced by a bill for furthering emancipation, which, in turn, was deferred in June to further consideration — which it does not seem to have ever received. In January, also, the Assembly received a petition from two hundred and four members of the Society of Friends, that such relief should be given the distressed slaves in the state as the rights of mankind and religion required. This was left on the table. But in February, 1787, slaves accused of capital offences were given the right of trial by jury in the county courts of Quarter Sessions, by the usual mode of procedure, and at public cost. All slaves over twenty-one years who had been set at large when not over thirty-five and not incapable of support, but whose masters had not given the required security, were declared free; and a master might thenceforth set free any healthy slave between eighteen and thirty-five, without security or other hindrance. Further, the act prohibited, under penalty of one hundred pounds, the exportation, or sale for exportation, of any slave to the Carolinas, Georgia, or the West Indies, without a permit from any three justices of the master's county. A person entitled to freedom at any time could not be exported, under the same penalty, to any place whatever; and the bill, as introduced, if we may judge from its first title, prohibited equally the exportation of slaves for life. The Society of Friends persisted in appeals for further legislation; and, following the advice of a committee of five members, appointed to consider these petitions, the Assembly of 1789 forbade exportation to Maryland and Virginia, as well as the places above mentioned, without leave from five justices meeting in open session.

It is interesting to note, in passing to Maryland, that the Declaration of Rights of that state, adopted in November, 1776, gives the speedy remedy for restraint or injury of person or property, to freemen only. In 1785, the House of Delegates of Maryland received several petitions from a number of residents of some half-dozen counties, for immediate or gradual abolition, and rejected them, on the second reading, by thirty-two to twenty-two. The vote of the members from these counties was by no means unanimous. Two years later, a petition of the Society of Friends for emancipation was rejected by thirty to seventeen. In 1789, the Senate requested the House to appoint a committee of conference to consider action for gradual abolition and against the exportation of negroes. Though a House committee of seven members — appointed to consider petitions from the Society of Friends and the Abolition Society — had just advised that no means be lost for bringing about gradual abolition with the slave-owners' consent, the House refused to join the Senate by thirty-nine to fifteen.

Later and earnest attempts at abolition met with no result; but many slaves were emancipated by deed. During this period, Maryland followed her sister slave-states, in forbidding masters to allow their slaves to go at large or hire themselves out. One other act is of interest to us, in showing the change that was growing in public feeling, by which the old, harsh punishments were to be largely put away. The governor was empowered to commute death sentences, in case of slaves, to exportation; and masters of slaves so punished were to be recompensed, as in the case of execution. It is probable, also, that slaves received the benefit of the act which, while directing most criminal cases to be tried in the county courts, allowed the right of removal to the general court to every person charged with a capital offence.[1] In 1780, slaves had been received, and set free, as recruits; and slaves belonging to confiscated British property were usually sold, for the state treasury — in one case, at least, with the proviso that families be not separated.

In Virginia, we remember, a master could manumit only by leave from the governor, as a reward for meritorious services by the slave. Here, as elsewhere, the Society of Friends desired emancipation. In December, 1780, the House committee on grievances reported — through Richard Henry Lee — that parts of a certain petition of sundry

---

[1] 1785, ch. 87; 14 Md. 135.

Quakers, for the manumission of some slaves already *de facto* free, were reasonable, but that the request for a general license to be given the Society of Friends, to emancipate all their slaves, should be rejected. This was thrice read and agreed to. A very similar petition from the Friends, in 1782, was answered in just the opposite way, that slaves already set at large by will or otherwise should not be declared legally free, but that it was reasonable that the Friends should manumit their slaves in future under proper restrictions. So it was enacted in May, 1782, that slaves might be freed by any instrument in writing, under hand and seal, duly attested, and acknowledged by the manumittor, or proven by two witnesses, in the county office. But all slaves manumitted, deemed by the county court to be incapable, or being under age or over forty-five, must be maintained by the manumittor or his estate; and the court might have a portion of an estate sold, for this support, if necessary. A certificate of freedom must be given the freedman. At the same time, the old penalty of fine against a master who let a slave hire himself out, was changed to sale of the slave by order of the court, and appropriation to the county of a quarter of the price.

The enlistment of negroes into the army had been prohibited, in 1777, unless they were shown to be free by certificates from justices of peace. It seems that some persons had enlisted their slaves as substitutes, representing to the officers that they were freemen, and had afterwards tried, when they were discharged, to enslave them. So, as it was just and reasonable, we read, that all who had faithfully contributed to American liberty, should enjoy as their reward the blessings of freedom, such discharged soldiers were declared free in 1783; and the attorney-general was ordered to bring action in behalf of any unjustly detained thereafter, who might recover damages for detention, as assessed by a jury. Several slaves were freed by the legislature, for public services. On the other hand, many slaves taken from Tory estates were sold for exportation.

In November, 1785, a petition was presented in the House of Burgesses from sundry persons, who, being firmly persuaded that the holding in slavery of so many of their fellow-creatures was contrary to the principles of the Christian religion and to the principles on which the government was founded, asked for a general emancipation under reasonable restrictions. Such action, they said, would strengthen the state by attaching the blacks to it by ties of interest and gratitude. Two days later, this petition was read, and rejected without an opposing voice. It could hardly obtain a reading, wrote Washington to Lafayette;[1] and a bill to take away the existing

[1] Sparks's Washington, ix. p. 163.

right of manumission, — reported by a committee in answer to petitions from several counties, — was supported by a strong minority.

In 1779, a distinguished committee had been appointed, to revise the laws of the State, and its report was printed and spread abroad in 1784. The proposed law on slaves was, in general, a simplification of existing laws, with the exception that manumission could be effected only with the consent of the slave, given in open court, and that all slaves thereafter freed should leave Virginia within a year, — unless too ill to depart, — or be deemed out of the protection of law. This innovation was rejected by the Assembly. Two members at least, of the committee on revisal, — Mr. Jefferson and Mr. Wythe, — desired to propose the emancipation of all slaves born after a certain time, and their removal from Virginia at a proper age, but public opinion was deemed too unfavorable for such measures.[1] Under the old laws, four justices of the county could form a court for trial of slaves for capital offences. By the new law, adopted in October, 1786, there must be five at least, and trials were to be held between five and ten days after commitment. The committee for revisal proposed that three fourths of the judges must agree in condemnation, but this was amended so as to require unanimity; and the Assembly added that thirty days,

[1] Jefferson's Writings, i. p. 48.

instead of ten, should elapse ordinarily before execution; and that no one having an interest in a slave should sit on his trial. The new law provided, also, that a slave who had begun an action for freedom should be tried, if arrested for any offence, as freemen were tried. Two years after, there was struck out of the code the old law which exempted from prosecution a master who killed his slave by accident or during correction, unless the killing was deemed wilful by the court, and declared that no person indicted for murder of a slave and found guilty of manslaughter, should be punished.

In North Carolina, — as there was some doubt, we read, as to the proper punishment, — it was enacted in 1774, that one who killed his slave, wilfully, so that, had he killed a freeman, he would be convicted of murder, should suffer imprisonment for a year. A second conviction was punishable with death. He who killed the slave of another was imprisoned for a year, for a first offence, and paid the value of the slave. Slaves could not be freed, we remember, in North Carolina, except for meritorious services, by leave of the county courts, under penalty of sale. This was reënacted in 1777, with the reward offered for the seizure of slaves at large, of a fifth of their price, — in order that the "evil practice" of freeing slaves might be prevented at such a critical time. This act, by its title, was aimed against domestic insurrections. We find by another act, two years later, that divers persons, minded wickedly to disturb the peace, had persisted in setting slaves at large, and the courts were again bidden to sell such slaves, not claimed duly by owners, except those who had enlisted into the army. Slaves confiscated in Tory estates were sold at auction or otherwise disposed of.

In 1779, also, further encouragement was given for the execution of the old patrol laws, in that members of the patrol were rewarded by the county and exempted, for the time being, from the jury, from work on the roads, and other duties, and could be fined, on the other hand, one hundred pounds, for refusing to serve. There was to be a monthly search for weapons among the blacks. These laws restricting the manumission of slaves were not deemed necessary in time of war only, for the sale of slaves illegally set free was continued by the practical reënactment of the act against Domestic Insurrections, in 1788. Slaves were tried, as we noted, by a court of three justices and four freeholders, for all offences. In 1783, as this method of trial for trivial offences had been found to cause slave-owners both delay and expense, single justices were empowered to try slaves in such cases, and to give the punishment of not over forty lashes. In 1786, the customary allowance to masters of executed or outlawed slaves was stopped, as the public had been put to much expense therein, and as slaves were often caused to commit crimes by cruel treatment. The period which we are studying ends, in North Carolina, with stricter police regulation of the blacks, particularly the free blacks: as to slavery, the movement of the State was plainly backward; but we may digress, to note that in 1791 the distinction between the murder of a white and of one who "is equally a human creature but merely of a different complexion" was done away in so far that the killing of a slave wilfully, without lawful provocation, was declared murder, to be punished as the killing of a freeman.

There seems to have been no change in the legal status of the slave, during these years, in South Carolina and Georgia. One act of Georgia is of interest, in passing. It was declared, in 1774, that the murder of any free Indian in amity with Georgia should be punished as the murder of a white person, as some friendly Indians had been killed — to the great scandal of society and the danger of involving Georgia in war — by some ill-disposed persons who did not consider such inhuman actions in a proper light, being not only ignorant of the dangerous consequences, but influenced by the ill-grounded prejudices which ignorant minds are apt to conceive against persons differing in color from themselves.[1]

[1] Coll. Acts of Ga., Wormsloe ed., p. 401.

Congress recommended, in 1779, to these two States, sorely straitened for troops, the enlistment of three thousand negroes, and offered to pay the owners. These negroes were to be fed and clothed by the United States, and each of them, when honorably discharged at the end of the war, was to be freed and given fifty dollars. Twice, at least, such a plan was before the Assembly of South Carolina, but was deemed dangerous, and, though the friends of it increased in number, was hopelessly defeated. The Assembly voted, instead, in 1782, to give to each man who might enter the army, the bounty of one able negro, at the time of enlistment, and another at the beginning of the second and of the third year of service. These slaves were taken from confiscated Tory estates. Some of their fellows were used in the army as servants and wagoners; others of them, to be sold for ready money for the public use, were ordered to be disposed of in families, so as not to separate parents from children. In the same year, the Georgia Assembly ordered the purchase by the State of all slaves belonging to Tories about to leave, that the labor of these, sold to citizens, might be kept for the development of the lands.[1] These Southern States, it is true, were especially liable to Indian attacks, and the great number of blacks in Carolina made

---

[1] South Carolina Statutes, iv. pp. 514, 520; Jones' Georgia," ii. p. 439.

any fears of insurrection most formidable. On the other hand, the delegates to Congress from Carolina thought that the enlistment of the ablest negroes, under the proposed plan, would lessen such dangers. It was on hearing of the failure of this plan that Washington wrote, that that spirit of freedom which had so strongly marked the beginning of the war, had subsided. It is private not public interest, he added, which influences the generality of mankind.[1]

We have noted that there were differences of opinion in Massachusetts and Pennsylvania over the status of the free blacks, and that emancipation in Virginia as planned by Mr. Jefferson — a zealous opponent of slavery — included the removal of the freedmen from the State. We shall not digress far, if, in closing, we call attention to the question that was then becoming linked to that of emancipation, namely, what was to be the condition of the freedmen. In the South, there were doubts as to whether two free races could live together. This question became one of the many influences, especially in Virginia and Maryland, which pulled the Gordian knot of slavery so tight that it could not be untied.

[1] Mr. George Livermore's Historical Research respecting the Opinions of the Founders of the Republic on Negroes, etc., — read before the Mass. Hist. Society, in 1862, — contains much valuable information; but we cannot see how Mr. Livermore can assume (p. 49) that the ideas of a few prominent men represented " the *prevailing principles of the people,*" in favor of abolition.

INDEX.

ABOLITION of slavery, measures taken (1775-1789) by Pennsylvania toward, 287-290; by Massachusetts, 290-292; by New Hampshire and Vermont, 292, 293; by Rhode Island, 293-295; by Connecticut, 296, 297; efforts toward in New York, 297-299; in New Jersey, 299; in Delaware, 300, 301; in Maryland, 302; in Virginia, 303-306.
Abolition Society, of Maryland, 302.
Active, case of The, 17-23.
Accounts, Treasury Office of, 130, 133; Chambers of, 134, 147.
Adams, John, 6; chairman of Board of War, 122-124; vice-president, 178; on ordinations, 194.
Adams, Samuel, 59, 112, 113; opposes the Constitution, 68-70, 73; is won over, 75-77; opposes single executives, 152.
Admiralty, Board of, 141, 142, 147, 160.
Admiralty, courts of, in the colonies, 5. See Prize Courts.
Adopting Act, 233.
Agents, colonial, 142.
Albany, churches of, 242.
Amsterdam, Classis of, 239-241.
Annapolis, Congress at, 36; Convention at, 41, 201.
Anti-Burghers (Presbyterians), 235.
Anti-federalists, 78, 79, 88, 91, 92, 95, 98, 108, 112, 249, 258. See Constitution, opposition to.
Antigua, Methodists in, 215.
Antonelli, Cardinal, 227-229.
Apostle, office of, 246.

Appeals in admiralty causes, 8; in England, 13, 14. See Committee, and Court of Appeals.
Arnold, Benedict, 19.
Articles of Confederation, judiciary as provided by, 2, 3, 16, 17, 27, 32, 44, 45; supersession of, 54, 56; insufficiency of, 68.
Arundel, Lord, 223.
Asbury, Francis, 211, 214-217, 252, 262.
Assembly, General, of Presbyterian Church, 237-239, 258; of Dutch Reformed Church, 242, 243.
Associate Presbytery, 235, 237.
Associated Reformed Church, 236.
Association, General, of Baptists, 246, 247.
Atherton, Joshua, 65, 66.
Auditor of the U. S. Treasury, 180.
Auditor-General, 130, 134.

Bache, Richard, postmaster-general, 169.
Baldwin, Abraham, 178.
Baltimore, Methodist conferences at, 214-219; Catholic see of, 229, 230; seminary and synod at, 231.
Bankson, Benjamin, 31, 41.
Baptists, 189, 243; "Separate," in Virginia, 244; their organization, 245-247; union with Regular Baptists, 248, 249; Free-Will, 249, 250; and Constitution, 249, 255, 259.
Barry, John, commodore, 224.
Bass, Edward, bishop, 207, 208.
Bassett, Richard, 216.
Bayard, Robert, 5.
Beach, Abraham, Rev., 200.
Beatty, John, 37.
Beaufort, collector of, 11.

Benson, Egbert, 178, 179.
Berkeley, George, bishop, 186.
Bill of Rights, Virginia, 291.
Bishops, for Protestant Episcopal Church, obtained, 192–196, 206; their constitutional position defined, 199, 202, 203, 205–209, 259, 260; of Methodist Church, 217, 218; of Catholic Church, 228–230.
Blair, James, Dr., 192.
Bland, Theodoric, 110.
Bloodworth, Timothy, 65.
Boardman, 211.
Boston, 5; convention at, 151; of Universalists at, 250.
"Boston Centinel," 75.
Boudinot, Elias, 32, 176.
Bowdoin, James, 69, 71, 76.
Bradford, William, 26.
Bray, Thomas, Dr., 192.
Briggs, Charles A., Dr., 231, 257, 259.
Brooks, Eleazer, general, 71.
Bucks County, petition of, 288.
Burghers (Presbyterians), 235.
Burke, Ædanus, 65.
Butler, Joseph, bishop, 187.

Cambridge, execution of slaves at, 269.
Carmelite nuns in Maryland, 231.
Carolinas, synod of the, 238.
Carrington, Edward, 78.
Carroll, Charles, of Carrolton, 224.
Carroll, John, priest, 220, 222–224, 226; prefect apostolic, 226–228; bishop, 229–231, 252, 256.
Catholics (Roman), 189; before the Revolution, 220–223; during it, 223, 224; Catholic Church in the United States organized, 225–227; acquires a bishop, 228–230; and the Constitution, 230, 256; first synod of, 231; further Union, 253.
Challoner, Richard, bishop, 221.
Chambre des Comptes, 147.
Chase, Samuel, 65; in Canada, 224.
Chester County, petition of, 288.
"Christmas Conference," 214, 216, 217.
Church of England, 188, 190. See, also, Protestant Episcopal Church.
Churches, constitutions of, 191–250; relations with Constitution of United States, 251–262.
Claims, Committee of, 129–131; Commissioners of, 131.
Clinton, George, 47, 109, 112, 113; opposes the Constitution of 1787, 64, 68, 73, 87; letter to Randolph, 88–90; leads opposition in New York, 92; his circular, 94–98, 100–104, 109, 110; his candidacy for vice-president, 107.
Clintonians, 92, 107.
Clymer, George, 164.
Codman, Capt. John, slaves of, executed, 269.
Cœtus party, in Dutch Reformed Church, 240, 242.
Coke, Thomas, 213, 214.
Commissioners of appeal in prize causes, lords, 14–16.
Committee, of Congress, for appeals, 12–16, 18–20, 22, 30, 31; for military affairs ("Secret," "Cannon," "Medical"), 119, 120, 122, 123; of War, 121; of Claims, 129–131; of Finance, 132; Naval, 138; Marine, 139; of Secret Correspondence, 143, 146; of Foreign Affairs, 144–148, 152; on the post-office, 169.
Committee of Safety, Massachusetts, 290.
Committee, General, of Baptists, 247–249.
Committees of Observation, 120.
Comptroller, office of, 147, 156, 180; of the Post-Office, 168, 169.
Confederation, 4. See Articles of Confederation, 4.
Conference, General, of Methodists, 212–220; of Free-Will Baptists, 250.
Conferentie party, in Dutch Reformed Church, 240, 242.
Congregationalists, 251, 252.
Congress, Continental, and prize courts, 6–11; its committees for appeals, 12–16, 18–20; resolutions on The Active, 22, 23; creates Court of Appeals, 27–32; fails to maintain it, 36–39; continues it, 40; transmits the Constitution, 54–56; sets it in operation, 96; establishes military committees, 119, 120; and boards, 121–126; appoints treasurers,

INDEX. 315

128; committee of claims, 129; establishes Treasury Office of Accounts, 130; office of Continental Treasurer of Loans, 131; remodels treasury system, 132–136; appoints naval committees, 138–141; committees for foreign affairs, 143–148; establishes single heads, 149–152, 155, 161; establishes post-office, 168–170; action respecting Catholics, 223, 226; and churches, 260.

Congress of Massachusetts, 6, 7.

Connecticut, Wyoming dispute of, 3; prize courts of, 9; ratifies the Constitution, 66; opposes second convention, 109, 110; religion in, 188; Episcopal Convention in, 195, 196; Episcopalians of, 202; Consociated Churches of, 234; laws respecting slaves in (to 1775), 266–268; measures for abolition of slavery in, 296, 297.

Consociated Churches of Connecticut, 234.

Constitution, of 1787, framed, 46–53; transmitted by Congress, 54–56; public opinion on, 58; the opposition to, 63–66, in Massachusetts. 68, 69, 71–73; in Virginia, 79–91; amended, 111, 112; on executive departments, 175, 176, 183–185; attitude of Catholics to, 230; relations of church constitutions to, 251–262.

Constitutions of the churches, 191–250; relations to Constitution of 1787, 251–260.

Controleur-Général, 147, 155.

Convention, brig, 18.

Convention of 1787, 42; its labors, 46–52; its adjournment, 53; discusses executive departments, 170–174.

Convention (proposed) of 1788, suggested, 51–53; advocated, 74, 87, 90; Clinton's circular respecting, 94–98; Harrisburg conference advocating, 98–100; Virginian efforts for, 100–105; efforts of New York toward, 106, 107; of North Carolina and Rhode Island, 107, 108; end of project, 109–112; its probable outcome, 112–115.

Conventions, of the Protestant Episcopal Church, 202–209, 261; of the Universalist Church, 250.

Conway, Moncure D., 89.

Conway Cabal, The, 125.

Corbin, Francis, 101.

Correspondence, Committee of, 143, 146.

Correspondence, General Meeting of (Baptist), 249.

Council, of Methodist Church, 217, 218.

Council of State, Privy Council, proposed, 173.

Councils of Safety, 120, 121, 124.

Court, of Appeals, see Committee of Congress for appeals, and 27–44; its constitution, 27–34; its business, 34–42; influence of, 43, 44.

Courts, Prize, see Prize Courts; special, for trial of offences of slaves, in Rhode Island, 268; in South Carolina, 270, 275; in Virginia, 270, 271, 274, 275, 306, 307; in Maryland, 271, 274; in North Carolina, 275, 308: in Georgia, 275, 276; in New York, 281, 282; in New Jersey, 283; in Pennsylvania and Delaware, 284.

Coxe, John D., 31.

Culpeper County (Va.), Baptists in, 244.

Cutler, Timothy, Dr., 188, 192.

Davies, Samuel, 233.

Davis, Hon. J. C. Bancroft, pamphlet on the Committees and Court of Appeal, 1, 2, 6, 12, 13, 20, 34.

Declaration of Rights, Massachusetts, 291.

Delaware, prize court of, 10; legislature of, 41; ratifies the Constitution, 66; laws respecting slavery in (in 1775), 284, 285; from 1775 to 1789, 300–302.

Denmark, King of, and ordinations, 194.

Deputies, House of (Episcopal), 209.

Dickinson, John, 17, 144.

Drayton, Wm. Henry, 18, 31.

Dublin, Presbytery of, 232.

Dutch Reformed Church, 237, 239–241; attains independence, 242, 243.

316 INDEX.

Elizabeth, case of The, 15.
Ellery, William, 18.
Ellsworth, Oliver, 18; on executive departments, 173.
Emancipation. See Abolition of slavery.
Embury, Philip, 210.
Episcopalians, 188, 191. See Protestant Episcopal Church.
Executive departments, development of, 116-185; under committees and boards, 119-149; under single heads, 150-165; post-office, 166-170; discussion of, in Convention, 171-176; in Congress, 176-183.

Falmouth (Portland), 168.
"Federal Farmer," 59.
Federalist, The, 63, 176.
Federalists, 93, 96.
Federal Republicans, 64, 106.
Finance, colonial, 127, 128; Standing Committee of, 132; Superintendent of, 137, 154, 155, 177, 180.
Fitzsimons, Thomas, 26, 33.
Flemins, George, 88.
Fletcher, Benjamin, governor, 239.
Folger, Timothy, 16.
Ford, Reuben, 247.
Foreign Affairs, Committee of, 144-148, 150, 152; Secretary for, 146, 160-165; department of, 176-179, 181, 182.
Foreign Applications, Committee of, 145.
Foster, Theodore, 16.
Franklin, Benjamin, 16, 144; in the Federal Convention, 46, 50, 51, 53; postmaster-general, 167, 169; on ordination, 194; in Canada, 224; and the Catholics, 226.
Fraunces' Tavern, meeting at, 106.
Freedmen, provisions respecting, in 1775, 279, 280, 284, 285; subsequently, 288, 289, 291, 296, 298, 299, 301, 304-306; problem respecting, 311. See Abolition of slavery.
Friends, 250, 251; petitions of, respecting slavery, 294, 300-304.

Gallatin, Albert, 98-100, 109.
Gardoqui, Don Diego de, Spanish ambassador, 229.
Garrettson, Freeborn, 216, 217.

Gates, Horatio, general, 124, 125.
Georgia, land case involving, 3; prize court of, 10; ratifies the Constitution, 66; laws respecting slavery in (in 1775), 272 -274, 279, 280, 286; special courts for offences of slaves in, 275, 276; legislation respecting slavery in, 1775 to 1789, 309, 310.
Gerry, Elbridge, and the Constitution, 52, 53, 57, 59, 74; on the executive departments, 177.
Gerrymander, Patrick Henry's, 105, 106.
Gillett, E. H., Dr., 234.
Gladstone, W. E., on American Constitution, vi, 46.
Glebe lands, in Virginia, 245, 249.
Goddard, Wm., 167, 168.
Gorham, Nathaniel, 71, 76.
Grayson, Wm., opposes the Constitution, 65; elected senator, 105.
"Green Dragon, The," 75.
Green, Jacob, schismatic, 258.
Grenville's Act, 44, 45.
Griffin, Cyrus, judge of the Court of Appeals, 30-32, 36, 39-41; letter of, 37, 38.
Griffith, Rev. Mr., 201.

Hamilton, Alexander, and the Court of Appeals, 35, 42; and the Constitution, 49, 50, 252; and The Federalist, 63; in the New York Convention, 92, 93, 96; on executive departments, 150, 151, 155, 156, 172, 176.
Hancock, John, 110; in the Massachusetts Convention, 69, 70, 73, 76, 77.
Hanover Presbytery, 234.
Harrisburg, convention at, 96, 98-100.
Harrison, Benjamin, 58, 59, 144.
Harriss, Samuel, Baptist preacher, 244.
Hartford, 27, 33.
Hatch, Nathaniel, 6.
Heath, William, general, 71.
Heck, Barbara, 188, 210.
Henry, John, 18.
Henry, Patrick, 58, 59, 109, 112, 113; opposes the Constitution, 60, 61, 65, 68, 78-82, 255; in the Virginia Convention, 83-90; labors for a second convention,

INDEX. 317

91, 95, 101–103; works against Madison, 104–106.
Home Affairs, secretaryship of, 179.
Hopkinson, Francis, 140.
Hosmer, Titus, 29, 30.
Houston, Capt. Thomas, 18, 26.
Hughes, James M., 106.
Huntington, Samuel, president of Congress, letters of, 29, 30.

Indians, laws respecting, 266–258. 276, 309.
Industry, The, case of, 6.
Insurrections, domestic, legislation respecting, 307, 308.

Jackson, Andrew, president, 182.
Jay, John, 144; and The Federalist, 63; in the New York Convention, 96; secretary for foreign affairs, 164, 165; on Catholics, 223.
Jefferson, Thomas, 48, 65, 164, 254, 255; on the Constitution, 83, 86, 87; the Baptists and, 249; proposals respecting slavery, 306, 311.
Jennings v. Carson, 34, 43.
Jesuits in America, 221–225.
Johnson, Samuel, Dr. (of Connecticut), 188, 192, 195.
Johnson, Wm. Samuel, 38.
Jones, Willie, 97, 107.
Judiciary, Federal, before 1789, 1–3; as then arranged, 43, 44.

King, Rufus, 37, 39, 71, 72.
Knox, Henry, general, 154.

Lafayette, 305.
Lamb, Gen. John, 64, 90, 91, 106.
Land cases, federal court for, 2, 3; its model, 44, 45.
Langdon, John, 70.
Lansing, John, 47, 57, 61, 93.
Lecky, W. E. H., 210.
Lee, Arthur, 146, 164.
Lee, Jesse, 188, 216.
Lee, Richard Henry, opposes the Constitution, 55, 56, 59, 60, 65, 67, 74, 78, 79, 81, 82; elected senator, 105; in Virginia House of Burgesses, reports on petition for manumission, 303, 304.
Lewis, John, Rev., vicar general, 225, 226.
Lincoln, Benjamin, general, 71; secretary at war, 153, 154.

Livermore, George, Historical Research respecting negroes, 311.
Livingston, John H., Dr., 241, 242.
Livingston, R. R., 37; secretary for foreign affairs, 161–164; chancellor, 163, 298.
London, bishop of, 191, 193; vicar apostolic of, 221, 223–225; yearly meeting, 250, 251.
Lowell, John, judge of the Court of Appeals, 1, 32, 36, 43.
Lowndes, Rawlins, 65.
Lowth, Robert, bishop, 193, 213.
Lulworth Castle, Bishop Carroll consecrated at, 230.
Lutherans, 188, 250.
Luzerne, Chevalier de la, 31.

Madison, James, 262; on the Constitution, 50; defends it in Congress, 54, 56; in letters, 61, 62, 70, 79; in The Federalist, 63; on Henry, 80–82; in the Virginia Convention, 85, 86; subsequent efforts for the Constitution, 92, 93, 95, 100, 252, 253; defeated for senate, 105; elected representative, 106; proposes amendments, 111; on executive departments, 176; opposes Established Church, 247, 254.
Maine, 71.
Makemie, Francis, 231.
Manumission, provisions for, in 1775, 280, 284, 285; subsequently, 287, 291, 293–297, 299, 301, 303–308, 310. See Abolition of slavery.
Marine, Agent of, 160.
Marine, Secretary of, 142, 160.
Marine Committee, 139–141.
Mark, slave, execution of, 269.
Marshall, John, chief justice, 21; in the Virginia Convention, 86.
Martin, Luther, 46, 48; on the Constitution of 1787, 57, 65, 66.
Maryland, prize court of, 10; and the Constitution, 65; ratifies it, 75, 79, 84; declaration of Episcopal clergy of, 196–198; Catholics in, before Revolution, 220–223; special courts for offences of slaves in, 271, 274; laws respecting slaves in (in 1775), 272, 273, 276, 277, 280; from 1775 to 1789, 302, 303.

Mason, George, on the Constitution, 51–53, 56, 57; opposes it in Virginia, 60, 65, 87; labors for a second convention, 91; on executive departments, 174, 175.
Massachusetts, land case involving, 3; prize courts of, 6, 9, 23; convention of (1788), 67–78; opposes second convention, 110; Baptists in, 243; laws respecting slavery in (to 1775), 267–269; extinction of slavery in, 290–292.
McDougal, Alexander, general, 151, 160.
McKendree, William, bishop, 220.
M'Clenahan, Blair. 26.
McTyeire, H. N., Dr., 211, 213.
Methodists, 188, 189, 210, 211; general conferences of, 212–219; delegated conference of, 220; in Canada and the West Indies, 215; final organization, 216–220; aid Union, 252; the Constitution and the, 256, 257.
Mifflin, Thomas, governor, 110; general, 125.
Mississippi question, 81, 82.
Monroe, James, 37, 106, 109.
Moore, Dr. Geo. H., on slavery in Massachusetts, 290, 291.
Moravians, 188.
Morris, Gouverneur, 50, 53; on executive departments, 172–174.
Morris, Robert, 26; chairman of Committee of Finance, 132, 151; Superintendent of Finance, 156–159, 177.
Moylan, Stephen, 224.
Murray, John, Universalist preacher, 250.

Naval Committee, 138, 139.
Navy, secretaryship of the, 117; department, in states, 137, 138; continental, 138–141, 160; commissioners of the, 140, 160; department of the, 183.
Neale, Thomas, postmaster, 166.
Negroes. See Slaves, Freedmen.
Nelson, Thomas, 59.
New Brunswick (New Jersey), conference at, 200, 201, 254, 255.
New England, religion in (1774), 187, 188; Episcopalians of, 196, 202, 203, 209; Methodism in, 216; Presbyterians of, 238, 239; slavery in, 264, 265; laws respecting slaves in (to 1775), 266–269; movements for abolition of slavery in, 290–296. See the names of the individual states.
New Hampshire, prize court of, 9, 10, 23; ratification of the Constitution by, 70, 78, 86, 90; Baptists in, 243; law of 1715 respecting slaves, 267; extinction of slavery in, 292, 293.
New Jersey, prize court of, 10; ratifies the Constitution, 66; Catholics in, 221; synod of New York and, 238; laws respecting slavery in (in 1775), 283, 285; from 1775 to 1789, 299, 300.
New Lights, 233.
Newport, Rhode Island, Indian and colored servants in, 267.
New York city, Court of Appeals sits at, 40–42; Episcopal conference at, 201; Catholics in, 221, 229; Dutch Reformed Church in, 242.
New York state, 3; assembly of, 61; opposition to Constitution in, 63, 64; convention of (1788), 67, 92–94, 102; religion in, 188; Associate Presbytery of, 235; synod of New Jersey and, 238; laws respecting slavery in (1775), 281, 282, 285; from 1775 to 1789, 297–299.
Nixon, John, colonel, 140.
North Carolina, prize court of, 10, 11; and the Constitution, 84, 97, 107; Baptists in, 243, 245; laws respecting slaves in (in 1775), 273, 277, 278, 280; special courts for offences of slaves in, 275, 308; legislation respecting slaves, from 1775 to 1789, 307–309.
Nova Scotia, Methodists in, 215, 216; Baptists in, 243.

O'Brien, Sir Lucius, 189.
O'Kelley, James, schismatic, 218.
Olmstead, Gideon, 17–21.
Orange County (Va.), 105; Baptists in, 244, 245.
Ordnance, Board of (English), 121, 122.
Oswald, Colonel, 91.
Otis, Harrison Gray, 43.
Otterbein, William, Rev., 214.

INDEX. 319

Oxford, Massachusetts, Universalist conference at, 250.

Paca, William, judge of the Court of Appeals, 1, 29–32.
Page, John, of Rosewell, 255.
Parsons, Theophilus, 76, 77.
Paterson, Wm., 47.
Penhallow v. Doane, 34.
Pennsylvania, Wyoming dispute of, 3; prize courts of, 9, 12; and case of The Active, 17–23; council of, 24; ratifies the Constitution, 67, 70; project of second convention in, 95, 96, 98–100, 110; Catholics in, 221; Associate Presbytery of, 235; laws respecting slavery in (in 1775), 284, 285; abolition of slavery in, 287–290.
Perry, Wm. S., bishop, 195, 197–199.
Peters, Richard, judge, 20, 21, 125.
Philadelphia, admiralty court at, 12; petition from citizens of, 24–27; court of appeals at, 27, 31, 33, 34, 36, 42; Episcopal conventions at, 202–209; Methodist conference at, 212, 213; presbytery of, 231–233; synod of, 238; General Assembly at, 238, 239.
Phillis, slave, execution of, 269.
Pickering, Timothy, colonel, 125.
Pilmoor, Joseph, 211.
Pinckney, C., 37, 52; on executive departments, 172.
Piracies, trial of, 3.
Pius, VI. pope, 229.
Pope (Pius VI.), correspondence of Catholics with, 228, 229.
Port Tobacco, Maryland, nunnery at, 231.
Postmaster-General, office of, 117, 168, 169, 183.
Post-office, colonial, 166; Constitutional, 167; Continental, 168; department established, 182, 183.
Potts, John, 31, 37.
Poughkeepsie, convention at, 92.
Prefect Apostolic, office of, 227.
Presbyterians, 188, 189, 231–236; General Assembly of, 237–239; see Presbytery, Synod; Associate, 235, 237; Reformed, 235, 236; further Union, 252; the Constitution and the, 257–259.
Presbyteries, in America, 231, 232, 234, 238, 257–259; Associate, 235, 237, 258.
President, relations of, to departments, 181, 182; veto of, 260.
Price, Dr. Richard, invited to America, 133.
Princeton College founded, 233.
Privateering, 4, 6.
Privy council, English, 14, 15.
Prize courts, before the Revolution, 5; in the states, 6, 9–11, 18–20, 27; federal, 7, 8, 12, 15, 18–20, 23, 27–44.
Propaganda, Congregation of the, 225, 227, 228.
Protestant Episcopal Church, in America, situation of, 190–196; constitutional development of, 196–209; established in New York, 239; in Virginia, 245, 247; furthers Union, 252–255; the Constitution and the, 259–262.
Provoost, Samuel, bishop, 206.

Quakers, 188.
Quebec, bishop of, 221, 227.
Quebec Act, 223.

Randall, Benjamin, Free-Will Baptist, 249.
Randolph, Edmund, 47, 57, 171; proposes a second Constitutional Convention, 50, 51, 53, 61, 62; supports the Constitution of 1787, 63, 87; letter to, from Clinton, 88–90.
Read, George, judge of the Court of Appeals, 1, 32, 33, 36, 39, 41.
Reed, Joseph, 24.
Reformed Presbyterians, 235, 236.
Register of the treasury, 156, 180.
Religion in America (1775-1789), 186–190.
Removals from office, debate on, 178.
Republican Club, 92.
Revere, Paul, 75, 76.
Revival, Great, 187.
Rhode Island, prize court of, 9, 11, 12, 16; and the Constitution of 1787, 57, 70, 108; laws respecting slavery in (to 1775), 267–269; from 1775 to 1789 (gradual abolition), 293–295.
Rice, importance of, 264.

Richmond, Va., 34.
Rittenhouse, David, 20.
"Rittenhouse, Fort," 21.
Robeson, Andrew, 30.
Ross, George, judge, 18, 26.

St. Mary's Theological Seminary, 231.
St. Omer, Carroll at, 222.
Santiago de Cuba, bishop of, 227.
Savannah, 168.
Saybrook Platform, 234.
Schuyler, Philip, general, 151.
Scottish bishops, consecrate Dr. Seabury, 195, 196; Church (Presbyterian), 231, 257; Associate Presbytery, 235.
Seabury, Samuel, bishop, 195, 196, 200, 203, 207–209.
Semple, Robert B., Rev., 244–246, 248, 249.
Sergeant, Thomas, on the federal judiciary, 2.
Seymour, Sir Edward, advice respecting souls of Virginians, 192.
Shays' Rebellion, 68, 71.
Shea, John Gilmary, 221, 223, 226, 230.
Slavery, Methodists condemn, 215; early history of, 263, 264; in 1775, 263, 265; early legislation on, 266–272; laws respecting, in 1775, in the Southern colonies, 272–280; in the Middle colonies, 280–287; laws respecting, how modified between 1775 and 1789, in New England, 287–297; in the Middle States, 297–302; in the South, 302–311. See Slaves.
Slaves, status of, in early colonial times, 263, 264; numbers of, 265; status in New England, before 1775, 266–268; trial of, in New England, 268, 269; growth of slave-code in the South, 271, 272; laws in force in Southern colonies in 1775 respecting, 272, 273, 278; trial and punishment of, 274–277; manumission of, 279, 280; laws in force in Middle Colonies in 1775 respecting, 281–285; operativeness of laws respecting, 285–287; Pennsylvania's measures for emancipation of, 287–290; those of Massachusetts, New Hampshire, and Vermont, 290–293; those of Rhode Island and Connecticut, 293–297; action of New York and New Jersey respecting, 297–300; of Delaware and Maryland, 300–303; of Virginia, 303–307; of the Carolinas and Georgia, 307–311.
Smith, Melanchthon, 39, 56, 93, 106.
Society for the Propagation of the Gospel, 192, 231.
Society for the Support of Clergymen's Widows, 200.
Sons of Liberty, 75.
South Carolina, land case involving, 3; prize court of, 9, 11; and the Constitution, 65; ratifies it, 79, 84,; navy department of, 138, 141; special courts for offences of slaves in, 270, 275; laws respecting slaves in (in 1775), 272–274, 277–280, 286; from 1775 to 1789, 309–311,
Spain, 23, 27.
Spottsylvania County (Va.), Baptists in, 244.
State, secretaryship of, 117, 179, 181, 182.
Stearns, Shubal, 243, 244.
Stono Insurrection, 286.
Strawbridge, Robert, 210, 212.
Strong, Caleb, 43, 71.
Sullivan, James, 76, 77.
Sully, duke of, 152.
Sulpitians in Maryland, 231.
Superintendents, Methodist, 213–217.
Superior, office of, 226, 227.
Supreme Court of the United States, 21, 34, 42, 43.
Surintendant, 154.
Susanna, The, case of, 6.
Synod, of Philadelphia (Presbyterian), 232; of New York and Philadelphia, 233–238; its letter to Congress, 236; of Presbyterian Church in general, 238, 258, 259; of Dutch Reformed Church, 243; of Lutheran Church, 250.

Taylor, Yelverton, 26.
Territorial Disputes. See Land Cases.
Thistle, case of The, 12.
Thomson, Charles, secretary, 15, 39–42.

Tobacco, importance of, 264; in opinion of Sir Edward Seymour, 192.
Tories, confiscated slaves of, 298, 305, 308, 310.
Treason, petty, executions for, 269.
Treasurer of Loans, the, 131, 136, 156.
Treasurer of the U. S., office of, 128, 134, 156, 180.
Treasury, secretaryship of the, 117, 180–182; board, 129, 131, 133–137, 147, 156; office of accounts, 130; new board, 159; department of the, 176, 177, 179–182.
Trenton, court for land cases sits at, 3; Congress at, 36.
Trumbull, Jonathan, 110, 164.
Trumbull, Joseph, 125.
Tryon, Governor, 5.
Tyler, Professor M. C., 80, 102.

Ulster, Synod of, 231.
Unitarians, 187.
United Baptist Churches, 248.
United Brethren in Christ, 215.
Universalists, 187; organization of, 250.

Vasey, 214.
Vergennes, Count de, 31.
Vermont, prohibition of slavery in, 293.
Vicar Apostolic, of London, 221, 223–225; in France, 226, 228.
Vicar-general, office of, 225.
Vice-admiralty courts, 5, 14.
Vining, John, 179.
Virginia, prize court of, 10, 23; assembly of, 41, 81, 101–104; its action respecting the Constitution, 60, 61; convention of (1788), 67, 83–90; project of second convention in, 95, 100–104, 110; navy board of, 137, 138, 141; Episcopal clergy of, 201, 209, 254; Methodists in, 213, 218; Catholics in, 221; synod of, 238; Baptists in, 243–249; special courts for offences of slaves in, 270, 271, 274, 275, 306, 307; laws respecting slaves in (in 1775), 272, 273, 276, 279, 280; from 1775 to 1789, 303–307.

War, Board of, 125, 126, 147, 153; secretaryship of, 117, 126, 154; secretary at (England), 121, 122, (United States) 153; department of, 176–179, 181, 182.
War and Ordnance, Board of, 121–126.
Washington, George, on prize courts, 6–9, 12, 42; on the Constitution, 50, 57–59, 97; persuades Randolph, 63; opposes a second convention, 74, 79, 98, 100, 101, 109; suggests Board of War, 121; on executive departments, 151; and the Catholics, 230; on slavery, 293, 305, 311.
Webb, Thomas, captain, 188, 210.
Webster, Daniel, 75.
Webster, Pelatiah, 151.
Weems, Mason L., 193, 194, 225, 226.
Wesley, John, 187, 188, 199, 200, 210–212; consecrates Coke, 213; subsequent relations to American Methodism, 214–217, 257.
Wharton, John, 140.
Whatcoat, Richard, 214, 217.
White v. The Anna Maria, 16.
White, William, Dr., 199, 200, 203; bishop, 206, 207, 252.
Whitefield, George, 233.
Whitemarsh, Catholic conferences at, 225, 229.
Williams, Robert, 210.
Williamsburgh, 28.
Wilmington, Delaware, Episcopal convention at, 206.
Wilson, James, 26.
Wirt, Wm., 80, 105.
Witherspoon, John, Dr., 235, 236, 252, 257.
Woodbury, Connecticut, convention at, 195.
Wyoming, dispute concerning, 3.
Wythe, George, chancellor, 29, 30; proposals respecting slavery, 306.

Yates, Robert, 47, 57.
York, Cardinal, 221.

ERRATUM.

On p. 174, line 9, for "The attention of Congress," read, "The attention of the Convention."

www.ingramcontent.com/pod-product-compliance
Lightning Source LLC
Chambersburg PA
CBHW021150230426
43667CB00006B/330